D1795175

Accelerating Japan's Economic Growth

The Japanese economy is beginning to show signs of recovery after years of stagnation/deflation, but many Japanese policymakers warn that this economic growth may be sluggish: slower than in the United States and certainly slower than in other East Asian countries. Japan faces significant economic problems, including an aging population, a large fiscal deficit, and the need to adjust to the IT economy and to competition with the rest of East Asia. A slow growth scenario would greatly reduce opportunities for new productive investment and would make it increasingly difficult to provide for Japan's growing social needs.

The authors of this book argue that Japan can and should grow more rapidly, and examine the reasons for the sluggish performance of the Japanese economy. For example, some Japanese economic sectors, particularly in distribution and finance, have failed to take advantage of new information and communications technology to accelerate the growth of productivity, as has happened in other countries, such as the United States. Production function studies and econometric model simulations suggest that with appropriate policies the Japanese economy can grow more rapidly and deal with its future problems. The book posits a number of policy proposals which would help to accelerate Japan's economic growth.

This book will be of interest to students of the Japanese economy, macroeconomics and international economies, and also to policymakers and professionals interested in Japan's economy.

F. Gerard Adams, Professor Emeritus, University of Pennsylvania, is an expert on model building and application.

Lawrence R. Klein, Nobel Laureate, is Benjamin Franklin Professor Emeritus, University of Pennsylvania.

Yuzo Kumasaka is CEO of IT Economy Advisers, an economic forecasting and consulting firm.

Akihiko Shinozaki, Professor, Kyushu University, Fukuoka, Japan, is an expert on the information economy and business investment analysis.

Routledge studies in the growth economies of Asia

Accelerating Japan's Economic Growth

Resolving Japan's growth controversy

F. Gerard Adams
Lawrence R. Klein
Yuzo Kumasaka and
Akihiko Shinozaki

Routledge
Taylor & Francis Group

LONDON AND NEW YORK

First published 2008
by Routledge
2 Park Square, Milton Park, Abingdon, Oxon, OX14 4RN

Simultaneously published in the USA and Canada
by Routledge
711 Third Avenue, New York, NY 10017

*Routledge is an imprint of the Taylor & Francis Group,
an informa business*

First issued in paperback 2011

© 2008 F. Gerard Adams, Lawrence R. Klein, Yuzo Kumasaka and
Akihiko Shinozaki

Typeset in Times New Roman by
Newgen Imaging Systems (P) Ltd, Chennai, India

British Library Cataloguing in Publication Data
A catalogue record for this book is available
from the British Library

Library of Congress Cataloging in Publication Data
    Accelerating Japan's economic growth : resolving Japan's growth
controversy / F. Gerard Adams ... [et al.].
        p. cm.—(Routledge studies in the growth economies of Asia)
    Includes bibliographical references and index.
    1. Japan—Economic conditions—1989– 2. Japan—Economic policy—
1989– 3. Japan—Economic conditions—21st century. 4. Japan—
Economic policy—21st century. I. Adams, F. Gerard (Francis Gerard),
1929–

    HC462.95.A24 2007
    338.952—dc22   2007007144

ISBN10: 0–415–43331–2 (hbk)
ISBN10: 0–415–66648–1 (pbk)
ISBN10: 0–203–94646–4 (ebk)

ISBN13: 978–0–415–43331–0 (hbk)
ISBN13: 978–0–415–66648–0 (pbk)
ISBN13: 978–0–203–94646–6 (ebk)

Contents

Figures

Tables

About the authors

F. Gerard Adams, Professor Emeritus, University of Pennsylvania, is an expert on model building and application. He has worked closely with Professor Klein. His most recent book, concerned with the implications of the IT revolution, is *East Asia, Globalization, and the New Economy* (2006).

Lawrence R. Klein, Nobel Laureate, is Benjamin Franklin Professor Emeritus, University of Pennsylvania. He is a pioneering developer of macroeconometric model building and forecasting in the United States. His current work involves short-term forecasting and policy prescriptions.

Yuzo Kumasaka is CEO of IT Economy Advisers, an economic forecasting and consulting firm. He has worked closely with political economists and policy makers in Japan and elsewhere in East Asia on the implications of the IT revolution for economic development and growth.

Akihiko Shinozaki, Professor, Kyushu University, Fukuoka, Japan, is an expert on the information economy and business investment analysis. He has written numerous influential papers on the relationship between IT and productivity growth.

Preface

This volume is based on studies of Japanese economic growth continuing on from the "Think Tank 2005 Japan," during the spring of 2006. It was produced in an effort to resolve a political controversy on the targets for Japanese economic growth.

At the time the research was carried out, the Japanese economy was showing signs of moderate recovery after almost 15 years of stagnation/deflation. In planning for the future, some government officials and experts have argued that growth will continue, but at a very slow pace. Japan is a mature economy with an aging population and a large public debt. As a result, it is said, that Japan can anticipate no more than very modest economic growth, perhaps 1.5–2% per year. Such a pessimistic perspective reflects the assumptions that productivity growth will follow recent slow trends and that growth will be checked by the constraints imposed by Japan's accumulated fiscal deficit. There is fear that seeking a faster growth path would revive inflationary pressure and impair the government's fiscal stability.

Accepting a slow growth scenario would lead to conservative fiscal and monetary policies that might greatly reduce opportunities for new productive investment and would make it increasingly difficult to provide for Japan's growing social needs as its population ages. We, as well as other experts and policy makers, believe that faster growth is possible, indeed, is necessary, if Japan is to continue as a vibrant economy. We expect that the "new economy" offers opportunities for increased rapid growth as demonstrated by the greatly improved productivity growth trend of other countries, like the United States. With appropriate policies, the information and communications technology (IT) revolution offers great opportunities for reviving the Japanese growth rate.

In studying these developments, it is important to recognize the impact of the IT revolution on the Japanese production function. Analysis based on a production function that fully recognizes the implications of new technology investments and applications on productivity is necessary. Such an approach would imply a higher rate of potential productivity growth, and would have implications for continued moderate inflation and for improving public revenues. It would depend on, and permit, more aggressive public policies.

In this study we estimate an improved production function appropriate to the new IT world. In the framework of an econometric model of Japan, simulation studies based on our theoretical framework demonstrate that higher growth rates are achievable making possible a more progressive policy strategy.

In Chapters 2–4 of this volume, we study the Japanese growth record, and its implications for projecting Japanese growth into the future. The potentials of the economy have been the subject of intense controversy among Japanese politicians and policy makers.

Chapter 5 is concerned with the theoretical underpinnings of the new increasing returns production function that is suitable for the study of the "new economy." We consider its implications for aggregate supply and demand and what may be required in terms of supply-side and demand-side policies. Then, we examine the nature of the new IT economy and how it might affect growth in Japan.

Chapters 7–10 look at experience with IT investments and applications in Japan and the United States.

Chapters 11–12 cover econometric modeling and simulation. A new increasing returns production function is introduced into the econometric model and other appropriate model revisions are made. We use this system to evaluate the impact of recognizing increased IT investment on Japanese growth.

A discussion of policy alternatives to encourage IT investment follows in Chapters 13–14. We suggest policies that will stimulate investment and applications of IT technology. We recognize the need for adjustments in the microeconomics of Japan and in fiscal and monetary policies to enable the economy to fully utilize its new production potentials.

This volume is a joint effort. All of the authors contributed to the text. Kumasaka coordinated the research and did the computer simulations. We appreciate Dr S. Ozmucur's help with the simulations. Adams integrated the separate studies into one consistent volume. We thank Professor Y. Inada for allowing us to adapt and use his model of the Japanese economy.

A note on terminology

Information and communications technology is central to the discussion of economic change in Japan. These terms cover a broad range of technological fields and their applications from hardware to software, from electronics to biology, from manufacturing to transportation and communication. Throughout this book the abbreviation **IT** has been used to refer to the entire field when there is no need for a narrower definition.

1 Introduction and summary of the book

After almost 15 years of deflation and recession, in Japan the issue of what is an attainable rate of growth consistent with price stability and equilibrium in the government budget has become a matter of political concern. Can Japan, like the United States, achieve a higher rate of output growth, or must the Japanese economy plan on continuing on a slow growth path? That is the focus of this research.

A Japanese version of a "Rising Tide Policy"

Several years ago, a Japanese high school student wrote a composition entitled "Japan Has Everything, except a Dream." We recalled that title when we recently read the official report of "Japan's Vision for the 21st Century," published by the Japanese Cabinet Office in April 2005 (Council on Economic and Fiscal Policy, 2005). It described a "Targeted Future State" that paints a picture of an economy where two things are essential:

- The ability to maintain a 1.5% annual economic growth rate until the year 2030.
- A growth rate of per capita real GDP of about 2%, a little higher than the growth of aggregate GDP reflecting a declining population.

Accelerating the growth rate of an advanced industrial country like Japan is a considerable challenge. Many of Japan's industries are mature and are already operating at the technological frontier. It is hard for a country to prosper if, as in Japan, its population shrinks and ages. Solving Japan's economic and social problems such as an excessive fiscal imbalance and growing public debt, an aging society, and growing pension demands cannot be accomplished without expanding the economic pie. Moreover, Japan is still adapting its industrial structure to the radical changes in its competitive position relative to other East Asian countries.

A pessimistic appraisal of Japan's prospects may turn out to be a self-fulfilling prophecy. Who will invest in a country whose likely annual growth rate is a mere 1.5–2%? Human and financial capital will flow out of a country with little or no hope for future expansion and profitability. Other Asian countries will not allow Japan to take a leadership role in the region if Japan is expected to grow at a glacially slow annual rate through the foreseeable future.

This pessimistic scenario implied by the government's economic projections should be considered a very serious warning, a wakeup call to the nation. Without a more aggressive forward-looking strategy, the people of Japan will suffer the effects of slow economic growth for many years in the twenty-first century. The increasing burdens of an aging population will be an unfortunate legacy for younger generations.

In the early 1990s, the Japanese were not the only ones taking a pessimistic view of higher economic growth. At that time, many people in the United States feared that the US economy had also reached maturity, and that there would no longer be great technological innovation to drive the economy. The consensus among economists about the US potential GDP growth rate was only about 2–2.5% per year, with productivity increasing only 1–1.5% annually. But, in the mid-1990s, some American economists began to recognize that the United States could grow at a faster rate than had originally been anticipated without accelerating inflation. One of those economists was Prof. Lawrence R. Klein, who noticed that the economic recovery that occurred after 1991 was characteristically different from past economic recoveries, as described in his 1995 paper, "The Re-Opening of The US Productivity-Led Growth Era" (Klein and Kumasaka, 1995). In that same year, Jerry J. Jasinowski, President of the National Association of Manufacturers, joined a small group of business economists who believed that the US economy could grow at a faster rate. Jasinowski collected about twenty professional papers that discussed economic policies detailing how this could be achieved. The papers focused on the New Economy, productivity, human capital, globalization, the role of government and fiscal and monetary policies. These papers were published as a book *The Rising Tide* in 1998 (Jasinowsky, 1998). The title was gleaned from a quote of President J. F. Kennedy during the 1962 GATT/Kennedy round of trade talks. He remarked that "a rising tide lifts all boats," that is, that all countries would be better off through growth generated by international trade. This notion also applies within a country, domestically. Rapid growth is likely to spread benefits broadly throughout the society. If growth is slow, some groups are always left behind and their incomes do not improve. A "Rising Tide Policy" that lifts all boats is essential for the general welfare of all.

It was fortunate for the United States that American economists recognized that their economy had the potential for faster growth in the mid-1990s. As Figure 1.1 shows, the productivity growth trend for the United States rose steadily since 1995. As seen in Figure 1.2, since that time economic growth averaged 2.5% (Figure 1.2), a rate that was, by general consensus among many economists, believed to be the potential growth rate for the period from 1995 to 2000. Luckier still, Alan Greenspan, Federal Reserve Chairman at the time, also recognized the increased productivity growth trend and resisted pressures to increase the interest rate in the early stages of economic expansion. The short term interest rate, which had been between 5% and 6% in the mid-1990s, was reduced from 2001 to the extraordinary low level of 1% in 2003, and was increased only very slowly in the 2004–2006 period, providing

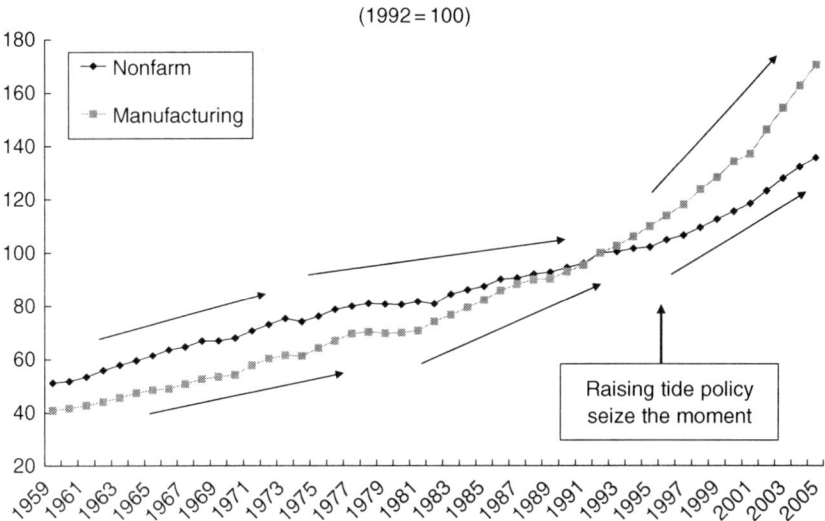

Figure 1.1 US productivity growth trend: nonfarm and manufacturing sectors.

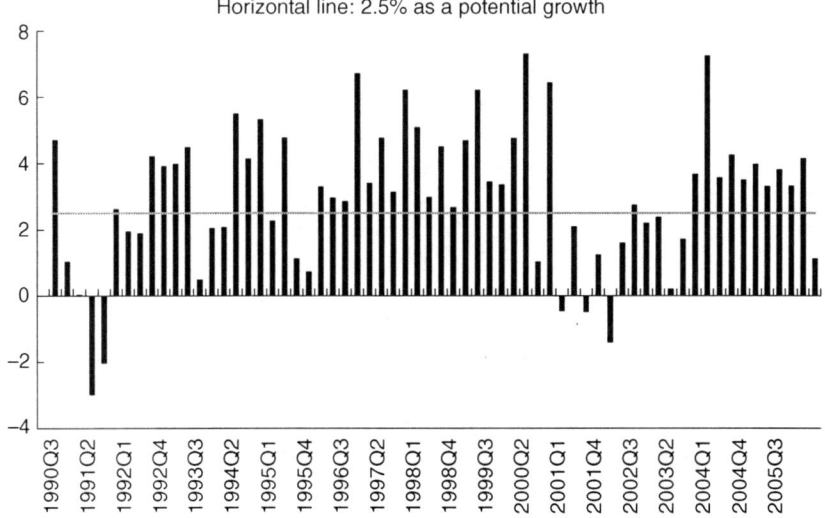

Figure 1.2 US real GDP growth rate (% per year).

continued stimulus to the economy over several years. Such an accommodative monetary policy stance, based on the assumption that productivity gains would offset increases in labor costs as the employment situation tightened, contributed to the long economic expansion seen in the 1990s and early 2000s (Figure 1.3).

Now, it is time for Japan to introduce her own "Rising Tide Policy." It has been unfortunate that many Japanese economists and business people misunderstood

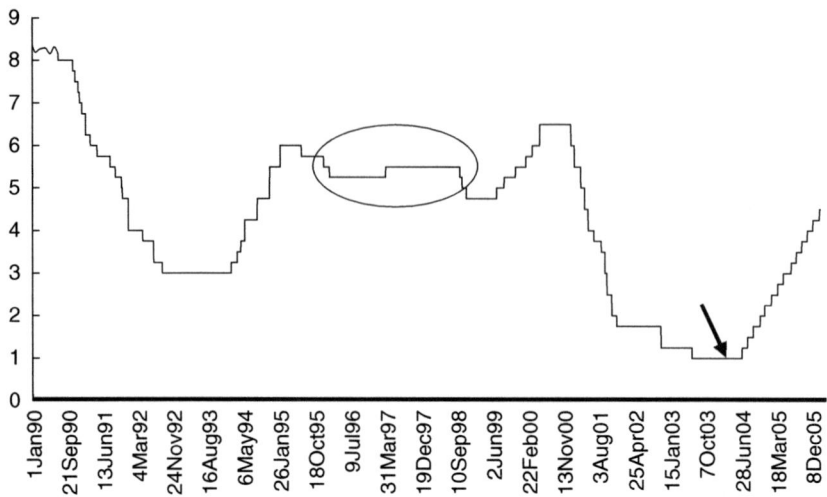

Figure 1.3 US federal funds rate (target rate after July 13, 1990) (%). (Dates on horizontal axis correspond to times when interest rate targets were changed.)

the potential of information technology in the 1990s, when the Information and Communication Technology (IT) revolution began. In view of the structural rigidity of the Japanese business scene and the fact that many business people viewed the IT revolution largely as a speculative bubble, they did not sufficiently adopt the new technologies in the 1990s. Japan did not see the increase in productivity growth through the IT revolution that was observed in the United States. It was not until after the bubble in the US stock market burst in 2000, that many Japanese businessmen recognized that IT was not a modern day tulip mania. Adam Cohen, writing in the New York Times expressed it best "... when the tulip bubble burst, nothing is left but soapy residue. But, the Internet revolution is really changing the world" (Cohen, 2002). Japan lost at least five years before trying to utilize IT effectively. As a result the Japanese economy found itself on a slow growth path, one that threatens long-term prospects.

In this project, we focus mainly on a theoretical and policy framework that will raise Japan's potential growth. In an earlier stage, Stage I (January–March 2006), we surveyed the effect of IT on economies in the United States and East Asian countries, and proposed a new theoretical structure for analyzing the relationship between IT and productivity growth. In the second stage, we applied this theory in a modified econometric model and carried out alternative forecast simulations. We use this work to propose fiscal and industrial development policies, particularly with regard to IT and its application, to raise Japan's potential growth.

The structure of this book is as follows:

–   Historical view of the performance of the Japanese economy over the long term and in the recent past.

- The nature of IT and its implications for a New Economy.
- A new theoretical framework to analyze the relationship between IT and the growth of potential GDP.
- The implications for fiscal and monetary policy of a faster growth path for potential output.
- Japanese development in the context of the East Asian growth process.
- IT and productivity growth in Japan.
- Industrial organization in Japan and the United States.
- A case study of the telecommunications industry in Japan.
- IT and productivity growth in the United States.
- A macroeconomic model for Japan, that embodies the "New Economy" production function.
- Simulation studies of Japan's higher economic growth.
- Policy recommendations to accelerate Japan's economic growth.

The Japanese economic growth policy controversy

The issue of establishing an appropriate growth target has become particularly important in recent years as Japanese economic performance has lagged. Japanese government officials have long found it difficult to reconcile the various aims of economic policy—rapid growth, price stability, international payments balance, and fiscal equilibrium—when different, often independently operating, government agencies have focused their responsibilities separately on one or another of these objectives.

For example, the Ministry of Finance has had great concern with regard to the fiscal deficit and the national debt, seeking when possible to reinstate taxes to minimize the current fiscal deficit. A good example of that was the premature reinstatement of the consumption tax in 1997 that drove the gradually improving Japanese economy back into stagnation. Today again, the Ministry of Finance is seeking substantial consumption tax increases, not only to improve budget balance on a current basis, but also in fear of a rising ratio between the public debt and national income, now at the high level of approximately 170%.

Similarly, the Bank of Japan is seeking to manage its monetary policy with focus on a narrow definition of inflationary objectives. For many years, in the face of deflation, the Bank of Japan followed a zero interest rate policy. Indeed, while nominal interest rates were at 0 or 1%, about as low as they could be, real rates of interest were somewhat higher, some 2 or 3%, because the price level was declining. Now that deflation has stopped and prices are rising at a modest rate, the Bank of Japan wants quickly to raise interest rates to ward off the risk of inflation. Unfortunately, rising interest rates at this time might not only slow gradually resurging Japanese economic growth. They might also impose added strain on fiscal balance as interest payments on the large outstanding debt would increase. Higher interest rates might also appreciate the Japanese yen again, as in the 1990s, reducing the competitiveness of Japanese goods in world markets.

Economic targets are necessary so that policymakers can make the critical policy decisions that guide the economy consistently toward its various objectives. They are particularly important in an economy like Japan's that remains on the edge between prosperity and recession and that greatly fears inflation.

Even during the long stagnant period 1995–2005, arguments were levied against a policy of fiscal expansion because of the public debt overhang, and a fear of inciting inflation, even though *deflation* was one of the problems that the economy faced. Fiscal stimuli were often brushed aside on two grounds:

i   The public deficit was too large, even though there was criticism that it was not properly measured[1];

ii   It was claimed that public works were already plentiful.

In 2006, the specifics of the economic situation have placed the policy controversy on the front burner. A political battle raged between two groups within the Japanese Council on Economic and Fiscal Policy concerning the prospect of Japan's post-Koizumi Administration economic growth over the next decade. The debate focused initially on how to reduce the government deficit.

The first group was led by Hidenao Nakagawa, Chairman, Policy Research Council in the Liberal Democratic Party and Heizo Takenaka, Minister of Internal Affairs and Communication. This faction, which we will call the "high growth" group, projected the future on the basis of a 3–4% growth rate for nominal GDP. Such a growth path translates into 3% annual growth of potential output in real terms, a substantial improvement over Japan's inadequate growth record of the past 15 years. Moreover, as we show later, such a growth path would yield increases in tax revenues sufficient to stabilize the government deficit without requiring immediate increases in the consumption tax.

The second group, which we will call the "low growth" group, was directed by Sadakazu Tanigaki, Minister of Finance, and Hajime Yosano, Minister of State for Economic and Fiscal Policy as well as Minister of State for Financial Services. This group insisted that Japan's potential growth was only 1.5%, a straightforward assumption because the average growth rate of real GDP in Japan was approximately 1.5% over the past decade. They did not expect higher economic growth and so they argued that an immediate increase in the consumption tax would be necessary to reduce government deficits.

The short term political impact of this debate was considerable since it was aimed at the very basics of tax policy decisions: whether, once again, to raise the consumption tax. Moreover, when economic policies are planned for the next decade, a difference of 1 or 2% in annual economic growth can give a very different picture of the future. Note, also, that adopting a low growth projection can be a self-fulfilling prophecy. In a complete dynamic economic system, an increase in taxes may have a depressing effect on GDP and on its growth path. Such a tax increase would be accepted by policymakers if its macroeconomic consequences are consistent with their underlying "low growth" plan. When the two groups failed to resolve their dispute, Prime Minister Koizumi asked

Nakagawa to prove that Japan would be able to achieve a 3% sustainable growth rate. That request was the basis for the present study.

Policy potentials for faster growth

Policies leading to a more rapid increase in growth rate involve a number of possibilities:

- More aggressive macroeconomic policies. Since it is anticipated that productivity growth will be faster, it would be possible to push macroeconomic activity more vigorously, with stronger fiscal policy and more accommodative monetary policy, without causing inflation.
- Market improvement policies. Removing the regulatory constraints that affect many service industries in Japan and improving the competitive functioning of markets may go a long way toward achieving improved productivity.
- Sector-specific industrial policies favoring IT industries. High-tech industries fit well with Japan's resource and skill endowments: skilled labor, abundant capital, and advanced high-tech engineering technology. There are also other fields, like distribution and financial services, where significant gains in productivity can be made. Policies that will promote Japan's development and application of IT technology and policies that will provide education, research and entrepreneurship will help to make a substantial contribution to more rapid growth.

The policy options for Japan will be considered at greater length in Chapters 2 and 13.

2 The economic growth record in Japan

After an extended slump, often referred to as a "lost decade," starting from the collapse of real estate and equity market prices in 1991, the Japanese economy is, at long last, showing signs of recovery. Although the growth rate, measured as the percentage change in real GDP, was very low during the 1990s, Japan retained its very high rank among the world's industrial countries as the second largest producer of real goods and services (real GDP) in *level* as distinct from *rate-of-change* measures of real GDP. Today, even that position is threatened if Japan continues to grow slowly, as other countries, particularly China, continue on their rapid growth paths.[1]

At the present time, it appears that a recovery in Japan to positive, but modest, growth has been reestablished, but there is still a lingering doubt about the sustainability of Japan's turnaround. Can Japan play a leading role in the world economy, especially in Asia? Japan's support will be needed at critical times, such as renewed currency crises as those of 1997–8 or in the face of natural disasters such as the *Tsunami* of 2004. Japan hopes to continue to play a dynamic *leading* role in the world economy during this age of globalization.

Perspective on Japan's long-term growth slowdown

First, we examine Japan's past performance over the long term, and then we try to assess where the Japanese economy is heading today, especially in terms of its potentials.

We confront the results of the East Asian Economic Miracle in Japan of the 1960s to 1980s and the extended slow period since the early 1990s. This deflationary time also contrasts with the high-growth performance of China and India in the 1990s and early 2000s, coming from economies that have much lower *levels* of income on a per capita basis and are at much earlier stages of economic development.

Japan grew at varying but typically modest rates from 1885 until postwar recovery set in during the latter part of the 1950s and through the early 1960s. (Table 2.1) Except for the war years, Japan has had (sustained) growth between 2% and 6% for significant stretches. This was not bad, but not sensational, though it should be noted that, until the 1970s, Japan was the only Asian country to become heavily industrialized and to achieve advanced country living standards.

Table 2.1 Growth rates of real GNP

Japanese cycles since 1885	Growth rates (%)
1885–98	4.3
1898–1905	2.3
1905–19	4.2
1919–31	3.6
1931–8	6.0
1938–54	0.5
1954–61	10.9
1961–73	9.4
1973–92	3.4
1992–8	1.2
1998–2007 (est)	1.3

Sources: Chapter 1 (Klein and Ohkawa, 1968; Saito, 2000; United Nations, 2006).

There was great satisfaction with the unusual success of the income-doubling decades of the 1950s and 1960s. This period demonstrated how the combination of high rates of investment and accumulated knowledge can produce an upsurge of growth—after all, Japan had been an industrial economy before the War and took advantage of vast technological development in the intervening period. An excellent work ethic and high-class products (textiles, appliances, cars, infrastructure expansion) created a surge in the late 1950s and 1960s, but the "Oil Shocks" of the 1970s and the collapse of the Bretton Woods exchange rate system called for a downgrade. There was, in fact, a lack of sustainability in Japan's rapid growth, so that in the 1970s and 1980s the Japanese economy grew more slowly and finally sank into a long period of stagnation/deflation in the 1990s.

As the 1960s were drawing to a close, some Japanese economists stated that their forecasts of Japanese economic growth would be 10% per year but the experience of the 1970s and 1980s called for a downgrade to 5% and as the 1990s approached, it was frequently said that this important potential growth rate was only 3%. Even that low figure was not plausible for the waning period of the twentieth century. It is notable how far off these growth forecasts turned out to be. Projections based on past experience, as were many of these forecasts, are often far from accurate in the future. The same is likely to be true today for forecasts based heavily on the slow growth of the past decade.

The entries in Table 2.2 show clearly the disappointing performance of the Japanese economy after its earlier growth spurt. During most of the 1990s and early 2000s real growth has been very modest. Repeatedly the economy has gone back into recession or stagnation towards zero growth, what has been termed a double-dip or even triple-dip recession. Unemployment rose to high levels. (On the basis of Japanese methods of measurement, 5% unemployment is a very high figure.) The rate of inflation has been very low, negative for some years. This is the basis for referring to this period as a time of deflation, though many observers use the word deflation in a more general recession or stagnation sense. Corporate earnings have remained flat or declined throughout the entire period.

Table 2.2 The Japanese economy emerging from the lost decade

	1992	1993	1994	1995	1996	1997	1998	1999	2000	2001	2002	2003	2004	2005
GDP growth rate % p.a.	1.0	0.2	1.5	1.9	2.6	1.4	−1.9	−0.1	2.9	0.4	0.1	1.8	2.3	2.6
Unemployment rate % of labor force	2.2	2.5	2.9	3.1	3.4	3.4	4.1	4.7	4.7	5.0	5.4	5.3	4.7	4.4
Consumer price index % change p.a.	1.7	1.3	0.7	−0.1	0.1	1.7	0.7	−0.3	−0.7	−0.7	−0.9	−0.3	0.0	−0.3
Earnings % change p.a.	2.2	1.9	2.3	2.1	1.9	1.5	−0.2	0.2	0.3	−0.6	−1.7	0.0	−0.1	0.7
Deficit % of GDP	−1.7	−4.6	−5.7	−6.6	−6.8	−5.6	−6.9	−8.3	−8.0	−6.2	−7.7	−7.4	−6.2	−6.1
Current account $billion	112.5	131.9	130.4	110.0	64.7	97.4	119.0	115.2	119.3	88.6	112.0	136.6	171.2	167.5
Investment–GDP ratio (%)	28.9	28.0	27.5	27.2	27.8	27.1	25.7	25.7	25.2	24.9	23.6	23.3	23.0	23.3
IT investment–GDP ratio (%)	2.3	2.2	2.3	2.7	3.2	3.2	3.2	3.4	3.7	4.0	3.9	3.9	4.0	4.1

Source: I & N data base.

The government deficit has consistently been between 7% and 8% of GDP for the past decade, a very high figure reflecting efforts to use fiscal policy to stimulate the economy. The trade balance has remained substantially positive. Business fixed investment as a share of GDP has declined in recent years to approximately 23% of GDP. While investment in IT has shown an increase in recent years, it continues to account for only a small share of GDP, only 4%.

A number of interacting factors explain what knocked the Japanese economy off its high-growth path and sent it into a long period of deflation. Some of these factors relate specifically to the boom and bust. But our special concern is to explain why the period of stagnation following the crash extended over so many years.

There is not a single cause, but much can be explained by Japan's growing maturity and changing competitive position. In the 1980s and 1990s, the economy of Japan had matured and faced increased competition from its neighbors in East Asia. Japan faded as a high-growth economy as it became increasingly difficult to compete in many consumer products with Taiwan and Korea and eventually with China. This was not only a matter of the rising exchange rate and increasing wages in Japan but also the result of the vastly improved production potential in other East Asian countries.

An interesting illustration of the adaptation that is required is as follows. Having involvement in the production of the *International Economic Review*, an economic journal operating as a joint venture of Osaka University and the University of Pennsylvania (backed by the Kansai Economic Federation), we followed the course of cost-pricing in the following phases.

1 Japanese printers (in English language) were every cost effective in the early 1960s through sheer effort, with low wage rates.
2 As wages and the yen exchange rate rose, gradual cost savings were achieved, through use of less expensive paper and fewer cycles of proof reading.
3 In the 1970s, printing was moved to the United States, at lower cost in spite of higher wage rates.
4 In the 1990s, management of production and printing was taken over by Blackwell Publishing of the United Kingdom with intensive uses of information technology.
5 Eventually, this transformed barely adequate income statements into highly profitable Western operations in the information age, able to cover all costs, including stipends for US editors and support for doctoral students at the University of Pennsylvania.

This example illustrates various dimensions of the adjustment of international trade as the economy becomes more globalized. On one hand, production activity shifted to lower-cost locations, locations where labor costs are particularly advantageous in the case of many labor-intensive consumer products. On the other hand, there is room for changing the mix of products and/or changing the nature of production methods to improve the competitiveness of goods being produced in the more mature country. In the case of Japan, such adjustments are most immediate with regard to East Asia and, particularly, to China which has become a production powerhouse for many products once produced competitively in Japan.

Japanese economic maturity with its concomitant increased labor costs and appreciation of the yen called for significant adaptations. In some areas of international competition, Japan adapted and remained profitable, leaders of world industry. For example, in the automotive group, Japan retained its earlier success and also in some electronic products. Japan became a leading producer of capital goods and high-quality consumer electronics. But in other fields, Japan has lost competitiveness compared to its neighbors.

In terms of contribution to the global world economy, it can be said that Japanese business practices like Just-In-Time inventory policy have been very effective, and quality circles for high business performance have worked well. But we will argue below that Japanese integrated business structure is more suited for stable industries than for highly competitive entrepreneurial ones. Japan had reached a high level of achievement in its advanced industries but relative costs were rising rapidly in conventional export production of consumer goods and other parts of the economy, like services and agriculture, did not maintain technological pace. Japan was becoming a two-tier economy: advanced high-tech sectors and much less sophisticated and less productive services and agriculture. Japanese industry is close to the best in the world; the Japanese automobile industry has higher levels of productivity and mechanization than even the industries in Germany and the United States. On the other hand, Japanese service industries are much less efficient. Retail trade remains in many cases the "mom-and-pop shop" and wholesale trade is scattered on too many levels of small size wholesalers. Japanese farmers produce high-quality products that require very high levels of protection and subsidy. This means that, while some industries are highly productive, indeed at the technological frontier, particularly those in international competition, in other activities there is much room for improved productivity.

In the 1980s, the bilateral trade surpluses with the United States led to upward pressure on the yen exchange rate. Under threat of trade sanctions from the United States and following numerous "voluntary restraint" agreements limiting Japanese exports, Japan agreed to yen appreciation, the 1985 Plaza Agreement. The yen appreciated all the way from 360 to the dollar in 1971 to 80 to the dollar in 1995 though it has remained in the 100 to 130 yen per US dollar range since then (Figure 2.1).

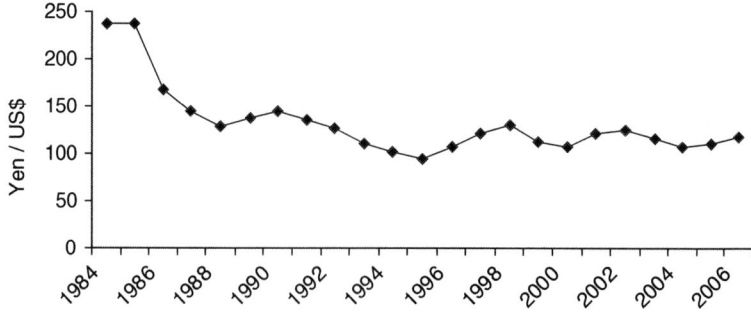

Figure 2.1 Yen/US$ exchange rate 1984–2006.

Source: I & N database.

For a time the appreciation of the yen impacted negatively on Japanese competitiveness leading to a shift of production to lower-cost subsidiaries in East Asia. This is responsible for what has been termed a "hollowing out," *kuhdohka*, of Japanese industry that took place over many years. At the same time, yen appreciation made possible the price deflation that is seen in Japan as damaging to the profitability and health of Japanese industries.

Total trade volumes (in US$) continued to grow during the past 20 years (Table 2.3), though the growth of both exports and imports slowed during the second half of the 1990s, the time of the East Asian financial crisis. Yet, Japanese export competitiveness was sufficient so that the current account balance remained steadily in surplus (Figure 2.2).

The increasing integration of the Japanese economy into the East Asian market is apparent in the statistics of destination and origin of Japanese trade (Table 2.4). The share of Japanese exports destined for the United States and Europe has been declining, while the share of exports going to China and other parts of East Asia has shown significant increase. A similar pattern is apparent with respect to imports, where products from the United States and Europe have been declining as a share and products originating in China have grown rapidly.

Finally we turn to product classification. It is more difficult to identify the changes, but we note, particularly, the declining share of exports and a rising share of imports of office and computing machinery and telecom products, mass-produced goods now increasingly produced elsewhere in East Asia (Table 2.5).

Table 2.3 Growth of Japanese exports and imports

	(% change per year)	
	Exports	*Imports*
1986–90	7.8	15.5
1990–5	8.7	7.2
1995–2000	1.6	2.4
2000–5	4.4	6.2

Source: Authors' calculation, I & N database.

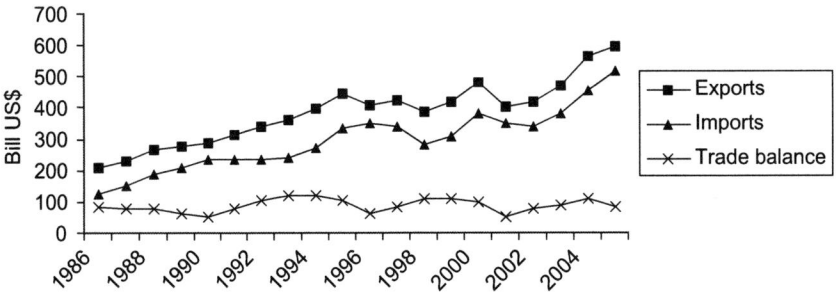

Figure 2.2 Japanese trade 1986–2005.

Source: I & N database.

Table 2.4 Destination and origin of Japanese trade

	(% of total exports or imports)			
	1990	*1995*	*2000*	*2005*
Exports to:				
US	31.7	27.6	30.0	22.4
Industrial Europe	21.7	16.7	17.1	14.3
China + HK	7.9	11.2	12.0	19.4
Other East Asia	18.4	31.1	28.2	27.9
Rest of World	20.4	13.5	12.7	16.0
Imports from:				
US	22.6	22.6	19.1	12.4
Industrial Europe	18.1	16.1	13.5	12.4
China + HK	6.0	11.5	14.9	21.4
Other East Asia	20.8	23.4	25.3	21.9
Rest of World	32.5	26.4	27.1	31.9

Source: I & N database.

Table 2.5 Product classification of Japanese trade, 1990–2005

	(% of total exports or imports)			
	1990	*1995*	*2000*	*2005*
Exports Machinery manufactures	70.9	70.3	68.7	65.7
of which				
General machinery	16.2	18.4	16.6	17.4*
Office + computing machinery	8.7	8.5	7.4	4.6*
Telecom	10.4	6.9	6.4	6.3*
Other elec. machinery	11.6	16.7	17.4	14.3*
Other manufactures	20.3	19.1	19.0	18.6
Other exports	8.8	10.6	12.4	15.8
Imports Machinery manufactures	15.4	22.5	27.9	26.6
of which				
Office + computing machinery	2.3	4.8	7.3	5.9*
Telecom	1.1	2.7	3.6	3.5*
Other elec. machinery	3.2	6.4	9.2	8.8*
Other manufactures of which	25.1	26.5	24.1	22.7
Apparel	3.8	5.6	5.3	4.8*
Fuels	24.2	16.1	20.4	25.3
Agricultural products	13.6	15.4	12.2	10.1
Crude materials	12.6	10.2	6.8	5.9
Other imports	9.1	9.3	8.5	9.5

Source: I & N database.

Note
* 2004.

These trends are similar to those occurring in other parts of the world. They reflect a vast improvement in the ability of East Asia, and particularly China, to meet the product specifications required in advanced countries like Japan. Increasingly mass-produced products can be sourced in China and sold in competition with home products in the Japanese market. While some sectors, like agriculture, remain excluded, the shift from costly production in Japan to low cost production in China, using inexpensive labor, allows Japan to focus its resources on products and fields where it has attained a high level of productivity like electronics, autos, and advanced equipment.

The integration of the Japanese economy with the economies of other rapidly growing East Asian countries will be a challenge during the coming years. It will require significant changes in the composition of production and employment in manufacturing industry. The production chains used in sourcing products in China may also call for significant developments in the Japanese distributions sectors, another possibility for productivity gains.

Turning next to financial issues, the collapse of asset values in the early 1990s following an entirely unrealistic stock market and property value "bubble" and the resulting difficulties of the Japanese financial system imposed a burden on the economy that did not lighten for many years (Figure 2.3). Stock prices collapsed in 1990 and land prices began to fall a couple of years later, more slowly than the drop of equity prices but continuing steadily throughout the 1990s. The decline of asset values reduced bank collateral holdings and affected bank capital ratios as new regulations in 1997 called for marking asset values to market (Deckle and Kletzer, 2003). Before the crisis, financial system lending had helped to magnify the speculative bubble. Krugman (1998) argues that lending continued even after

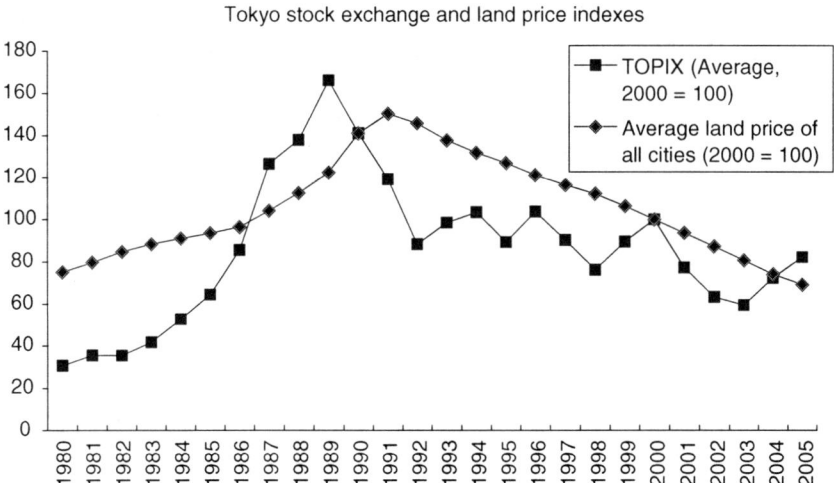

Figure 2.3 Japanese asset values during the lost decade.

Source: Topix data: Tokyo stock exchange land price data: Ministry of land, infrastructure, and transport.

the crisis, but, once the decline in asset values affected capital ratios, undercapitalized financial institutions restrained lending in order to meet capital adequacy standards. There are differences of opinion, however, about whether tight money, that is, unwillingness to lend, was a source of the problem, since for a long time banks simply continued to hold their nonperforming loans (NPLs). On the other hand, some authors conclude that after banks began to "mark-to-market," that is when they began to apply realistic values to their asset holdings in their accounting statements, there was a significant shortage of funding in 1997 and 1998 (Motonishi and Yoshikawa, 1999; Woo, 1999).

Others have explained the persistence of stagnation on the basis of organizational/ cultural factors, the difficulty of the "integrated" Japanese system of business organization to adapt to the new economy as readily as more modular organizations operating in the United States or elsewhere (Shinozaki, 2004). A view that links closely with our own work is in the analysis of Hayashi and Prescott (2002) and Wolff (2001) who compute a sharp decline of total factor productivity (TFP) during the 1990s. The implication is that Japan did not fully take advantage gains in IT to increase productivity in many sectors. That may be, particularly in view of the two-tier structure of the Japanese economy that we have discussed above with the service industries and agriculture lagging far behind industry (Weinstein, 2001). But we note that Hayashi and Prescott use a traditional constant returns to scale production function. As we show below, an alternatively formulated function will yield somewhat higher potential output estimates.

Comparison of Japanese growth and United States growth

How does the growth of Japan compare with that of the United States? In the past decade, the US economy has performed quite well, better than in previous decades. This has been a period not only of rapid growth in labor and capital inputs but also in productivity. Labor productivity in the nonfarm business sector rose from 1% per year in 1987–95 to 2.5% in 1995–2001 and 3.3% from 2000 to 2005, as we have noted. Total factor productivity increased from 0.6% to 1.4% in the 1995 to 2001 period (Bosworth and Triplett, 2004; Jorgenson *et al.*, 2005). Even in mid-2006, when revisions of the statistics suggested the need for downward revision of productivity growth by approximately 0.25% annually, many experts were projecting productivity for the nonfarm business sector at 2.5% and for the US economy as a whole in the neighborhood of 2% per year (*Financial Times* July 18, 2006, p. 7).

A number of recent empirical studies seek to explain the US growth phenomenon[2] so that comparisons can be made with Japan. They tend to follow the multifactor productivity approach, accounting first for the increase in the quantity and quality of inputs and then focusing on the residual or multifactor productivity component. Jorgenson *et al.* (2005) have been concerned with the American growth resurgence over the long period from 1975 to 2000. Their results are summarized in Table 2.6. The corresponding Japanese figures are shown in brackets.

Table 2.6 Sources of United States (Japanese) output growth (% per year)

Source of growth	1980–9	1989–95	1995–2001	1995–2003*
Output	3.38 (3.98)	2.43 (2.39)	3.76 (1.89)	3.56 (1.28)
Labor input	1.33 (1.29)	0.98 (0.00)	1.12 (−0.32)	0.67 (−0.32)
IT capital	0.45 (0.47)	0.49 (0.37)	0.99 (0.79)	0.88 (0.54)
Non-IT capital	1.08 (1.21)	0.70 (1.29)	1.11 (0.57)	1.01 (0.62)
Total factor productivity	0.52 (1.01)	0.26 (0.83)	0.55 (0.90)	0.99 (0.45)
Total factor productivity from IT production	0.23 (0.19)	0.23 (0.20)	0.49 (0.43)	0.46 (0.36)
Total factor productivity from non-IT production	0.29 (0.82)	0.03 (0.63)	0.06 (0.42)	0.53 (0.10)

Source: Jorgenson *et al.*, 2005, table 3.15; * from Jorgenson and Motohashi, 2005, tables 4 and 5. Japanese data in ( ).

It is apparent that in the United States output growth had begun to accelerate in 1995. This contrasts sharply with Japan where the growth rate declined in the latter half of the 1990s. Particularly notable is that in the United States labor inputs grew at approximately 1% per year whereas they declined in Japan.[3] Capital inputs, both IT and non-IT, grew more rapidly in the second half of the 1990s in the United States than in Japan. In recent years, total factor productivity has taken opposing paths in the United States and in Japan. Between 1995 and 2003 total factor productivity increased sharply in the United States to an annual rate of 0.99, more than twice that of Japan. The principal difference is in total factor productivity associated with the non-IT sectors where the figure for the United States is only 0.53 while in Japan it is only 0.10. Jorgenson *et al.* (2005) conclude "that a powerful surge in investment in information technology and equipment after 1995 ... accounts for a large portion of the resurgence in U.S. economic growth" and that there was after 1995 "a jump in total productivity growth of the IT producing industries" (p. 84). Oliner and Sichel (2000) also found that the productivity gains of the 1990s could be explained as a result of increased capital inputs, much of this undoubtedly in the form of IT equipment, and as a consequence of gains in factor productivity.[4]

Jorgenson *et al.* (2005) find it useful to distinguish between three categories of industries—the IT-producing industries including computers and computer services, the IT-using industries including services, and the non-IT industries that include most manufacturing industries and retail and wholesale trade.[5] They point out that the four IT-producing industries produce only 3% of national output but have been responsible for about one quarter of the 1990s' growth resurgence in the United States. The IT-using sectors account for a quarter of GDP and a corresponding fraction of the growth resurgence, while the non-IT sectors account for 70% of GDP but only half of the growth resurgence. The distinctions between the groups of industries are useful, particularly between IT-producing industries and the others. Much recent progress in the United States has been from gains in productivity in the non-IT industries. This has involved use of IT and logistical methods in trading and service activities that have not been traditionally related to information technology. These are particularly the fields of banking, finance, and retail and wholesale trade.

Where the information technology industry was directly important in US economic progress throughout the period, the explanation appears to change materially in recent years. In the 1990s gains in multifactor productivity were associated with production of IT equipment. There was, moreover, heavy investment in ever more productive new IT equipment (Jorgenson and Stiroh, 2000; Oliner and Sichel, 2000; Basu *et al.*, 2003). Bart van Ark, a professor at Groningen University, is quoted with an interesting distinction between the 1990s and the years since 2001: "Looking back at the late 1990s, it was more of an investment boom... from 2000 onwards, it is not an investment story—it is a productivity story" (*Financial Times*, August 18, 2006, p. 7).

Moreover, the differences between rapid growth in United States and less rapid growth in Europe (a story similar to that in Japan) are being explained by productivity improvements in just three sectors: retail, wholesale, and finance.[6] Such findings are implicit in the work of Basu *et al.* (2003) who show recent productivity growth rates of around 5% per year in these fields, much faster than in other service or industrial activities, except for the IT-producing industries.[7] This is not altogether surprising since these are the fields where modern logistic and merchandising methods and e-business have become increasingly widespread. It is important to stress that because of the large size of the service fields relative to the IT producing industries, services play a predominant role in the growth of aggregate multifactor productivity. In this regard Bosworth and Triplett (2004) note that "The retail trade sector has been the largest single contributor to the post-1995 resurgence of productivity growth" (Chapter 4, p. 1). That may not have happened to the same degree in Japan.

The role of policy in Japanese economic performance

The need to accelerate cyclical recovery and, indeed, to speed up the long-term growth of the Japanese economy is the fundamental challenge of policymaking. We consider Japanese economic policy during the stagnation period and beyond.

Revisiting Japan's policy of the 1990s

In the 1990s, the results of Japan's macroeconomic policy seemed completely opposite to what happened in the United States. In Japan, business investment grew slowly and public works expenditures increased rapidly in contrast to reductions in government spending (in defense expenditures) and rapid growth of business investment in the United States (Table 2.7). The Japanese national government expanded its fiscal size, while private business sectors contracted their investment. In fact, from 1992 to 1999, the government enacted supplemental

Table 2.7 Annual % changes of selected GDP components in Japan and the United States

	Japan				*United States*			
	GDP	*Business investment*	*Government expenditures*	*Public works*	*GDP*	*Business investment*	*Government expenditure*	*Defense expenditure*
1980s	3.8	7.8	1.3	−0.2	3.0	3.3	3.0	4.7
1990s	1.7	0.8	3.1	4.7	3.0	6.9	1.4	−2.4
2000–6	1.0	−0.5	2.2	2.9	3.6	9.0	1.4	−2.5

Source: Authors' calculation.

Table 2.8 Growth of nominal investment in information technology (annual % changes)

	1981–5	*1986–90*	*1991–5*	*1996–2000*
Investment in IT	18.7	14.5	2.2	7.2
Hardware	17.6	10.0	2.6	5.3
Software	34.0	40.0	2.0	12.9
Investment in IT	14.0	5.6	8.7	13.2
Hardware	12.8	2.5	7.6	10.8
Software	19.2	14.5	10.8	17.0

Source: Selected data from Shinozaki (2003), p. 94, tables 5–7.

budgets 11 times for additional public works, aiming at rebooting the economy. The government, however, could not attain its policy goal nor bail the economy out of its economic slump in the 1990s.

The Japanese government did not have clear visions of the information age.[8] A combination of macroeconomic public works policies and lack of appropriate industrial policy in Japan gave business sectors an incorrect signal so that the government encouraged businesses related to public works instead of high technology venture businesses. Moreover, private business sectors embraced the incentives for receiving easy money from the government rather than earning profits from market competition by producing goods and services that met consumers' and industries' updated demands.

Consequently, Japanese private sectors missed dynamic business trends in the midst of the information technology revolution and hesitated to take business risks and invest in the new technology. The statistics on Japanese business investment in information technology (Table 2.8) show that the growth of investment in the IT fields fell to low levels between 1991 and 2000. It seems that economic resource allocation in the "lost decade" was more focused on conservative sectors promoted by government spending than on innovative private business sectors.

While industrial development during the period of rapid growth of the 1950s and 1960s was clearly policy driven with focus of government plans on particular critical industries, at a later time Japanese economic policy was more strongly directed to macroeconomic rather than industrial objectives. Fiscal and monetary policy responses to the slowdown in the 1990s sought to use traditional Keynesian policy stimulus. But these policies showed a surprising lack of success and, indeed, created additional difficulties that, in part, lie behind continued stagnation.

Krugman's (1998) view that Japan's monetary policy problem represented an old-fashioned liquidity trap has gained considerable acceptance.[9] The basic facts are that the Bank of Japan could drive the nominal interest rate only down for a very low level, 0–1%. At the same time, prices had begun to fall in view of recessionary conditions and the appreciation of the yen. The real interest rate, equal to the nominal interest rate less the expected rate of price decline, remained positive, indeed it increased. The result was, on one hand, the lack of the desired monetary stimulus and, on the other, a lack of profitability for the banking system, due to extremely low interest rates. As Krugman points out, in a liquidity trap monetary policy actions are ineffective because there is no way to reduce real interest rates in the absence of inflationary expectations.

Inadequate regulation of the banking system and a reluctance to consolidate insolvent banks was another failure of monetary policy. It was not until 2001 that Japanese authorities sought the cleanup of bank balance sheets and the consolidation of banks.

With respect to fiscal policy, as we have noted, Japanese authorities repeatedly introduced new fiscal packages that followed a strategy of public works spending on building bridges, roads, and municipal facilities at a rapid rate. On the revenue side, the consumption tax was reduced in 1996, but temporarily. These policy actions have minimum payout in terms of productivity though clearly they seem to have had some impact on aggregate output, first positive then negative in 1998 and 1999. Since expenditures exceeded revenues by more than 5% of GDP, they rapidly raised the ratio of outstanding public debt to nominal GDP to 170%. The Ministry of Finance became increasingly anxious in an effort to increase taxes and reduce expenditure. Seeking to improve the situation, the consumption tax was returned to its earlier level in 1997. As many economists predicted, the Japanese economy followed with another dip of recession.

High levels of public works expenditures account for a large national internal fiscal deficit. The large public debt that has been accumulated is often seen as an obstacle to further fiscal stimulus. There is concern about the ability of the Bank of Japan to find financing for this debt and for the growing burden of the interest payments.

Other dimensions of policy, focused on industrial and/or structural elements, must also be considered. During the 1990s, Japan extended its deregulation policy to cover a broad range of industries that had previously been partially or fully regulated. These included transportation, communication, energy, finance, insurance and real estate. A significant program restructuring the banking system, the Big Bang, was introduced in the period since 2000 and strong efforts were made at the behest of then Finance Minister Heizo Takenaka to deal with the banks' NPL problem.

Blomstrom *et al.* (2001) suggest that "deregulation in Japan has followed a uniquely Japanese model, just as regulation assumed uniquely Japanese forms" (p. 8). Privatization of large public service enterprises was left incomplete in many cases, allowing the government to continue to hold part interests and probably also, control. While firms' ability to adjust prices and to enter new markets increased, some of the mechanisms for administrative guidance still exist. "While the heavy hand of the regulator has been lifted from the controls, the administrative apparatus still works in the background" (Blomstrom *et al.*, 2001). La Croix and Mark (2001) survey the substantial deregulation that occurred during the 1990s in transportation, telecommunications, electricity, and retail sales. Japan followed other countries in breaking up its national monopolies in transportation and communication. Nevertheless, large fractions of these activities are still controlled by one or a small number of national firms that are not subject to strong competitive pressures.

Retail trade is an entirely different question because so much of Japanese retail trade is in the hands of small companies with fewer than five employees. The Large-Scale Retail Store Law was originally intended to protect small neighborhood stores from competition of large firms with scale economies. It was eliminated in 1997 under pressure from the United States. Some have argued that regulatory change has accelerated discounting and stimulated imports (Fahy and Taguchi, 1995) but others (La Croix and Mark, 2001). feel that barriers to entry remain high in many fields. There remain many possibilities for privatization and/or for increasing competition that may pay off in increased efficiency and productivity.

The current situation and prospect

In the period since 2000, there appear to be signs of modest recovery with GDP growth averaging 1.5% per year. But this is clearly not a fast enough growth path

Table 2.9 Long-run forecasts for major countries

	Five year averages % per year				
	2001–5	*2006–10*	*2011–15*	*2016–20*	*2020–5*
Real GDP					
Japan	1.5	2.1	1.6	1.1	0.9
United States	2.6	3.0	2.8	3.0	2.9
United Kingdom	2.3	2.7	2.5	2.3	2.3
Eurozone	1.4	1.9	1.6	1.7	1.6
Russia	6.1	4.6	3.9	3.6	3.3
China	8.5	8.6	7.2	6.4	6.1
GDP Deflator					
Japan	−1.4	1.1	2.0	1.1	2.7
United States	2.3	2.0	1.8	1.9	2.0
United Kingdom	2.5	2.5	2.3	2.2	2.2
Eurozone	2.1	1.8	1.7	1.6	1.6
Russia	17.1	13.6	5.1	4.0	3.5
China	3.2	3.8	3.3	3.3	3.3

Source: Global Insight *World Overview*: First Quarter 2006, Waltham MA: Global Insight.

and there is fear that even this modest growth cannot be sustained. Only in the past couple of years has the unemployment rate shown a modest decline. Prices *fell* in a deflationary mode and hourly earnings were weak though, again, there have been modest increases in the past couple of years. These developments occurred despite substantial policy stimulus and the fact that the current foreign account surplus continued to be large and even growing.

In 2006 with signs of economic recovery and a return to price increase, albeit very modest, the Bank of Japan began again to increase interest rates and the Ministry of Finance began again to consider raising the consumption tax, the controversy to which we have referred.

Looking ahead, the Japanese slow growth scenario has been widely adopted. Recent forecasts for Japan and for other major world countries are summarized in Table 2.9. These are forecasts prepared on the basis of standard procedures by Global Insight Inc., a major US econometric forecasting firm. They suggest that, in the absence of significant policy changes, the Japanese economy will continue on a slow growth path with low inflation compared to significantly higher growth elsewhere in the world. While it is not surprising that growth projections for less advanced countries, like China and Russia, are high as compared to Japan, we note that the long-run forecast for Japan is low even compared to mature countries like the United States, the United Kingdom, and the European Union.

3 The challenges to Japanese economic growth

There are a number of important challenges to Japanese economic growth. If the Japanese economy is to grow more rapidly, public policy must take these into account.

- The Japanese economy is mature and must seek to adapt to the new technologies.
- The Japanese population and labor force is aging.
- Japan has a heavy public debt burden.
- Japan's role in the world economy is changing.

Japan's economic maturity and the new technologies

Economic maturity has its advantages and disadvantages. In the case of Japan it means that many Japanese industries are operating at the technological frontier, that Japanese per capita incomes are very high, and that Japan has a stable urban living pattern. Important dimensions of the "new economy" are already in place in Japan. On the other hand, further rapid progress becomes difficult as Japanese labor costs are high and non-competitive in many fields, as opportunities for automation have already been exhausted, and as large established business firms lack flexibility in their operations. Moreover, as we have noted, the Japanese economy has sectors that have failed to attain the scale of operation or the technological skills that are available to twenty-first-century business.

Japanese business sectors must seek out and employ the technologies at the most advanced frontier. We would anticipate that technological change will contribute to productivity, though these effects have sometimes been difficult to quantify. Further progress can be expected not only in IT hardware and high-tech technology but particularly in applying IT systems in the service fields. While these are sectors where it is difficult to achieve productivity improvements, they are also fields where much potential remains.

Demographic trends and economic growth

The aging of the Japanese population and labor force is a very serious issue. In Japan birthrates have been low for many years. The labor force is aging rapidly.

Moreover, Japan has not had the influx of young immigrants that have augmented the labor force in Europe and North America.

Due to the demographic trends of an aging and decreasing population, pessimistic perspectives prevail about the long-term economic outlook for Japan. According to *Population Projections for Japan: 2001–2050*, prepared by the National Institute of Population and Social Security Research, total population will be decreasing at a rate ranging from 0.3% to 0.5% annually over the next few decades. The working-age population, ages 15 to 64, is estimated to decrease faster—at a pace ranging from 0.7% to 0.9% annually (Table 3.1). This demographic trend affects the annual growth rate of the economy, which will be reduced by as much as 0.9%.

The Japanese government places great emphasis on the importance of policy packages that raise the declining birth rate, but it is unlikely that any measures can quickly mitigate and reverse this trend. Moreover, it takes a generation for new-born babies to become a productive workforce even if the birth rate rises immediately. In the end, it is productivity improvement that must compensate for the declining demographic trend. Based on the medium variant of population projections, productivity would need to grow 3.5–4.0% annually to make up for the 0.5–0.9 percentage point contraction of the demographic trend and to achieve a 3% growth target for the entire economy.

Immigration could also contribute to the growth of the labor force, as it does in the United States and Western Europe. While Japan could gain by attracting immigrants with high levels of education and/or significant capital, as do many other countries, it is unlikely that such people would be numerous enough to make a large contribution to the growth of the labor force. Indeed, problems of language and social adjustment stand in the way of securing and accommodating a large inflow of such immigrants. Immigration of unskilled workers would be more feasible from populous countries in East Asia, like China, but it is unlikely

Table 3.1 Demographic trends in Japan

Periods	Mean age (years)	Total population (annual % change)	Working-age population (annual % change)
1960s (actual)	30.3	1.1	1.8
1970s (actual)	32.7	1.2	1.0
1980s (actual)	35.8	0.6	0.9
1990s (actual)	39.5	0.3	0.0
2000s (projection)	43.0	0.0	−0.5
2010s (projection)	45.9	−0.3	−0.9
2020s (projection)	48.2	−0.5	−0.7

Source: Shinozaki (2005a), National Institute of Population and Social Security Research (2002).

Note
Projections of the mean age and annual percent changes of both total and working-age population are based on the medium variant estimation.

for social and political reasons that Japan would want to draw in large numbers of such an immigrant labor force.

As the population ages, the ratio of retired population to working population increases so that the burden of pension payments and health benefits becomes heavier. This problem is aggravated as life expectancy becomes longer. Thus, the demographic cycle leads toward a declining labor force, an aging population, and a heavy retirement benefit and health care cost burden of older people. This is happening much earlier in Japan than in other mature countries, light years ahead of other East Asian countries.

The fiscal challenge

The heavy social burden of an aging population further complicates the already difficult fiscal position of the Japanese government. Slow growth of nominal GDP means slow growth of tax receipts. In turn, that makes it difficult to provide social benefits and/or public works expenditures which in the past have been used to support a laggard economy. The fiscal deficit has been running between 6% and 8% of nominal GDP. As a result, as we have noted, the outstanding public debt represents close to 170% of GDP. It is not clear whether this represents a significant burden, in view of the fact that the outstanding bonds are held in many cases by public institutions. But there is a strong feeling among government officials that the growth of the public debt must be kept in check and that, if necessary, taxes should be raised to control the fiscal deficit. The challenge to accomplishing the budgetary objective is complicated by the fact that increasing taxes may result in a lower nominal GDP, thwarting the objective of a lower debt to nominal GDP ratio.

Japan's changing trade pattern

As we have noted in the previous chapter, Japan has maintained a competitive position in many of its export markets, though we have some evidence of change. The rapid growth of low-wage competitors in Asia threatens to change Japan's position in the world economy. Japan can compete as a producer of mass production consumer products only with considerable difficulty. Most of these are produced more competitively in Korea and Taiwan and, most recently, in China. Indeed, the Japanese economy is readjusting to import products from these countries, many of them produced by affiliates of Japanese firms. This trend is likely to continue so that Japan will become principally an exporter of the very highest tech products and capital goods.

The challenge for Japan's future development internationally lies in securing its role as the dominant supplier of high-tech capital goods to other countries of Asia and as an importer of consumer products produced in that part of the world. The integration of the Japanese economy with the East Asian market promises significant dividends.

The Japanese economy going forward: the alternatives

For the long-term future, we can visualize a Japan that continues on its current policy track. This is likely to be a Japan that is growing slowly, that is falling behind in the race with other East Asian countries. In the short-run, this may be an acceptable situation as Japanese incomes are high, unemployment has moderated, and the level of urban amenities has been greatly improved. Unfortunately, this weakens the case for policy change. Politicians who are concerned about the current status of their constituents and bureaucrats who worry about the outstanding government debt may seek to avoid new policy measures. Unfortunately in the longer run, the demographic, budgetary, and trade challenges that we have noted earlier are likely to further reduce Japanese economic growth. In the absence of new policies, heavy burdens will fall on the younger generations who will be the principal workers and earners in the middle of the century.

Alternatively, we may see policies that will accelerate Japanese growth, taking advantage of the new potentials being developed in the IT industry and in the application of their products. This will require, as we have noted, new aggregate fiscal and monetary policy, new approaches to market and competition policy, as well as possibly some industry-specific targeting. A more detailed discussion of specific measures follows in Chapter 13.

4 The IT/E-business revolution and globalization

Implications of the New Economy for Japan

Technical change, the IT revolution lies behind the developments that are fundamentally changing the economy of Japan and of its trading partners. In this section, we discuss the nature of the IT/E-business revolution. We shall see that the transformation is far greater than simply the development of new technologies and their application to production processes in the IT industries. The revolution influences *what* is being produced, *where* it is being produced, and *how* it is being produced. It affects many conventional industries and service activities. It is a driving force in the global reallocation of production of many products from the advanced countries to the less-developed countries and, particularly, to East Asia.

These forces have had profound implications. In the domestic Japanese economy some firms are world leaders. Japanese firms like Sony and Matsushita have actively participated by developing advanced products and by selling them in world markets. But the IT revolution has also produced serious competitors elsewhere in East Asia in electronics and autos, for example—Lenovo in China, LG, Hyundai, and Kia, in South Korea, and so on. Moreover, in Japan, the IT revolution has not been translated fully into productivity improvements. Some important domestic Japanese sectors, like distribution and financial services that account for a very large share of Japanese GDP, have lagged behind developments elsewhere.

Defining the IT revolution

There had been numerous definitions of the IT revolution. Perhaps the most comprehensive summary is that of Lester Thurow (2003):

> We now live in a period of time historians of the future will call the third industrial revolution. Leaps forward and interactions between six key technologies (microelectronics, computers, telecommunications, man-made materials, robotics, and biotechnology), are once again sending the economy off in new directions. Collectively, these technologies and their interactions are producing a knowledge-based economy that is systematically changing how we conduct our economic and social lives. (p. 30)

Other definitions have emphasized brain work in place of manual labor, rapid technological change, applications in conventional commerce and E-business and increased international competition (Friedman, 2005). The essential features of the revolution, that apply in Japan as well as in other countries, can be listed as follows:

- Creation of new technologies and their application.
- Network communication.
- Expanded range of competition, nationally and internationally.
- Change in international comparative advantage.

In the last 15 years, the period of slow growth and deflation in Japan and the crash of the dot.com bubble in the United States have cooled some of the initial enthusiasm for investments in new technologies and industries. But the underlying technological trends in hardware and software are worldwide and have proceeded in Japan as elsewhere in the world. In some production activities and, certainly, in the world of wireless communication, Japan has continued to lead the way. The rest of East Asia has largely been a follower in these developments, albeit a very rapid one. East Asian countries are rapidly integrating their economies with Japan and other advanced countries. Some of the smaller East Asian countries like Singapore, Korea, and Taiwan have become IT leaders and specialized producers of IT products like chips and flat screens but the most populous countries in the region, like China and Indonesia, have focused on traditional consumer goods like clothing and small electronics where they have comparative advantage since they are low-wage countries and still lag behind in the technological revolution. They play a massive role in the changes that are affecting trade with Japan and the other industrial countries.

Characteristics of the IT revolution

Before we introduce a new type of production function as a new framework to analyze the effect of the IT revolution on the economy, we should distinguish IT progress from traditional technological progress brought on by inventions such as electricity and the internal combustion engine.

Traditional technological progress is often called "muscle strengthening" technological progress. This is because the new technology enables people to lift heavier things and to go farther more quickly. In contrast to traditional technological innovation, the IT revolution is "brain strengthening" technological progress enabling the user to communicate, count, and act, often without human interaction, more quickly and over longer distances.

It took many years for traditional inventions to be widely disseminated and used as new capital replaced old machinery during each stage of the industrial revolution. The IT revolution has introduced changes much more rapidly than past industrial revolutions. An example of the speed of IT technological change is "Moore's Law" discovered by Intel co-founder Gordon E. Moore. He found that the number of transistors embedded in a chip was likely to double every 18 to 24 months suggesting that output would increase with incredible rapidity.

While improvements in computer performance have not been nearly as rapid as Moore's Law might suggest, once the basic framework is in place, progress is often radical and astonishingly fast. Moreover, the IT revolution is still in full swing.

Intellectual material, often termed *knowledge*, is a central ingredient of new economy products. It may take the form of technical advances embodied in machines or production processes. It may also be in the form of computer programs or "content" such as video or music. It may involve communications, logistics, and business processes.

Many IT developments represent disruptive innovations (Christenson, 2000) rather than gradual adjustments. One can well imagine the radical changes in business operations—technology, organization, management procedures—that are required when production changes from electromechanical products to microelectronics or from analog devices to modern digital systems. The changes involved in switching back-office operations or order-taking from human staff interactions to automatic web-based computer operations are enormous. This is not just a small adjustment, particularly if an enterprise already has a working legacy system. This has important implications for competition, in that small nimble new firms have found it more easy to compete by adopting technological innovations than large successful organizations whose plant and equipment make use of an earlier generation of technology. As we will discuss at greater length in Chapter 8, there may be implications as well for the optimal organizational structure. Integrated organizations, as are often seen in Japan, may find adjustment more difficult compared to more modular organization types found in other countries like the United States.

The IT business fields offer opportunities for dynamic Schumpeterian competition (Schumpeter, 1942). For many products, technological innovations or refinements are being made continually. Standard specifications have not yet been finalized. This is an invitation to product differentiation and what Schumpeter called "creative destruction." New products or new features compete with existing products, driving their producers out of business or forcing them to upgrade their products in turn. There are, however, also cases where dominance of the market by existing producers or by public regulatory standards impedes competition.

Many of the products of the new economy have been initiated by new entrepreneurial companies. These require venture capital and involve a high degree of risk. The availability of risk-bearing capital from venture capital firms and an entrepreneurial spirit have been an advantage for new IT and E-business firms in the United States.

The IT revolution has brought about the dramatic decline in the price of high-tech equipment such as PCs and chips and computing power. That is the basis for the rapid proliferation of the IT revolution. The best example is the dramatic decline in the price of memory chips. If the price index of a memory chip is assumed to be 1.0 in 1992, going backward in time, the comparative price index in 1974 would have been 1778 and, going forward in time, by 1996 the price index was 0.47. Imagine the combination of this dramatic decline in the price of memory chips with the rapidly improving speed of the microprocessor. In 1997 Denis Gauthier said "If the same technological progress occurred with automobiles for the past 20 years, the price of a car would only be $5 and it would run 250,000 miles on a gallon of gas."[1] Significant cost reductions and increases in speed have also occurred in transportation and communications. These have been critical considerations in the development of an international supply chain where parts are produced in one country, assembled in another, and sold in still another country.

The new technologies have important applications in conventional fields as well as in high-technology products. The use of computers and Internet connections greatly increases efficiency and reduces the cost of distributing conventional products. In many cases, like banking, stock trading, even the purchase of movies and books, the transaction can be carried out electronically. But even when physical delivery is required or when physical products are being manufactured and assembled, the applications of IT can greatly increase productivity in non-IT sectors. Many such applications have increasing returns to scale.

"Metcalfe's Law" is as important as "Moore's Law" in the IT revolution.[2] Metcalfe's law is "The more people there are on a network, the greater the value of the network to each user." The law was named after Robert Metcalfe, a founder of 3Com, who said that the value of a network is proportional to the square of the number of users. For example, an additional PC in a network system increases benefits more than the last PC. This means there is the possibility that the marginal product of IT has increasing returns. This characteristic may reflect externalities and "economies of scale."

The IT revolution must change some assumptions that are usually made when we analyze the traditional economy. Marginal cost usually increases in the old economy as volume increases. On the other hand, although it may initially cost a lot to develop new software, it is not costly to make an additional copy and costs do not increase when more copies are made. On the contrary, the additional cost is in copying the original software and packaging the copy. The more the software is copied, the lower the average cost to produce and, often, to use the software. And the more widely the software is distributed and used for communication, the greater the benefit of each additional copy. Economies of scale and increasing returns in IT producing or using sectors are a central part of the present stage of the IT revolution.

Externalities are also typical of knowledge acquisition from R & D or from learning by doing. The knowledge embedded in the new technologies, sometimes termed the "ideas," is a non-rival good in the sense that, once developed, an idea can be used by many users without reducing the available supply. In contrast to ordinary economic goods, one person's use of new technology does not reduce its availability to others. While some ideas are public goods, available to all with little or no restrictions, others are the intellectual property of the patent holders (Warsh, 2006). A vast and rapidly growing body of knowledge, some originating in Japan as well as in many other countries, can be drawn on to make technical improvements. Once an initial high-tech base has been established, externalities and learning by doing (and large scale) will promote efficiency and further growth.

The IT revolution spills over worldwide, from one country to many others. Once new equipment or software is developed, it will be used in many countries. But there are some basic requirements in order to use the new IT equipment effectively. Appropriate IT infrastructure must be available and there must be a sufficiently skilled labor force to set up and maintain the system. For technological progress to be effective, people must be trained to utilize the new technologies. Unskilled people without computer training will not make effective use of advanced IT though, perhaps surprisingly, standardized programs may make it possible to carry out sophisticated functions with limited training and skill. That means that high levels of education are required only in industries that seek to adapt themselves to the frontier of the IT revolution. It is possible to extend the advantages of IT to sectors like services and agriculture that traditionally have operated with low levels of technology, though the availability of skilled technicians may be essential to set up and maintain the operating system.

Culture and business organization may also play an important role. The ability of business people and business organizations to adapt their way of working to the IT revolution is a key to success.

The IT revolution has dramatically changed the transactions between businesses, known as B2B (business to business) and between businesses and consumers (B2C). Information services have become an important input factor in producing output.[3] Automatic computer equipment can frequently handle transactions that previously required human intervention. This has significant implications for productivity. Electronic communication can greatly reduce the costs of carrying out transactions—selecting, ordering, payment. It may also affect the organization of production, in that reduced transaction costs facilitate outsourcing (Coase, 1937). The modern supply chain between independent organizations located in different parts of the world is greatly facilitated by the reduced costs of communications and shipment.

Traditionally, technological progress has been treated as an exogenous factor. This is called "disembodied technical progress," which applies equally and alike to all resources of workers and machines in current use. This means such technological progress represents technical know-how "falling, like manna, from heaven." This view of technological progress measures gains in productivity as a residual that cannot be explained by capital stock and labor inputs. IT innovation, however, is often embodied in new IT equipment. Therefore, IT technological progress should be explicitly related to measurable input factors such as capital intensity, human capital, IT capital stock, and should include allowance for increasing returns.

Steps of the IT/E-business revolution

The IT/E-business revolution involves a number of distinct steps. It is important to note that the steps need not be followed consecutively in each country where IT developments are employed. Often what happens in one country can serve as the basis for new developments elsewhere in the world. But the development of

IT industries and/or the application of IT technology calls for a setting, both organizationally and policy-wise, that will encourage the use of advanced techniques.

Technology is an essential ingredient of many new economy operations in modern economies. This means that the technology must be developed first. Technology is geographically mobile and can originate anywhere in the world. Important new IT technologies have been developed in Japan. Much technology that was developed in the United States and Europe is used in Japan. And, in turn, important technological developments that originated in Japan are used in Europe and America. Some of these technologies involve new sophisticated products, some apply to production methods, and some are software. New technology can originate in the research laboratories of large companies, or, as frequently in United States, it can come from independent entrepreneurs financed by venture capital.

The educational level and culture in a country are important considerations in whether a particular country can utilize the IT revolution effectively.[4] Since the IT network connects globally, English-speaking countries have more benefits than do non-English speaking countries. Flexibility in a firm's organization as well as in the labor market is also important in adapting to and taking advantage of the new technologies.[5] For example, can a company cut costs dramatically by laying off workers and introducing IT? Or, if two companies merge to gain economies of scale with IT, and if workers from each company still stick to their own company's culture and do not meld with each other, the merged company can neither cut costs dramatically nor increase productivity growth.

Application of new technology involves creation of new high-technology products: digital cameras, advanced laboratory equipment, aircraft, and so on. Japanese industry has been a leader in many of these products, though in the case of many consumer products other East Asian countries have already assumed important positions. New technology has been the basis for establishing sophisticated new industries in Japan and in the other advanced East Asian countries. These developments have contributed to productivity, but in view of changing product specifications the gains attributable to them have frequently been difficult to measure.

The production of conventional products has also gained from the application of high technology. Even when conventional labor-intensive manufacturing techniques are used, advanced IT applications in logistics, inventory control, and transportation have the potential to greatly improve productivity in retail and wholesale distribution activities. Numerous examples such is the use of RFID tags, computerized logistical techniques developed by express carriers, containerization of shipments, simplified customs procedures, and so on, illustrate the potentials. The application of modern logistical techniques by large scale transport companies (FedEx) or marketers, pioneered in the United States by Wal-Mart, yields tremendous gains in productivity.

The ultimate step in this direction is, of course, E-business. The use of computer networks to permit transactions business to business and from consumers to business directly over the Internet has been growing rapidly and has reduced manpower requirements in fields like finance, wholesale and retail trade transactions, travel tickets and reservations, and some aspects of entertainment. In most countries, E-business is at an early stage but growing very rapidly. It promises further gains in measured productivity.[6] The potential for further development of these activities in Japan remains large.

Globalization and international trade patterns

Another way to look at recent developments is in terms of the vast changes in trade patterns that have been summarized with the term *globalization*. Globalization is the word for the increasing integration of world markets.

What are the relationships between the IT revolution and globalization? International trade has been a part of the world economy for many centuries. Tariffs and other barriers have been reduced gradually in the post-Second World War years. What has changed radically is the cost of communication and transportation. Not only have improved logistics greatly facilitated shipments of goods from one country to another. Perhaps, even more important, is the transfer of knowledge and finance from the advanced countries to the less-developed countries that have become important producers of consumer goods.

The critical consideration for participation in the world market is whether a country is able to produce goods that are competitive, both cost-wise and in terms of design and quality, with those produced in the advanced world. The vastly increased interaction between countries that has been made possible by the IT revolution means that today the knowledge and technology to produce high-quality products, meeting specific market requirements, are available in many parts of the world. Advanced logistic controls and inexpensive container transportation, or air transport, make possible direct shipments from sources in developing countries to markets in the rest of the world. The result is an increasingly broad competitive playing field (Friedman, 2005).

Off-shoring of intellectual service activities is the latest step in IT-based globalization. With the help of electronic networks, many firms are finding that they can place routine, and sometimes not so routine, intellectual service activities in low-cost foreign countries. In the United States, the classic example is the call center that responds to consumer inquiries from India rather than from Indiana. Recently off-shoring has been used to accomplish far more sophisticated tasks. A computer software firm in Boston sends its programming tasks to India at the close of the working day and receives the answers in the morning when work in Boston resumes. Some American hospitals are sending their x-ray pictures for medical evaluation in foreign countries. The availability of broadband communications on a worldwide basis makes these links possible. In each case the cost of achieving the work is much lower, sometimes only 1/10 of the cost of the United States. Typically, off-shoring operations call for use of the English-language. This gives Japanese firms a measure of protection since few foreign countries are able to deal in Japanese. However, low-cost competition by foreign technologists may ultimately affect the Japanese economy as well.

The impact of globalized competition on a mature economy like Japan takes several directions. These forces have some positive as well as negative implications.

- Increased competitive pressures on conventional consumer goods industries producing products that can be produced worldwide and that call of labor-intensive manufacturing.
- Reduced costs of imports and reduced inflationary pressures (particularly as measured by the CPI), permitting a higher rate of domestic utilization without excess inflationary pressure.
- Substitution of imported goods for conventional consumer products in which Japan is no longer competitive with neighboring East Asia.
- Increased opportunities for advanced high-tech products and sophisticated technological services to improve productivity at home and to serve export markets.

While Japan has been a late-comer in participating in the effort to import consumer goods, in recent years Japan has joined other countries in seeking a growing share of its needs for consumption products from foreign sources. In turn, other countries in East Asia have imported high-tech machinery, parts, and other necessary supplies from Japanese manufacturers. This is the basis for mutually beneficial East Asian trade. Japan is rapidly taking its place in the regional and global economy not only as a producer but also as a consumer.

The changes in the world economic environment involve important developments, some of them very costly for existing industries and some of them offering important opportunities. On one hand, low-cost foreign labor displaces domestic workers. On the other hand, consumers find that many imported goods are less expensive than corresponding domestic products. It is difficult sometimes to balance the interests of these two groups. There is much resistance to change. Policy decisions are often made on the basis of political judgments rather than in terms of realistic appraisal of economic alternatives. Public policies are needed to facilitate adjustments from "old" industries that are losing competitiveness to "new" industries whose position is improving and whose outlook is promising.

The challenge of a "new economy"

These developments mean that we are living in a new economy to which Japan, like the other developed countries, is adjusting. Whether this is really a new economy depends greatly on what is meant by the term. We can argue that the developments fundamentally change the economy in terms of its growth potentials, its application of technology and its geographic scope. As a result, we must visualize the economy in very different terms; a world of rapid productivity growth and increased dynamics and a broader scope of worldwide competition. But the basic rules of economics have not been revoked. Indeed, as the scope of competitiveness has increased, the rules of free market economics may be more important than they once were. The world economy is more wide-open and competitive then ever. (The implications of various organizational structures in this respect are considered in Chapter 8.)

This means that the challenge of the next decade for Japan will be to take advantage of the changes in the world economy and to use them to achieve a faster rate of growth than in the recent past. This calls for expanded participation of Japan in new economic environments. Internally, as we will explain later, this calls for further educational, research, and development spending and, importantly, entrepreneurship and financing. Japanese industry must be competitive in a dynamic world market. This calls for further development of the high-tech capital-intensive industries in which the Japanese economy has become a leader. Improving national productivity also requires improving the productive ability of conventional industries, those providing consumer goods and services and distributing them. These are precisely the fields where the pressures of labor requirements are the greatest and where the potential for productivity improvement is also greatest. Gains in productivity can also be achieved, by reducing production in low productivity fields or in fields where productivity potentials are limited such as some consumer goods, personal services and agriculture. The potentials of E-business need also to be further explored. Improved growth of total output and total factor productivity will allow the Japanese economy to expand more rapidly in the future.

5 IT and productivity growth
Theoretical and empirical framework

A framework of economic theory helps to explain the impact of IT on economic growth. It is important to integrate IT into the potential output side of the theoretical model since the new technology has impacts that are not taken into account in traditional production function models. This is particularly important in the case of Japan where reliance on new IT technology rather than conventional inputs is likely to be the heart of a rapid growth strategy.

Of course, output is not only determined by the supply potential. One must also consider aggregate demand considerations, but these are not materially different in the "new economy" than in conventional models. In this chapter, we first focus on the theory of production and then we will briefly take into account demand side considerations.

First, we present the traditional framework for measuring the potential output, which concludes that the growth of Japan's potential output is 1.5%.

Second, we show how the IT revolution is different from traditional technological development.

Third, we present a new framework that incorporates the characteristics of the IT revolution. This new framework suggests the possibility that IT will result in a higher potential output.

The traditional framework for measuring potential output

The growth of potential output means the highest sustainable economic growth rate without accelerating inflation. This is a supply-side concept in the sense that available productive inputs such as labor and capital stock are fully utilized.[1] In addition, technical progress plays an important role because technical progress itself can increase output with constant input of both labor and capital stock.

Potential output is traditionally measured as follows:

Real GDP (Y_t) is produced by two productive input factors such as capital stock (K_t) and labor (L_t) at time t. K_t consists of machines, telecommunication equipment, computers, structures and so on. L_t is labor input such as employed workers or man-hours. Then, the following relationship among Y_t, K_t, and L_t is assumed to hold; this is called an aggregate Cobb–Douglas production function.

$$Y_t = A_t * K_t^\alpha L_t^\beta \tag{1}$$

where A_t represents the level of technical progress at time t. But, there are no explicit time series data for A_t. Therefore, A_t is calculated as a residual in Eqn (1), given Y_t, K_t, and L_t. A_t is also termed "Total Factor Productivity" (TFP) because it measures productivity on a basis that allows for all inputs, that is, K_t and L_t.

α is termed the output elasticity with respect to K. It means that when K increases by 1%, output (Y) will increase by α%. Likewise, β is the output elasticity with respect to L. When L increases by 1%, output (Y) will increase by β%. In most cases, $\alpha + \beta = 1$ is assumed, that is, an assumption of "constant returns to scale." This means that if inputs of K and L double to $2K$ and $2L$, then output Y also doubles to $2Y$. If $\alpha + \beta > 1$ holds, it is termed "increasing returns to scale." This is because when input of K and L double, output Y will increase, more than doubling. The concept of the economies of scale will play an important role as the IT revolution develops.

Dividing real GDP (Y) by labor input (L) in Eqn (1) defines labor productivity, Eqn (2).

$$y_t = \frac{Y_t}{L_t} \tag{2}$$

We can transform Eqn (2) into the relationship among the growth rates of variables in Eqn (3). The dot on the variable means the growth rate of the variable.

$$\dot{Y}_t = \dot{y}_t + \dot{L}_t \tag{3}$$

Equation (3) shows that economic growth rate (real GDP growth rate) is expressed by the labor productivity growth rate and the growth rate of labor input. To be precise, we can calculate potential output by assuming the long-run labor productivity growth rate and the growth rate of the labor force.

Table 5.1 shows the growth rates of the real GDP, labor productivity, employed workers and the labor force for the 1995–2004 period in Japan. The last row is the average rate for each variable for the 10 years. The average growth rate of labor productivity is 1.43%. Although the average growth rate of the labor force is 0.0% over the entire period, the labor force has been declining since 1999. The average labor force growth rate during the period of 1999–2004 is -0.4%. According to Table 5.1, we have to conclude that Japan's potential output has averaged 1.43% and, pessimistically, we may project it near this rate. This is approximately the same as the 1.5% growth of potential output that the Japanese government, Cabinet Office, described in a report "Japan's Vision for the 21st Century" published in April 2005.

We should remember, however, that the past 10 years were a stagnant period for the Japanese economy. Although we take the average of the labor productivity growth rate for the 10 years, it is reasonable to assume that the cyclical factor in labor productivity growth was not excluded in the average growth rate.

Table 5.1 Growth rates of GDP, labor productivity, employment, and labor force (% per year)

	Real GDP	Labor productivity	Employed workers	Labor force
1995	2.01	1.96	0.06	0.32
1996	3.43	2.97	0.45	0.67
1997	1.81	0.71	1.09	1.13
1998	−1.04	−0.39	−0.65	0.09
1999	−0.14	0.66	−0.80	−0.20
2000	2.39	2.65	−0.25	−0.19
2001	0.21	0.75	−0.53	−0.21
2002	−0.30	0.99	−1.27	−0.93
2003	1.36	1.59	−0.22	−0.34
2004	2.67	2.47	0.20	−0.36
Average	1.24	1.43	−0.19	0.00

Source: Authors' calculation.

As Eqn (3) shows, in order to obtain higher potential output, we must raise labor input and/or labor productivity.

Increase in labor input

There are many possibilities for increasing labor input in Japan. These could involve drawing on the important share of Japan's population that is not in the labor force, for example, retired workers, non-working women, or young people. Alternatively Japan could draw on immigrants, low skill workers or, preferably, highly qualified professionals. These alternatives will be discussed at greater length in Chapter 13. A 0.5–1.0% annual increase in labor force may be possible.

It is important, also, to improve the quality of workers through training and education. The IT revolution makes the labor market borderless. A country operating in a globally competitive world needs an education strategy.

Raising labor productivity

As Eqn (3) shows, another way to raise potential output is to improve labor productivity. In order for Japan to achieve a higher potential output, labor productivity must be raised from 1.5% to 2.5%:

Labor productivity growth is written as Eqn (4) from Eqns (1) and (2).

$$y_t = A_t(k_t)^\alpha (L_t)^{(\alpha+\beta-1)} \tag{4}$$

Then,

$$k_t = \frac{K_t}{L_t} \tag{5}$$

k_t is called the capital intensity, which shows the capital stock to labor input ratio.

Transform Eqn (4) into Eqn (6), which shows the relationship among the growth rates of variables.

$$\dot{y}_t = \dot{A}_t + \alpha \dot{k}_t + (\alpha + \beta - 1)\,\dot{L}_t \tag{6}$$

Since we assume constant returns to scale, $\alpha + \beta = 1$ holds. Equation (6) is rewritten as Eqn (7).

$$\dot{y}_t = \dot{A}_t + \alpha \dot{k}_t \tag{7}$$

Equation (7) says that labor productivity is raised by the technical progress rate (or TFP) ($\dot{A}_t$) and α times the increase in capital intensity ($\alpha\,\dot{k}_t$).

We show Eqn (7) in Figure 5.1. Before technical progress occurs, a unit of product is made by labor input ($L1/Y1$) and capital stock ($K1/Y1$) at A. When technical progress occurs, isoquant I shifts to isoquant II by moving toward to the origin. And the product at B is made by fewer inputs, such as ($L2/Y2$) and ($K2/Y2$), than at A. Then, labor productivity improves from $Y1/L1$ to $Y2/L2$. But, capital intensity does not change. In addition, when more capital stock is used to substitute for labor inputs, the production point moves from B to C. Then labor productivity improves from $Y2/L2$ to $Y3/L3$ and capital intensity increases from k_1 to k_3.

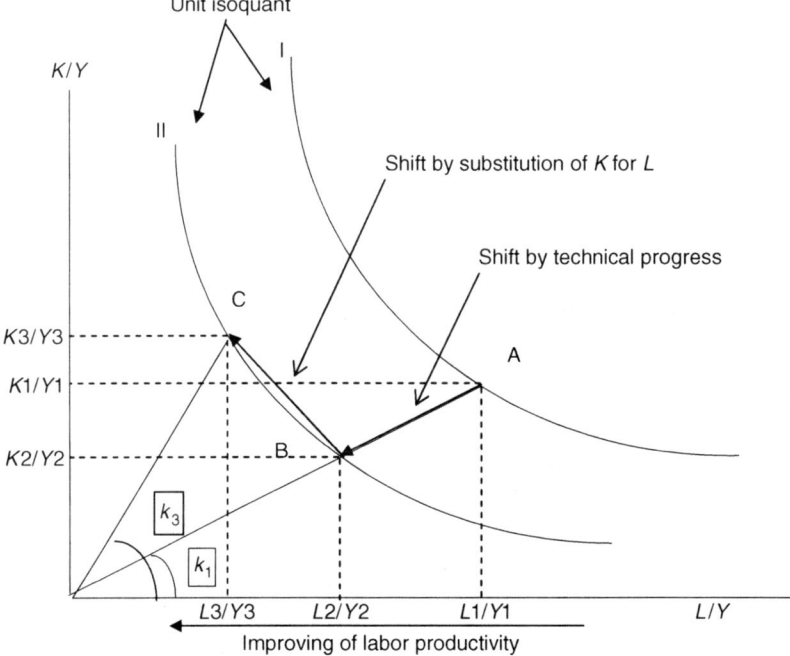

Figure 5.1 Shifts of unit isoquants by substitution and technical progress.

According to Jorgenson *et al.* (2005), the average TFP growth rate in the US economy was 0.26% for 1989–95 and 0.71% for 1995–2002. In short, technical progress in the United States every year after 1995 was faster by about 0.5% than before 1995. In addition, as seen in Figure 5.2, real investment in information processing grew at more than 15% per year during the period of 1995–2000. This contributed to increased capital intensity.

The method used to calculate TFP or technical progress as a residual in an aggregate production function is called the "Growth Accounting" approach. However, this approach may miss something important about the effect of the IT revolution on the economy.

An "S" type production function

When we consider the characteristics of the IT revolution, we consider the possibility of "economies of scale" when IT capital stocks or IT input services increase as well as when a new economy develops and people become accustomed to the IT revolution. Also, we have found that the United States has benefited more from the IT revolution than has Japan. We illustrate these points in Figure 5.3. And this figure will be very useful in determining how IT policies can raise potential output in Japan.

Figure 5.3 presents the relationship between IT capital stock and output. Other inputs such as labor and other capital stock are assumed to be constant. This is called an S-type production function because the curve looks like the letter "S." An S-type production function is more realistic than a traditional production function of Eqn (1), especially when new IT capital stock is being created and applied due to the invention of PCs, software and so on.

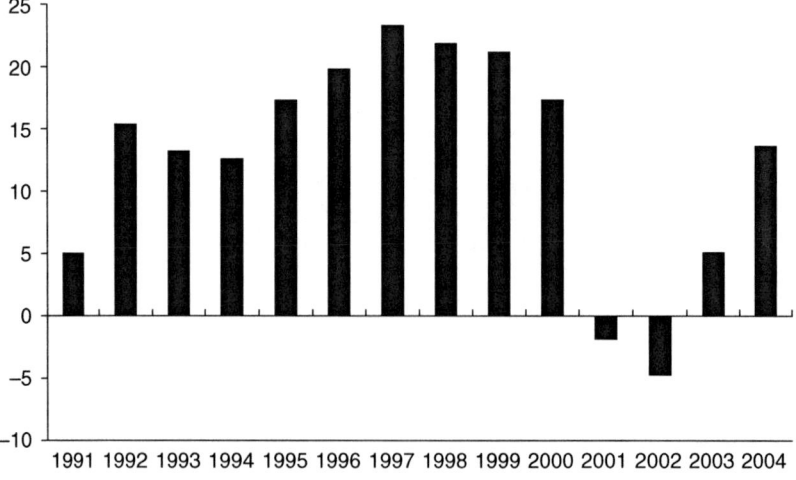

Figure 5.2 Real investment in information processing in the United States (%).

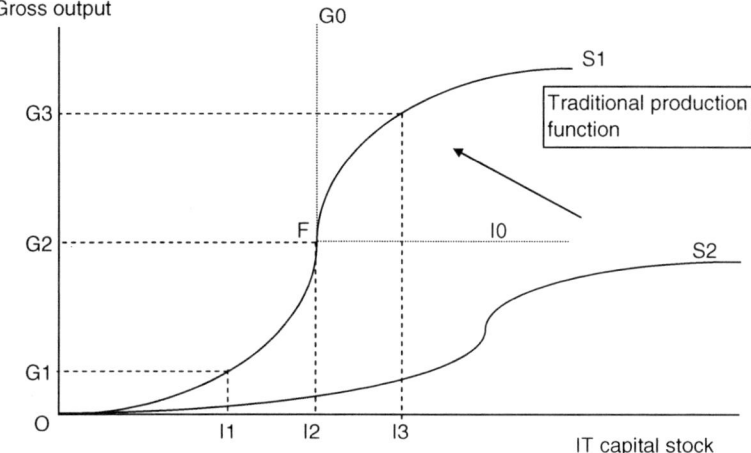

Figure 5.3 "*S*" type production function: relationship between output and IT capital stock.

This S-type production function can present the situation that when IT capital stock passes a threshold, its effect on the economy increases quickly. In Figure 5.3, this is apparent between I1 and I3 on a curve S1. But its effect will be small again after the curve reaches I3 where IT progress starts to mature.

A traditional production function of Eqn (1) shows the relationship between output and input in the phase of G0–F–I0. In this phase, marginal product always encounters decreasing returns. This is reasonable in an old economy. However, as Metcalfe's law implies, the marginal product of IT capital stock has increasing returns over a certain range of IT capital stock.

Without doubt, IT affects the economy significantly and will do so even more in the future. The question is how much does the introduction of IT affect productivity and the growth of potential output? The new economy will lead to economies of scale and raises the productivity growth rate. How many years the economy takes to take full advantage of IT depends on the specific situation in each individual country. In this respect, policy, industrial structure, and even culture may be important considerations. How quickly the marginal product starts to increase depends on the country. How wide is I1–I3, meaning how long the IT revolution takes to proliferate among people and to become fully established, may also differ between countries.

In Figure 5.3 one may assume that the S1 and S2 curves represent the US and the Japanese economies, respectively. Productivity growth in the United States started to rise in the late 1990s while it did not in Japan. The US economy has had more benefit from the IT revolution than Japan, suggesting that S1 is much steeper than S2. If we consider the S curves for South Korea, Singapore, and Taiwan, their S curves may be between S1 and S2.

Although people in both the United States and Japan use the same quality PCs and broadband, why is there such a difference between S1 and S2? The answer will explain the fact that labor productivity growth rose sharply in the United States in late 1990s but did not do so in Japan.

Estimating a new framework to analyze IT revolution

In order to analyze the effect of the IT revolution on the economy more correctly, Prof. Klein (2000) replaced a Cobb–Douglas production function (Eqn 1) by a generalized KLEM production function.[2]

$$X = K^{c(2)}L^{c(3)}M^{c(4)}\exp[t^{c(5)}]\exp[c(6)*K/(ITS*L)]$$
$$\exp[c(7)*(ITS)(I) - c(8)*L/(ITS*I)]\exp[c(1)] \tag{8}$$

where
X: Real Gross Output
K: Real Gross Total Capital Stock
L: Labor Input
M: Real All Intermediate Inputs, excluding Information Service Input (I)
ITS: Real Net Capital Stock of IT
I: Real Information Technology Service Input (B to B)
t: Time trend to proxy Disembodied Technology Change
He considered the following characteristics of the IT revolution in the generalized Cobb–Douglas production function:

1   Constant returns to scale $(\alpha + \beta = 1)$ is not assumed. We can therefore measure the economies of scale.
2   Both α and β are not assumed to be constant. Variable elasticity of production and variable elasticity of substitution over the range of inputs are permitted.
3   Real gross output is used for the real GDP. Information service flow as an intermediate input plays an important role in the production function.
4   Not only disembodied technical progress but also embodied technical progress is explicitly defined. Embodied technical progress is endogenously determined.

Prof. Klein applied this production function to the US automobile and parts sector and financial sector respectively (Klein *et al.*, 2003). Kumasaka and Tange applied a closely similar type of production function to the Japanese macroeconomy (Kumasaka and Tange, 2004)

$$X = K^{c(2)}L^{c(3)}M^{c(4)}\exp[t^{c(5)} + c(6)*K/(ITS*L) + c(7)*(ITS)(I)$$
$$- c(8)*L/(ITS*I) + c(1)] \tag{9}$$

In this form, one might consider technological change as having both disembodied and embodied elements. Disembodied technological change is indicated as exp $[t^{c(5)}]$ in Eqn (9). The functional form exp $[t^{c(5)}]$ for the time trend is used instead of the more common exp. $[c(5)*t]$ because it allows for a non-constant growth rate over time and is more likely to yield trend stationary dependent variables.

The functional form, $\exp[c(6)*K/(ITS*L)+c(7)*(ITS)(I)-c(8)*L/(ITS*I)]$, reveals embodied technological change. $[c(6)K/(ITS*L)]$ shows that embodied technological change depends on the capital/labor ratio with labor weighted by the information technology capital stock. $[c(7)*(ITS)^*(I)]$ means the interaction of ITS and I. $[-c(8)*L/(ITS*I)]$ indicates that the increase in ITS or I enhances the marginal productivity of labor. Embodied technological change would increase or decrease, depending on the interaction of the values of $c(6)$, $c(7)$, $c(8)$, K, ITS, I and L. The functional form for the information service input and information capital stock, depending on the coefficient value $c(7)$, specifically allows for an increasing marginal product of I and ITS over some initial range of I and ITS values.

By forming the natural logarithm of Eqn (9) we have the structural equation to be estimated:

$$\ln X = c(1)+c(2)*\ln K+c(3)*\ln L+c(4)*\ln M+t^{c(5)}+c(6)*K/(ITS*L)$$
$$+c(7)*ITS*I-c(8)*L/(ITS*I) \tag{10}$$

Thi. functional form was developed to remove the drawbacks in Eqn (9) in order to analyze the effect of IT on the economy. This is one of the several functional forms used to generalize the Cobb–Douglas production function (see Intriligator *et al.*, 1996). The implication of this generalization allows for the possibility of a variable returns to scale coefficient, as well as a variable elasticity of substitution. The estimation results of Eqn (10) are presented in Table 5.2.

We summarize the most relevant findings as follows:

(i) Marginal product of output with respect to IT capital stock is increasing returns. Figure 5.4 presents the two-period marginal product relationship, with all other variables at their 1995 values. Low values of information technology capital stock have a negative marginal product. But a threshold amount is required to reap the productivity benefits. Once that threshold is reached, further increases in IT capital stock generate increasing returns. Since Japanese IT capital stock probably exceeds this threshold, IT investment in the 2000s is likely to increase marginal productivity.

(ii) Output elasticities with respect to IT capital stock and IT service input increase as time passes and as inputs increase. In a traditional production function of Eqn (3), output elasticities with respect to both capital stock and labor input are assumed to be constant. But the output elasticity with respect to any input factor is variable in a generalized Cobb–Douglas production function. Table 5.3 shows the empirical result of the output (X: gross output) elasticity with respect to IT service input, which consists of software except customized software, data processing services and computer rental.

Table 5.2 Estimation result of Eqn (10)

Dependent Variable: LOG(X)
Method: Least Squares

Sample (adjusted): 1972–99
Included observations: 28 after adjusting endpoints
Convergence achieved after 14 iterations
LOG(X) = $C(1) + C(2)*LOG(K) + C(3)*LOG(L) + C(4)*LOG(M) + T^{\wedge}C(5)$
$\quad\quad + C(6)*K/(ITS*L) + C(7)*ITS*I - C(8)*L/(ITS*I)$
$\quad\quad + [AR(1) = C(90), AR(2) = C(91)]$

	Coefficient	Std. error	t-statistic	Prob.
$C(1)$	−0.276084	0.260899	−1.058203	0.3040
$C(2)$	0.145974	0.062030	2.353269	0.0302
$C(3)$	0.574868	0.104955	5.477281	0.0000
$C(4)$	0.493465	0.019587	25.19340	0.0000
$C(5)$	0.135757	0.050440	2.691475	0.0149
$C(6)$	0.035426	0.014596	2.427054	0.0259
$C(7)$	3.75E–05	1.74E–05	2.152280	0.0452
$C(8)$	0.015006	0.008011	1.873018	0.0774
$C(90)$	0.734080	0.214982	3.414610	0.0031
$C(91)$	−0.334931	0.206157	−1.624640	0.1216

R-squared	0.999783	Mean dependent variable	6.516679
Adjusted R-squared	0.999675	S.D. dependent variable	0.276268
S.E. of regression	0.004981	Akaike info criterion	−7.493724
Sum squared residuals	0.000447	Schwarz criterion	−7.017936
Log likelihood	114.9121	Durbin–Watson statistic	2.069789

Inverted AR Roots	0.37 + 0.45i	0.37 − 0.45i

Source: Authors' calculation.

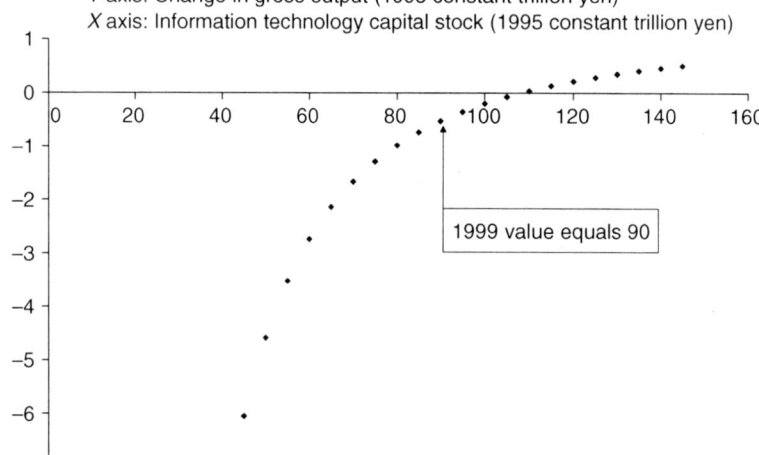

Y axis: Change in gross output (1995 constant trillion yen)
X axis: Information technology capital stock (1995 constant trillion yen)

1999 value equals 90

Figure 5.4 Two-period change in output given a 5 trillion yen increase in information technology capital stock: the Japanese Case.

Table 5.3 Output elasticity of gross output (X) with respect to IT service input (I)—the Japanese Case

All other variables held at actual values in 1985 and 1995

I	*Elasticity in 1985*	*Elasticity in 1995*
1	0.0086	0.0051
2	0.0055	0.0057
3	0.0050	0.0074
4	0.0052	0.0093
5	0.0056	0.0112
6	0.0061	0.0133
7	0.0068	0.0153
8	0.0074	0.0174
9	0.0081	0.0195
10	0.0088	0.0216
11	0.0096	0.0237
12	0.0103	0.0258

Source: Authors' calculations.

Note
Actual values of I are I (1970) = 0.68, I (1975) = 1.02, I (1980) = 2.04, I (1985) = 4.99, I (1990) = 5.08, I (1995) = 6.45, and I (1999) = 8.84.

Excluding the result of 0.086 in 1985, we find the following findings from Table 5.3:

- The elasticity of X with respect to IT service inputs becomes greater when IT service input becomes larger.
- The elasticity of X with respect to IT service inputs in 1995 is larger than that in 1985 even if the IT service input is unchanged.
- The elasticity of X with respect to IT service inputs will be larger as time passes.

Likewise, we can conclude the same things about IT capital stock (ITS) from Table 5.4.

ITS consists of information-related equipment, computer and peripheral devices, communication equipment and telecommunication facilities construction.

We make the following findings from Table 5.4

- The elasticity of X with respect to ITS becomes larger when ITS becomes larger.
- The elasticity of X with respect to ITS in 1995 is larger than that in 1985 even if ITS remains unchanged.
- The elasticity of X with respect to ITS becomes larger as time passes.

Prof. Klein's studies of the automobile and parts sector and of the financial service sector found similar results to those of the study about the Japanese macroeconomy.

Table 5.4 Output elasticity of gross output (*X*) with respect to IT
capital stock—the Japanese Case

All other variables held at actual values in 1985 and 1995

ITS	Elasticity in 1985	Elasticity in 1995
10	0.0088	0.0216
20	0.0165	0.0428
30	0.0245	0.0641
40	0.0325	0.0855
50	0.0406	0.1069
60	0.0486	0.1284
70	0.0567	0.1500
80	0.0648	0.1716
90	0.0729	0.1932
100	0.0810	0.2149
200	0.1626	0.4344
300	0.2449	0.6586

Source: Authors' calculation.

Note
Actual Values of ITS are ITS (1970) = 1.30, ITS (1975) = 6.23, ITS
(1980) = 11.14, ITS (1985) = 21.59, ITS (1990) = 35.03, ITS (1995) =
56.65, and ITS (1999) = 89.90.

Economies of scale

Although constant returns to scale are assumed in a traditional production
function, we can measure the economies of scale in a new production function.
We already found that the marginal product of *X* with respect to IT capital stock
(ITS) will increase in the 2000s in Japan. Also the elasticities of *X* with respect to
both ITS and IT service inputs (I) will be greater when ITS and I become larger
as well as when time passes. These findings imply that the Japanese economy
may show increasing returns to scale in the 2000s.

Figure 5.5 shows how much in percentage terms X (real gross output) grows
when all inputs grow at an annual rate of 10% from 1995.

*   Economies of scale in Japan have been increasing gradually since 1996. The
    Japanese economy had scale economies of 2–3% in the late 1990s. We might
    say that the Japanese economy had almost constant returns to scale before
    2000. The elasticity of X with respect to input factors would be a little bit
    smaller when we assume cost minimization.
*   Scale economies will be 7.4% in 2010. But this result will be small, as
    compared to the US economy, whose scale economies are presently 10–15%,
    as Klein and Kumasaka concluded.[3]

In conclusion, as a "new"economy develops, IT plays an increasingly important
role. Therefore, the traditional analysis about the effect of IT on the economy

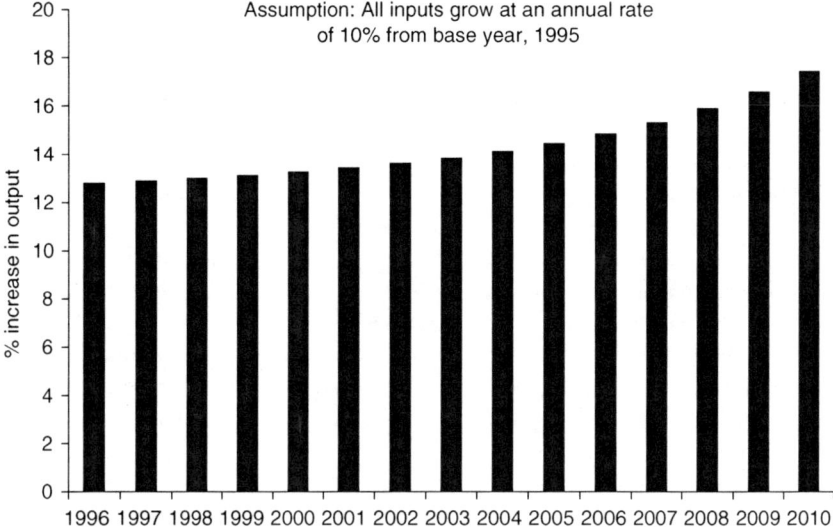

Figure 5.5 Economies of scale for Japan.

underestimates the effect of IT on the economy. But the US economy had more benefits from the IT revolution and received them much earlier than did the Japanese economy.

In conclusion, we should consider the economic policies that shift the S2 curve to S1 in the macroeconomy. As for industries, it is important to find out when their marginal product with respect to IT capital stock and IT service input will have increasing returns.

Macromodels for measuring the impact of IT and IT policies

Impact of IT and policies designed to encourage new technologies must be seen in a broad framework encompassing the entire economy rather than just the production function. Macroeconometric models are promising tools for evaluating policy alternatives in a comprehensive way. In this section we consider possibilities for modeling IT and its impact on growth in a macroeconometric model framework.

Production function, potential output and demand

The production function with inputs of labor force and capital stock and various ways to deal with productivity measures the supply, the potential output, of the economy. However, whether the potential output is achieved depends greatly on demand considerations, whether aggregate demand is sufficient to absorb the product produced at full employment. It is important, consequently, to extend the theory to incorporate demand as well as supply considerations.

Indeed, the relationship between demand and supply in the context of a rapidly changing economy is at the heart of the Japanese growth controversy. The fear that demand will exceed available supply constraints, causing a resumption of inflation, is one of the arguments that lie behind conservative policies seeking to limit the expansion of demand in line with low expectations of productivity growth. The impact of the government deficit on the large and growing national debt is another concern. It is important, consequently, to look closely at output potentials in an IT economy. The anticipated growth of the supply potential will influence the nature and amount of demand stimulus required. If potential output growth is greater than had been planned for, that is, 3% instead of 2%, there will be room for more aggressive macro demand stimulus policy.

Moreover, it is also important to recognize the relationship between demand and potential supply as increased demand may provide the incentives for investment and increased supply. The point is that there are frequently relationships between the forces that affect the demand and supply sides. The statistical evidence suggests that over the business cycle there are close links between the expansion of demand and the growth of productivity and supply (note the discussion in Chapter 7). Productivity shows strong cyclical patterns. Productivity grows in the expansion phase of the business cycle and stimulative fiscal and monetary policy advances not only demand but also productivity. There are many specific policies that will help advance demand and provide a productivity dividend as well. For example, increasing investment will increase aggregate demand. As investments are put in place, they increase the economy's supply potential by increasing productivity or production capacity or both. Similarly, expenditures on R&D represent demand impact that ultimately will have effects on a supply-side. Policymakers must take these relationships into account.

Long-term versus short-term model

The traditional econometric model is focused on short-term variations of the economy over the business cycle. To visualize the impact of technological change and of the new economy, it is important to take a longer time perspective. An annual model or even an analysis based on a five year time interval can serve the purpose. It can recognize many of the policies associated with the introduction of IT that are likely to have a gradual impact on the economy over a fairly extended period of time

Disaggregation

There are advantages and disadvantages to using a highly disaggregated model to study questions associated with productivity growth and IT. It may be possible to study behavior in sectors that are growing rapidly or declining and between sectors closely associated with the introduction of new technology, hardware and software, and to evaluate their contribution to productivity. It may be appropriate to provide a detailed sector breakdown, one that would distinguish between sectors that benefit from IT and those that do not. Such a breakdown may also help to establish the sources of productivity growth in the economy.

Disaggregation of the inputs into production may also be appropriate. In our discussion of the production function, we have considered IT capital and IT services. We also take into account the improvement of the labor supply due to education and learning-by-doing.

On the other hand, disaggregation imposes considerable costs. The required effort rises by more than the number of sectors, and it may increase the difficulty of making reliable estimates of the coefficients of the underlying functional relationships. In some cases data may not be available. In others, the data may be imprecise, or the data series may not be sufficiently long to establish firm behavioral relationships.

Conclusion

Modern econometric models integrate the demand and the supply sides of the economy. To fully evaluate the potential growth of an economy, it is necessary to integrate a new economy production function into a macro econometric model that includes income flows, the demand elements of the economy, prices, and the government budget. Such a model can be used to carry on computer simulations of the probable future trend and of alternative policy possibilities. We do such calculations on the basis of a relatively simple macroeconometric model in Chapter 12. In the Appendix, we present a proposal for a disaggregated econometric model designed to study the important issues of policy formulation and new IT economy.

6 The East Asian growth process and IT

Implications for Japan

For many decades, Japan was the lead economy in East Asian development. Today, as the East Asian countries have developed modern manufacturing industries of their own, the relationship between Japan and East Asia is very different. Japan is a mature economy, with developed country living standards, advanced technology, and high costs. The East Asian countries are at a very different stage of development and have very different resources, technologies, and exchange rate parities than Japan. Except for Singapore, Taiwan, and South Korea, they are at an earlier level of development. Some, like China, have a large, almost unlimited, supply of cheap low skill labor that can be drawn from agriculture and, as a result, they have low wages and a large competitive advantage in conventional manufacture of consumer goods for world markets.

The competitive position of Japanese industry has changed. Many Japanese manufacturing industries making consumer goods have had to upgrade their products or seek to manufacture them abroad since Japan is at a competitive disadvantage in labor-intensive activities in comparison with producers in China and other East Asian countries. On the other hand, Japanese high-tech and capital goods industries continue to compete successfully. Japan is the prime producer of high-technology capital goods in East Asia, and perhaps in the world. As a supplier of high-tech products, Japan has symbiotic and complementary relationships with East Asia that offer much potential for trade and for gains in productivity.

This section investigates the changing position of Japan in East Asia and its implications for Japanese growth policy. First, we focus on the essentials of the East Asian growth process, in particular, the "flying geese" theory and the linkages between the East Asian countries that represent a "growth ladder." Then we consider the differences in the rate of development and productivity between Japan and other countries of the East Asian region. We consider the role of IT in these developments.

The East Asian growth process

Postwar Japanese growth has largely been attributed to a mix of industrial policies developing export-oriented industries that have advanced Japan's technological potential. From the perspective of the rest of East Asia, these policies represented the leading edge of the flying geese formation (Kojima, 2000). This notion visualizes

Japan as the policy leader of East Asia. And indeed, some East Asian countries, like South Korea, successfully followed the Japanese example. But, early on, Japanese scholars, like Akamatsu (1962), saw the development of East Asia as greatly dependent on the linkages between countries with different factor endowments and at different levels of technology and development.

The various stages of development are described in Table 6.1. The initial point of development is, of course, the agricultural economy (Stage 1). The basic notion assumes that relatively low wages and favorable exchange rates initially provide competitive advantage in labor-intensive products like apparel and consumer electronics exports to the world market (Stage 2).[1] As development advances, rising wage levels and appreciating exchange rates reduce competitiveness in labor-intensive products. At this stage of development, production of traditional products is shifted to countries that still have lower costs and the more advanced East Asian countries turn to more sophisticated and, typically, more capital- and technology-intensive products (Stage 3). As the required technology comes closer to the technological frontier, growth is somewhat slower. Finally, we can envision a still more advanced stage of development with emphasis on sophisticated services like finance, management, and high technology (Stage 4).

The East Asian development ladder hypothesis (Adams, 2006) follows this pattern suggesting that as countries mature, and income and cost levels rise, some industries lose their competitive advantage and are shifted to neighboring countries in East Asia that are at a lower stage of development. The advanced countries turn to higher technology industries and high level services (Table 6.2). Thus, we see that in 1950–80 Japan was predominantly a producer of labor-intensive products (Stage 2), and then moved toward high-tech manufactures (Stage 3) in the 1980–95 period, and may increase production in the direction of high-tech services in the years to 2010. In other words, as production has shifted geographically, the advanced countries readjust their output away from mass production consumer goods to sophisticated high-tech products, sometimes sophisticated parts for assembly into finished goods abroad, or more complex products like capital goods, tools, and luxury items. Management, finance, and design and entrepreneurial functions also frequently concentrate in the more advanced countries. The advanced activities rely heavily on IT software and hardware. The shift to high value-added products and application of IT technologies is greatly improving productivity in some of the most advanced countries.

In East Asia, Japan remains a leader in Stage 3 of the development ladder process though South Korea, Taiwan, and Singapore are growing more rapidly as

Table 6.1 The development ladder—stages

Stage 1	Primary Products	Abundant cheap land and labor
Stage 2	Labor Intensive Manufactures	Low Cost Labor
Stage 3	Hi Tech Manufactures	Capital Intensive, Technically Sophisticated Products
Stage 4	Services (high level)	Educated Labor Force

Table 6.2 The stages of the product cycle process

	1950–65	1965–80	1980–95	1995–2010
Stage 1	Indonesia Philippines Thailand Malaysia China Taiwan Singapore Korea	Indonesia Philippines Thailand Malaysia China	Indonesia Philippines Vietnam	Laos Combodia Myanmar
Stage 2	Hong Kong Japan	Taiwan Singapore Korea Hong Kong Japan	Thailand Malaysia China	Indonesia Philippines Vietnam Thailand China
Stage 3			Taiwan Singapore Korea Hong Kong Japan	Malaysia Taiwan Korea Japan
Stage 4				Singapore Hong Kong

they focus their activities on the IT fields and Singapore, in particular, increases its reliance on high level services. While Japan already has many Stage 4 high level service activities, it may retain an important role in the production of high-tech manufactures, typical of a Stage 3 economy, rather than to become primarily a service center for smaller East Asian economies such as Singapore.

The role of IT in East Asian growth

The economics of IT and e-business in East Asia depend on the setting prevailing in each country and the East Asian countries are quite heterogeneous. They range across very different levels of development from incomes per capita of $29,400 in Japan to $410 in Vietnam in 2005. Wages range correspondingly. The East Asian countries are spread across the so-called digital divide with high rates of computer ownership and connectivity in Japan, Singapore, Taiwan, and South Korea and very little, relatively, in China and Vietnam (Adams, 2006).

Similar differences are apparent with regard to higher education. The countries may also be ranked approximately from the perspective of technology from simple assembly on one extreme to advanced R&D on the other. Japan, South Korea, Taiwan, and Singapore are already leaders in modern technology. China is taking advantage of its low wages and vast scale to provide a setting for developing industry. Other East Asian countries have also made substantial progress but some are still very much at the "apparel and assembly" stage of industrialization (Table 6.3).

Table 6.3 Technological stages of East Asian industries

	Japan	S. Korea	China	Singapore	Taiwan	Malaysia	Thailand	Philippines	Indonesia	Vietnam
1960s	Assembly Process Engineering	Assembly		Assembly	Assembly					
1970s	Assembly Product Engineering & Development	Assembly/ Process Engineering		Process Engineering	Assembly	Assembly	Assembly			
1980s	Product Engineering & Development	Assembly/ Product Development	Assembly	Product Development	Process Engineering	Assembly	Assembly	Assembly	Assembly	Assembly
1990s	Product R and D Management & Finance	Product Development/ R & D	Assembly/ Process Engineering	Product Development/ R & D Management & Finance	Product Development/ R & D Management & Finance	Process Engineering	Assembly/ Process Engineering	Assembly	Assembly/ Process Engineering	Assembly

While IT technology has only recently influenced East Asian development, it has played an important role in advancing Japan's position as a high-tech producer and exporter and in facilitating Japan's integration into the East Asian economy.

The growth of modern industry in East Asia has been going on for many years and is largely, but not entirely, independent of the IT industries. Only in recent years have electronic consumer goods played an increasingly large role in East Asian exports. Even today, a large share of the goods originating in China and in other East Asian developing countries are traditional consumer products like clothing and apparel produced by labor-intensive methods. In these cases the role of changing communications and transportation technologies has been to facilitate the geographic separation between production in East Asia and consumption in the developed world. Communications technologies also permit offshoring intellectual tasks such as computer programming.

Japan has been a leader in the production of IT products, particularly advanced high-tech capital goods, and supplies many of the inputs that go into assembly in other East Asian countries. IT technologies have greatly facilitated the development of Japanese subsidiary companies in China and in other East Asian countries. Perhaps because of language differences, while Japan is active in international software development and e-business, it is not as competitive in the software and business fields as it is in high-tech hardware.

East Asian growth and multi-factor productivity

The phenomenally rapid growth of real GDP in other parts of East Asia, interrupted briefly by the 1997 financial crisis, is shown on Table 6.4. Rapid growth resumed after the 1997 East Asian crisis period, though it is apparent that the most advanced countries, Singapore, Hong Kong, Taiwan, and Korea are growing somewhat more slowly than the less advanced countries. These figures compare with growth of real GDP in Japan at an annual rate recently of 1.5–2.0% (only 0.76% in 1999–2002).

Table 6.4 Growth of real GDP in East Asia

	(% per year)			
	1987–91	*1991–6*	*1996–9*	*1999–2003*
Japan	4.88	1.55	0.20	0.76*
China, People's Republic of	8.00	12.10	7.90	8.20
Hong Kong, China	6.60	5.30	1.17	3.90
Korea, Rep. of	9.10	7.00	2.43	5.60
Indonesia	7.50	7.60	−2.53	4.00
Malaysia	8.60	9.60	2.00	4.50
Philippines	3.90	3.50	2.67	4.10
Singapore	9.30	9.30	4.87	2.80
Thailand	10.90	8.10	−2.50	4.80
Taipei	8.40	6.80	5.57	2.60

Source: ADB, OECD data bases.

Note
* 1999–2002.

Japanese economic growth during the recent decade has been far slower than in other parts in East Asia that have gained greatly as countries have advanced from a lower stage of economic development to a higher one.

To appreciate the contributions of technical change to economic progress in Asia, we show in Table 6.5 estimates of inputs into production in East Asia and we compare the growth of total factor productivity of Japan and of the other East Asian countries in Table 6.6. These calculations are based on the traditional Cobb–Douglas production function with constant returns to scale discussed in the first part of Chapter 5. This allows us to segregate all of the increase in output that occurs

Table 6.5 Inputs of labor and capital in East Asia

Inputs	(Growth of inputs % per year, capital weight 0.4, labor weight 0.6)			
	1987–91	*1991–6*	*1996–9*	*1999–2003*
Japan	1.75	0.75	0.18	0.20*
China, People's Republic of	6.10	4.50	4.50	4.10
Hong Kong, China	2.10	3.50	2.97	2.00
Korea, Rep. of	4.60	5.00	3.17	3.70
Indonesia	2.30	4.20	3.53	1.30
Malaysia	4.10	7.10	4.87	3.20
Philippines	2.10	3.40	1.90	3.30
Singapore	5.20	4.90	5.53	3.60
Thailand	4.70	4.70	2.17	1.50
Taipei, China	1.90	3.10	3.13	2.10

Source: Authors' calculation.

Note
Computed * 1999–2002.

Table 6.6 Growth of total factor productivity in East Asia

TFP	(% per year, assuming weight of capital 0.4, labor 0.6)			
	1987–91	*1991–6*	*1996–9*	*1999–2003*
Japan	3.13	0.80	0.02	0.05*
China	1.90	7.60	3.47	4.10
Hong Kong, China	4.50	1.80	−1.80	1.90
S. Korea	4.50	2.00	−0.73	1.90
Indonesia	5.20	3.40	−6.07	2.90
Malaysia	4.40	2.50	−2.83	1.30
Philippines	1.90	0.10	0.77	0.80
Singapore	4.10	4.40	−0.70	−0.80
Thailand	6.30	3.40	−4.63	3.30
Taiwan	6.40	3.80	2.40	0.50

Source: Authors' calculation.

Note
Computed * 1999–2002.

beyond the factor inputs. As we have noted, total factor productivity represents the increase in output that cannot be explained by increases in inputs. This is not simply technological change. It may also represent the shift from low productivity to high productivity industries; and it may represent increasing returns to scale. These are essential ingredients as countries move from low levels of development to advanced status. The data shows that total factor productivity gains have been less accessible to advanced countries like Japan than to the developing countries. We anticipate that increased reliance on IT products and their application will provide new benefits to Japan and other advanced countries, as well.

These tables show that the inputs of labor and capital have been rising very rapidly in East Asia, but there remains a very large component of total factor productivity, for example, 4% per year in China in the 1999–2003 period. In comparison, the growth of inputs and growth of total factor productivity in Japan has been much slower, inputs at approximately 0.2% a year and total factor productivity at an average of 0.05% per year in the 1999–2002 period. Averaging the figures over a longer period, 1991–2002, Japanese inputs increase 0.8% per year and total factor productivity increases by 0.2% annually, still very low numbers compared to other East Asian countries.

Slow growth in Japan reflects many forces, macroeconomic as well as microeconomic. Various dimensions of the IT revolution and the New Economy may have had an effect, as we discuss later.

The new economy and the development ladder

The IT revolution represents a further step in world technological and economic progress. It offers new opportunities for the development ladder process. Many entrepreneurs are taking advantage of the new technological developments to advance themselves and their businesses. This is taking place in East Asia as well as in Europe and the United States.

The underlying economic considerations may be different than they used to be, but they are not eliminated in the new economy. Competitive advantage still depends on the ability to produce products more cheaply and/or with higher quality than elsewhere. If the product calls for high level skills or high quality, the product or its high-tech components will be produced in the most advanced countries. On the other hand, if it calls for cheap labor, manufacturing or assembly, then some of the East Asian developing countries are ideal low cost sources. Increasingly, businesses are producing products in a transnational production chain, carrying out each segment of the production process where it can be done most economically. The international supply chain and the relocation of production, are integral to the new economy.

The role of Japan and the IT revolution

What are the potentials for Japan in East Asia in connection with the IT revolution? Japan has played an important role in East Asian development. The IT revolution has changed the position of Japan relative to other East Asian countries. Being the most advanced country in the region, and with a limited and aging population, Japan's labor costs are and will remain considerably higher than those of other countries in the region. This means that Japan must compete in the high-tech fields in which its industries excel. The further development of high-tech industries is an essential for an advanced country.

Second, Japan must more widely apply IT methods to improve the efficiency of retail and wholesale distribution operations and other services that must continue to be done in the home economy. The service activities make up a large component of the GDP of advanced economies. Significant gains in productivity can be accomplished by improving productivity in service activities. Progress in this direction, as illustrated in other countries like the United States, suggests that important gains can be made by applying further IT and e-business methods in the service and trade fields.

Finally, in an international context, Japan is assuming a role of management and financial support for subsidiary companies located elsewhere in East Asia. These can produce products for the Japanese market and for export more cheaply than production in Japan. Moreover, this makes possible a complementary interaction between Japan and other East Asian countries, one in which the supply chain takes advantage of regional specialization and trade. Further international specialization and opening to world trade can enable Japan to import low cost consumer goods and to focus domestic production on the high tech and luxury products in which Japan has high and potentially increasing productivity.

7 Information and communications technology and productivity growth in Japan

Over the last two decades, there has been controversy about the impact of information technology on the Japanese economy. Some analysts claimed that information technology contributed to the improvement of productivity while others argued it did very little. Studies by the Japanese Economic Planning Agency and by the Ministry of Economy, Trade, and Industry find that IT capital deepening contributed ¼ to ½ of 1 percentage point to labor productivity during the second half of the 1990s (Callen and Ostry (eds), 2003).

Intensive academic research and business case studies suggest that investment in information technology pays off when it is combined with business process reengineering and institutional reforms. An example of such a case is the macroeconomic impact in the United States. The annual productivity growth rate in the United States has accelerated 1.6 percentage points, or doubled from an annual growth rate of 1.5–3.1% (Jorgenson *et al.*, 2004). This productivity acceleration is one of the most important benefits of the information technology revolution.

In Japan, however, the dynamic impact of information technology appears to be smaller so that it has been frequently disregarded, at least in the national government's long-term economic projections. The Council on Economic and Fiscal Policy at the Cabinet Office describes two kinds of scenarios: one to be avoided and another to be welcomed. Surprisingly, even in the positive scenario, the economy is slated to grow at a mere 1.5% annually.

What makes the Council members so pessimistic? One is the demographic trend of an aging and decreasing population. The other is the underestimation or neglect of the positive impact of the information technology revolution. Although the advantages of information technology and globalization are mentioned in the scenario, their ability to vitalize the economy is not reflected in the form of productivity resurgence and the resultant economic growth in the projection.

In this chapter, we consider how productivity and IT investments will contribute to the growth rate of the Japanese economy over the next few decades. We will then measure the fundamental productivity trend or structural growth rate of productivity since this measurement is necessary to examine whether higher economic growth is feasible in Japan.

Measurement of a fundamental productivity trend

In this section, we add the effect of business cycle variation and the distinction between IT and non-IT assets to our earlier calculations of the productivity trend of the Japanese economy in order to better grasp the macroeconomic clues needed to examine the feasibility of higher economic growth. We can measure the lowest productivity growth rate as a minimum baseline by focusing on the 1990s in light of the long-run trend over the last three decades. The economy experienced the deepest slump in the 1990s. This measurement is necessary to distinguish the structural trend of productivity from the business-cycle changes of productivity since productivity is pro-cyclical. For this purpose, we employ the following formula based on the growth accounting method

$$Q = M(pK_0)^\alpha (pK_i)^\beta (\text{hr}L)^\gamma$$

where α, β, and γ represent income shares for each input respectively, $\alpha + \beta + \gamma = 1$, Q is output, M is multifactor productivity, p is the utilization rate of capital assets assuming that the utilization rate is homogeneous in each asset, K_0 represents non-IT capital assets, whereas K_i is IT capital assets, hr is work hours per employee, and L is the number of employees. (Note that the discussion here is based on an adaptation of the Cobb–Douglas production function with constant returns framework discussed in the first part of Chapter 5.) The utilization rate of capital assets is used as a proxy for the business cycle effect in this equation.[1] Then, the equation mentioned earlier can be transformed as

$$\dot{Q} - \text{hr}\dot{L} = M + \alpha(\dot{K}_0 - \text{hr}\dot{L}) + \beta(\dot{K}_i - \text{hr}\dot{L}) + (\alpha + \beta)\dot{p}$$

where a dot over a variable indicates the rate of change expressed as a log difference. In this equation, $\dot{Q} - \text{hr}\dot{L}$ represents changes in output per hour or labor productivity, M represents changes in multifactor productivity, and $\dot{K} - \text{hr}\dot{L}$ represents changes in capital assets per hours worked, which is referred to as capital deepening. The capital deepening portion is further divided into the contribution from IT assets $(\dot{K}_i - \text{hr}\dot{L})$ and non-IT assets $(\dot{K}_0 - \text{hr}\dot{L})$.

Based on the aforementioned formula, we can measure a fundamental productivity trend separate from the business cycle effect, using the data sets that are published officially by government ministries for output, total capital asset input, labor input, and utilization rate as well as the data sets in Shinozaki (2004) for information and communications technology assets input.

Table 7.1 shows the results of the productivity trend calculation. The first line in the table represents the growth rate of the entire economy and the third line shows the productivity growth rate computed as the first line (growth rate of output) minus the second line (growth rate of labor input). The fourth and fifth lines allocate this productivity growth rate to the business cycle effect and the fundamental trend.

Japanese macroeconomic performance has changed drastically over the last two decades. The statistics in the first line illustrate this transformation well.

Table 7.1 Productivity trends in Japan (annual % changes)

	1976–8	1981–5	1986–90	1991–5	1996–2000
Growth rate of output	4.81	3.65	5.21	1.56	1.45
Growth rate of labor input	1.37	0.92	1.29	−0.27	−0.83
Output per hour	3.44	2.73	3.92	1.84	2.28
Business cycle effect	1.15	−0.02	0.29	−0.81	0.00
Fundamental trend	2.29	2.75	3.63	2.64	2.28
Capital deepening	1.66	1.62	1.83	1.76	1.35
of IT assets	0.09	0.17	0.48	0.38	0.53
of non-IT assets	1.57	1.45	1.35	1.38	0.81
Multifactor productivity	0.63	1.13	1.80	0.88	0.93

Source: Selected figures from Shinozaki (2004) table 3, p. 10.

As we saw in Chapter 2, the economy enjoyed a powerful boom in the late 1980s and plunged into a slump in the 1990s. The economy grew at a healthy 3.7% annually in the early 1980s and at a vigorous 5.2% annually in the late 1980s. Conversely, it grew at a mere 1.5% annually in the 1990s. The economic growth rate in the 1990s was less than one-third of the rate in the late 1970s or late 1980s, and less than half of the rate in the early 1980s. On the whole, the 1990s growth rate fell drastically from earlier periods.

For the fundamental productivity trend, however, the changes in the 1990s were not as drastic. The fundamental productivity trend was relatively moderate due to the sharp decline in the entire growth rate, which resulted mainly from the decrease in labor input and the business cycle effect on productivity. Even in the "lost decade" of the 1990s, the fundamental productivity trend grew at around 2.5% annually; at 2.6% in the first half and at 2.3% in the second half of the 1990s. Although an approximate 2.5% growth trend is about 1 percentage point less than 3.6% trend in the late 1980s, the second half of the 1980s might be considered an exceptional period of overheating boom. For this reason, in comparing fundamental productivity trends of the 1990s with those in the late 1970s or early 1980s, we find the figures were almost the same, ranging from 2.3% to 2.8%. It therefore seems appropriate to conclude that an annual productivity growth rate of around 2.5% is the fundamental trend that the Japanese economy still represents a potential minimum.

This calculation lends support, from a somewhat different perspective, to our earlier consideration of the production function. Since this calculation focuses on fundamental versus cyclical elements in growth and uses constant returns to scale, much of the benefit associated with technological change is incorporated into the cyclical factor, a negative one during the past decade. It emphasizes the need for a cyclically buoyant economy in order for IT investments to be made and to have impact on growth and productivity.

Feasibility of a 3% GDP growth rate

For 3% economic growth under the diminishing demographic trend discussed above, productivity should grow at 3.5–4.0% annually. Thus, it is necessary for the Japanese economy to attain an additional 1.0–1.5% annual productivity enhancement on top of the approximate 2.5% fundamental productivity trend. The matter in question in this argument is whether a mature economy such as Japan's, not an emerging economy like the BRICs, can revitalize and push its productivity upward again.

An answer lies in the remarkable macroeconomic performance in the United States since the late 1990s (Table 7.2). As Chandler (2000) states, the US economy underwent "the transformation from the Industrial [Age] into the Information Age in the last decades of the twentieth century" (Chandler, 2000, p. 3). There was intensive investment in information technology and it surely paid off. The US economy has reaped the full benefits of technological innovation in the form of achieving productivity resurgence. Assuming that the annual percentage change of labor productivity will continue at 3.1%, one may compute that the living standard in the United States will double in 23 years rather than 47 years, a generation faster than before. The most important implication of the acceleration in the US growth rate is that even a mature or developed financial system such as the US economy can raise its productivity growth rate even after a long economic slump, if it can successfully ride the waves of the information technology revolution.

At the other side of the Pacific Ocean, in Japan, a different state of affairs has existed since the 1990s. We have reviewed Japan's experience in the 1990s and learned that roughly 2.5% of the annual productivity growth constitutes a fundamental trend or a minimum baseline of the economy. We also learn from that time period that Japan failed fully to transform its economy from the Industrial Age to the Information Age and that it missed the chance to take advantage of the information technology revolution.

As Jorgenson (2001) pointed out, capital deepening of IT assets represents the effects on the user side of information and communications technology whereas multifactor productivity represents efficiency gains from either the user or

Table 7.2 Sources of US productivity growth (annual % changes, percentage point)

	1959–73 (a)	1973–95 (b)	1995–2003 (c)	Changes	
				(b)–(a)	(c)–(b)
Labor productivity	2.85	1.49	3.06	−1.36	1.57
Capital deepening of all assets	1.41	0.89	1.75	−0.52	0.86
Capital deepening of IT assets	0.21	0.40	0.92	0.19	0.52
Labor quality	0.33	0.26	0.17	−0.07	−0.09
Multifactor productivity	1.12	0.34	1.14	−0.78	0.80

Source: Selected figures from Jorgenson *et al.* (2004) table 1, p. 3.

the producer side of technology, or both. Table 7.2 demonstrates that there were no accelerations in either IT capital deepening or multifactor productivity in the period until 1995 and that the Japanese economy missed the chance to benefit from them. (Reasons for and some background to this failure are considered in the following chapter.)

Looking at the positive side of this issue, it can be argued that there remain potentials in Japan. In other words, it seems reasonable to believe that the Japanese economy could attain a 1.0–1.5% productivity bonus on top of the 2.5% minimum baseline if it manages to embrace the Information Age and take full advantage of the dynamism of the information technology revolution. Given the Japanese macroeconomic fundamentals, advanced assets of R&D, social and political stability, high level of education, and so on, this is not an unrealistic scenario for Japan.

Higher growth, perhaps 3% economic growth, seems feasible if Japan takes advantage of the information technology revolution. Japan will then be able to reap the full benefits through structural reforms that allow innovation and competition. This step into the future will require appropriate macro policy and a market friendly microeconomic policy, with reforms in the private business sector to regain competitiveness.

8 Revisiting Japanese industrial organization and the corporate system

In this chapter, we provide an example of how social/cultural factors might account for the difference in information technology investments and productivity gains between Japan and the United States. The example, which is focused on information technology and business organization, is only one of the various forces that may explain the disparity with regard to the productivity growth path between Japan and the United States. Numerous other factors, some related to culture, some related to government regulation, and some related to the state of the economy and financial markets may be taken into account in explaining the Japanese situation.

Information technology, the Internet in particular, began to deeply affect economic performance world wide in the 1990s. At the same time, a clear contrast emerged on both sides of the Pacific Ocean: the longest and vigorous economic expansion in the United States and a dawdling slump in Japan. This contrast was partly, but significantly, caused by a difference in corporate attitudes about investment in new technology. The "IT capital deepening" figures in Tables 7.1 and 7.2 clearly illustrate this disparity. Managers in the United States invested intensely in technology while in Japan they seemed to take a wait-and-see position.

Why were the implications of information technology lost on Japanese management? To address this question, we consider the features of Japanese industrial organization, or Japan's corporate system, which produced a prosperous economy through the 1980s and conversely caused it to stagnate in the 1990s. We analyze possible impediments preventing the Japanese economy from reaping the benefits of the information technology revolution. We then consider the best ways for Japan to realize a productivity resurgence and resultant economic growth.

First, we will review the strengths of Japanese industrial organization, and then we will analyze how those strengths became weaknesses when it came to leading the economy into the Information Age.

The integrated system in Japan versus the modular system in the United States

According to the Economic Planning Agency (1990), which analyzed the strengths of the 1980s Japanese economy, corporate Japan's organizational structure had several principal features. These characteristics facilitated success in technological improvement and in transforming the economy from energy-consuming heavy industries into well-advanced R&D manufacturing through the 1970s and 1980s. The features were: (1) intensive face-to-face communications based on an intimate human network; (2) shared business information through informal communication; (3) some overlap in jobs under a flexible organizational structure and unrestricted job descriptions within a firm; and (4) the extension of these characteristics to transactions between the firms and the creation of long-term relationships in an industrial organization.

We refer to the aforementioned characteristics as an "integrated organization" or "integrated system" (Policy Research Institute, 2000). In an integrated organization, information circulates by means of informal traffic and is shared in a tacit manner. Accordingly, an integrated system is appropriate for technological improvement through "learning by doing" (Arrow, 1962) because invisible and tacit skills can be shared and transferred easily among employees or a group of companies and are accumulated within a group day by day.

For that reason, corporate Japan has performed well through continuous improvement such as *kaizen* or total quality management in its production lines. As Arrow mentioned, "knowledge is growing over time" (Arrow, 1962, p. 155). Learning by doing is an important engine of R&D activities in an integral organization, which is characterized by its continuous improvement, known but tacitly held skills, long-term relations, integrality, common culture, gradual progress, and so on. That is one reason why Japanese business maintains excellent performance in such organized industries as automobile and liquid crystal display manufacturing, even in the Information Age.

In contrast, corporate America has different features in its organizational structure (Figure 8.1), we refer to them here as a "modular organization," or "modular system" (Langlois and Robertson, 1992). In a modular organization, formal job descriptions define the mission of each job position. Moreover, borders that separate job units or divisions are much clearer than in an integrated organization. However, a modular system sometimes makes it difficult to understand

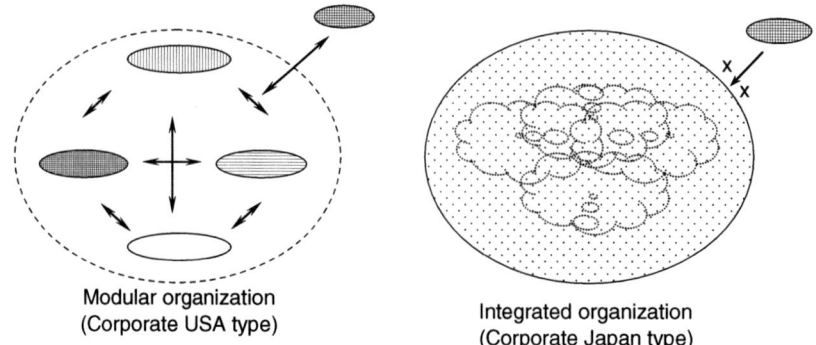

Modular organization
(Corporate USA type)

Integrated organization
(Corporate Japan type)

Figure 8.1 Modularity versus integrality.

the internal activities of other job units and to share information that involves the entire organization. Therefore, a standard format for an open interface is created to promote smooth formal communications among the units. This common interface and simple protocol ease communication, even with newcomers or outside participants, in a modular organization. This is in sharp contrast to communication outcomes in an integrated organization.

As mentioned earlier, one type of activity that improves the R&D payoff is what Arrow calls "learning by doing" which is suitable for an integrated system. Another type of activity that improves the R&D payoff is what Joseph Schumpeter refers to as "innovations." Innovations are characterized as disruptive changes, new combinations, open source relations, modularity, novelty and variety, random (or leapfrog style) progress, and so on (Christenson, 2000). These characteristics are more suitable for the modular system of the United States rather than the integrated system of Japan.

Transformation from the Industrial Age to the Information Age

Progress and diffusion of information technology seems to cause dynamic changes in the economic environment. In fact, it seems reasonable to assume that economies are going to change from those favoring an integrated system to those favoring a modular system.

The reason for this presumption is that, with the networks and digital technology that typify the new economy, there are externalities, that is, "network effects" and "economies of outsourcing."

Table 8.1 clarifies the notion of "economies of outsourcing" and incorporates it into other concepts of economies; "economies of scale," "economies of scope," and "network externalities." Economies of outsourcing are the opposite of economies of scope just as network effects are the opposite of economies of scale.[1] Under economies of outsourcing, economic benefits arise from resources outside the organization, rather than from in-house resources as under economies of scope,

Table 8.1 Economies in the Information Age and the Industrial Age

Types of merit	Emerging information age	Matured industrial age
Scale merit	Network effects (externalities)— consumers' scale merit	Economies of scale—producers' scale merit
Resource merit	Economies of outsourcing –outside resources –multiple organizations –synergy effect –innovations (new combinations)	Economies of scope –in-house resources –single integrated organization –cost saving –learning by doing
Desirable industrial organization	Multiple small players Competitive market Compatibility Modularity	Larger organization Oligopoly, or monopoly Continuity Integrality

Source: Shinozaki (2004), p. 18, table A-2, with some modifications.

inducing a synergy effect of dynamic "new combinations," which is the key concept of what Joseph Schumpeter refers to as a driving force of innovation.

In the new economy, organizational modularity has an advantage over integrality. Some of the strengths of an integrated system turn into weaknesses. This is what may have happened in the 1990s, the period of transformation from the Industrial Age into the Information Age.

Challenges to the Japanese system in the Information Age

Information and communications technology has progressed and changed its nature from simple high-performance automatic transaction machinery to an effective business communications tool. The challenges involved in adopting such radical new technology are considerable under any circumstance. But a modular organization can more easily adapt its operations to a standard format of formal communications and reap the benefits of that technological change in the form of a productivity resurgence.

In contrast, integrated organizations find it more difficult to adopt a new technology. Their intimate human networks have performed so efficiently and effectively that management cannot easily accept the importance of using the new technology and so makes less use of it.[2] For this reason it takes a long time for integrated organizations to fully implement new technologies. Even if integrated organizations recognize the importance of using the new technology, they need drastic business process reengineering and business unit restructuring in order to gain its benefit.

Take intensive face-to-face communication as one example, wherein preference represents a locational constraint at a time when organizations are expanding their business globally. Too much dependence on face-to-face and informal communications in the human network implies less, perhaps even inadequate, attention to creating a formal means of information traffic flow and a consequent reluctance toward building and using an information technology network as the main tools of business processes communication. Lacking appropriate technology, a global organization will fail to make prompt decisions.

Another problem arises from the overlapping missions and unclear job unit borders that gave Japanese firms an advantage in the 1980s. Such complexity or obscurity makes it more difficult to reap the benefits of outsourcing or the more recent trend of offshoring because it is so hard to identify the job units that *should be* outsourced. Moreover, when outsourcing occurs, a new and different form of communication is required to negotiate with arm's-length suppliers than to deal with internal sources. The complexity or obscurity in integrated organizations must be confronted during any restructuring of the organization resulting from mergers and acquisitions.

The arguments here are not intended to reject all the features of the Japanese system. The integrated system works quite well with some businesses such as high-quality consumer products industries that depend heavily on technological improvement through "learning by doing." Nevertheless, the integrated system of the Japanese economy, which performed excellently in the 1980s, may be less suitable for the emerging phase of the Information Age.[3] In some cases information technology performs far more efficiently and effectively than intimate human networks. Unfortunately, corporate Japan has been hesitant to introduce such technology in fear that it might erode its human network advantage. This appears to have been a factor in their failure to accelerate their productivity through intensive investment in the technology.

Cultural characteristics and business organization

An alternative view would relate the differences in business organization to underlying cultural differences between Japan and the United States. The classic research of Geert Hofstede suggested that there are important cultural differences between Japanese and American managers (Hofstede, 1980, 1984, 1997). His survey studies suggest that Japanese score higher on uncertainty avoidance and lower on individualism. They are more careful in the face of change and work more closely with one another than Americans. These cultural attributes might be seen as consistent with the organizational difference, integrated rather than modular business.

Culture carries the discussion into rather tenuous territory, away from management toward business psychology. Moreover, the cultural surveys were carried out many years ago. There is controversy about whether such cultural factors should be seen as permanent attributes. There is reason to think that the cultural—business organization relationship has some flexibility. As managers are exposed to international contacts and as businesses from various countries work more closely together, there appear to be tendencies toward international convergence. Business organizations are being changed to meet the requirements of new technologies and more widely distributed international business (Inkeles, 1998; Porter, 2000). This means that the Japanese business of tomorrow, especially firms exposed to international competition, may find it easier to adapt to the changed requirements and opportunities of the new economy.

Private sector reforms for the Information Age

There is no need to be pessimistic about prospects for technological change in Japan. As we have noted, radical technological development and transformation involving disruptive and radical innovation is often easier to accomplish in a modular than in an integrated industrial organization system. The technological changes associated with Silicon Valley in United States illustrate how modular firms, many independently small and beneficiaries of venture capital, first introduced and developed the new IT products and services. Large firms then apply the newly developed systems, a process that calls for radical organizational change and favors the modular firm model. Visualize, for example, the dissemination of a cell phone system on a nationwide basis. Or consider the application of inventory control systems by such giant retailers as Wal-Mart and Home Depot. Paradoxically, once these firms mature and the products became standardized, the optimal formal organization may well again be a more integrated system. These are clearly large successful integrated firms. Also, where Japanese integrated firms may have been at a disadvantage at the early stages of the transition is the 1990s and early 2000s, a time of product development and change, they may have some advantages once the technologies are standardized and disseminated on a nationwide basis.

This suggests that Japan can go both ways. Many Japanese firms are becoming modular. At the same time, now that the technologies are more standardized, many integrated firms are now in a position to take advantage of them effectively.

There is an upside potential since investment in technology in Japan seems to be on the increase recently. In addition, private business sectors have finally realized the importance of business process reengineering and business unit restructuring for the Information Age although they are still at the halfway mark. To facilitate this momentum, we must clarify what kinds of efforts are needed.

Based on a nationwide survey of 9,500 firms (effective response from 3,141 firms), multiple comparison analysis revealed that reforms in organizational structures and human resource management significantly affect the outcome of investment in information technology (Tables 8.2 and 8.3). That is, the results of IT investments are better in firms that simultaneously engage in business process reengineering and that put greater emphasis on human resource management. Yet, it was also found that small firms have difficulties in their use of technology, particularly with regard to staffing, and that some industries such as medical and educational services are less enthusiastic than manufacturers about the use of information technology (Shinozaki, 2005b).

Logit model analysis revealed that reforms such as paperless transactions fairly quickly make the business process efficient, both internally and between the firms. On the other hand, drastic and fundamental organizational reform, such as changes in the top management's decision-making process, business unit restructuring through mergers and acquisitions, and the revision of long-term relationships with suppliers and customers, do not pay off quickly (Shinozaki, 2006a). The analysis also found that human resource management is more effective and

Table 8.2 Business process reengineering and investment in IT (investment outcome score)

		Business process reengineering	
		Intensive effort firms	*Less effort firms*
Investment in IT	Massively investing firms	3.6	2.6
	Less investing firms	3.0	2.0

Source: Shinozaki (2005b), table 7, p. 30.

Note
The higher score represents a better outcome of investment in IT. Score differences between the categories are statistically significant.

Table 8.3 Human resource management and investment in IT (investment outcome score)

		Human resource management	
		Intensive effort firms	Less effort firms
Investment in IT	Massively investing firms	3.4	2.6
	Less investing firms	2.9	2.0

Source: Shinozaki (2005b), table 8, p. 30.

Note
The higher score represents a better outcome for investment in IT. The difference of scores between the firms of less invested and intensive human management efforts (score 2.9) and those of massively invested and less human resource management effort (score 2.6) is not statistically significant. Other differences of scores are statistically significant.

important than organizational reform in reaping the benefits of information technology, but that, so far, the major effectiveness in human resource management appears in training the *existing employees* within the firms rather than in hiring *new experts* from outside the firms.

Japanese companies on the whole tend to plan gradual corporate reforms rather than drastic reforms. This tendency implies that the inertia of Japan's integrated system persists in the midst of information technology innovation. In this sense, it still may be necessary for Japanese private business sectors to continue their intensive efforts for drastic business reforms that will lead to their transformation.

Japanese companies are definitely making progress and are far ahead of where they were in the 1990s. They made all-out efforts to deal with reducing holdover debt, selling off nonperforming assets, and eliminating excess employment over the past decade. Thus, the 1990s period was not only the "lost decade" but also the "born-again decade." Japanese private business sectors have been struggling with transformation and now they seem to be managing successfully.

But the challenge of adapting organizational structure and culture to a more dynamic and high-tech world remains a problem, particularly for some of the more traditionally oriented sectors of the Japanese economy. As we will later elaborate at greater length, this is not a problem that can readily be handled by government policy action, though some public policies are not irrelevant. Much change is the result of competitive pressure. This means that the more competitive and open the economy, the greater the pressure to invest in IT, and to reorganize business to meet the needs of the new technologies. Smaller companies, particularly in retail and wholesale distribution, a particular concern in Japan, find the adjustments difficult. Government support may be necessary for training employees particularly in small-sized companies. Medical and educational service industries will need help to institute institutional reforms along with business process reengineering and investment in information technology. We are hopeful, however, that private business sectors in Japan are getting ready to ride the wave of the information technology revolution and to reap its benefits on their own terms.

9 Case study of government policy and the telecommunications market in Japan

In this chapter, we present a case study of the Japanese telecommunications industry and the role of government policy in its development. We use this as a basis to discuss industrial organization policy potentials in Japan.

The characteristics of the Japanese communications market are compared with communications markets in other countries in Table 9.1. It is notable that, in comparison with another high income country like the United States, Japan has approximately the same frequency of telephone lines, mobile subscribers, and Internet users. On the other hand, Japan has considerably fewer personal computers, reflecting the fact that Japanese IT is much more based on mobile telephony than

Table 9.1 IT sector characteristics in Japan and other economies (2004)

	Japan	*US*	*China*	*Korea*	*Singapore*	*HK (China)*	*Thailand*
Telephone lines (per 1,000 people)	531	608	241	457	430	552	106
Mobile subscribers (per 1,000 people)	669	615	258	760	901	1,192	420
Internet users (per 1,000 people)	606	569	73	656	559	508	112
Personal computers (per 1,000 people)	425	760	40	558	565	453	74
Broadband subscribers (per 1,000 people)	141	129.1	16.5	247.6	118.2	216.9	0.2
Secure internet servers (per million people)	160.2	674.9	0.2	18.6	226.3	141	4.1
E-government readiness (scale 0–1)	0.63	1.00	0.41	0.95	0.97	n.a.	0.53
ICT expenditure (% of GDP)	7.4	8.8	5.3	6.6	10.4	8.4	3.5
Price, fixed line (US$ per month)	26.0	25.0	3.6	7.3	6.7	15.1	8.3
Price, mobile (US$ per month)	29.1	10.8	3.7	2.1	5.7	3.4	6.8
Price, internet (US$ per month)	21.1	15	10.1	9.7	11	3.9	7.0

Source: World Bank, 2006.

in the United States. This appears to be true even though the price structure for mobile connections is considerably less favorable than in the United States.

The readiness of government in Japan for e-government operations is judged by the World Bank to be somewhat behind the United States. For purposes of comparison we also show data for some other East Asian countries.

The smaller advanced countries of East Asia are far advanced in telecommunications and computer use, particularly Hong Kong (China), Singapore, and Korea. Again there appears to be heavier reliance on mobile communication than, even, in the United States. The cost of mobile service in these countries is relatively low. Lower income countries like China and Thailand remain far behind in fixed telephone lines and in Internet users and computers, though these countries have leapfrogged ahead in the mobile communications field.

Turning now to Japan, during the 1990s, Japanese private business sectors faced several impediments that prevented them from fully reaping the benefits of the information technology revolution. These include government policies with regard to fiscal expenditures, privatization of state-owned companies, regulations in the telecommunications industry, enforcement of competition policy, legislation on technology, business friendly laws, and so on.

Appropriate government policy packages are necessary for transforming the economy and achieving a higher growth rate in the Information Age. To determine relevant policies, in this section we will review Japanese government telecommunications policies over the last decades.

Revisiting Japan's industrial policies in the telecommunications market

Japanese policy toward the telecommunications industry provides a good illustration of the impact of public policy constraints on an industry faced with large-scale technological change.

Privatization/deregulation began in 1985 when the Nippon Telegraph and Telephone Public Corporation was privatized as Nippon Telegraph and Telephone Corporation (NTT) and the market was liberalized for new startups. This was not a full privatization but a kind of quasi-privatization because NTT has a special semi-governmental status under the NTT Law that obliges the government to hold at least one third of NTT's shares. Besides, NTT does not have a free hand in its business but has several constraints in its management under the law. Constraints include not only the obligation to provide universal service but also the need to seek government approval regarding business plans, organizational structures, corporate governance, appointment of top management, and so on.

Right after deregulation, several new common carriers started their businesses and many new information network service companies joined the market. Accordingly, investment in information and communications technology had increased throughout the 1980s.

The Japanese investment boom in the 1980s ended suddenly in the early 1990s, whereas the investment boom in the United States had just begun at that time.

Coincidentally, information and communications technology has progressed further and changed its nature from simple high-performance automatic transaction machinery to effective business communications tools. Driving forces for this change were the Internet or the underlying digital technologies of Transmission Control Protocol/Internet Protocol (TCP/IP) and the router network system, which called for drastic transformation in the information network system architecture.

An older form of data communications network, an expensive switched network system using analog technology, became a legacy system. In its place the new network system based on an inexpensive router technology dominated the data communications network all over the world. This technological change inevitably affected market conditions in the telecommunications industry (Table 9.2). In this table we show the changes from an analog system to a digital system and finally to a network age in their implications for communication and computing. With the changing technology come new high volume uses, changes in payment algorithms, and new business structures.

Unfortunately, Japanese government policies did not keep up with this transformation. Arguments about the policy for the telecommunications industry were mainly focused on issues about the reorganization or breakup of NTT and its group of companies and the reform of the NTT Law that had been enacted in 1985 when NTT was privatized. One of the major reasons for these continued discussions is that, in accordance with the reorganization or breakup of NTT, the NTT Law should have been reviewed in 1990 to facilitate a pro-competitive market. The deadline, however, was extended twice: in 1995 and then in 1997. These arguments wasted precious time in the quickly changing digital age.

Table 9.2 Change in the state of technology and network business

	1980s Legacy network age	1990s 2000s Transforming age	2010s?~ Ubiquitous network age
Technologies	Analog	Digital	
	wired only		wired + wireless (FMC)
	Narrow Band		Broad Band
	Copper Cable Line	(xDSL)	FTTH
	Switched network	TCP/IP, Router	(Next Generation?)
	Telephony	Internet	
Major Contents	Voice	Low Volume Data (text) / Medium Volume Data (picture)	Extra-high Volume Data (video)
Charge	Charge on Access Time & Distance	Flat Rate (Stay Online)	New Business Model?
Remarks	Business Oriented Computing → Ubiquitous Computing		

Source: Shinozaki (2006b) with some modifications.

The resultant reorganization (not breakup) of NTT in 1999 still seems imperfect and tentative, while market conditions have been changing forcefully.

Government policy allowed NTT and its group of companies to dominate the telecommunications market even after the market was liberalized. Thus, NTT's business strategies dominated markets that involved information and communications technology. This state of affairs significantly slowed down the transition into the Internet-based information age because NTT adhered to the switched network system instead of the router network system of TCP/IP technology. NTT had invested heavily in the expensive switched network system for a long time.

The Japanese government's policies in telecommunications industry were not exactly appropriate either for NTT or for its competitors. As for NTT, many constraints were imposed by the NTT Law designed specifically only for NTT, although NTT kept an advantageous position as a gigantic quasi-private company. Under the law, NTT could not manage its business flexibly and speedily because it had to negotiate with a government ministry and/or Diet members for approval whenever NTT tried to transform its business in accordance with changes in the market conditions or demands of users. That made NTT conservative with respect to innovation. As for competitors, they were still tiny and handicapped challengers but forced to confront a gigantic and conservative competitor. They were clearly at a competitive disadvantage.

As a government company with a fine-tuned charging formula based on its switched network system, NTT kept charging its subscribers on the basis of listed tariffs that depended on access time and distance (Figure 9.1). These business strategies, however, were a huge impediment that prevented Japanese

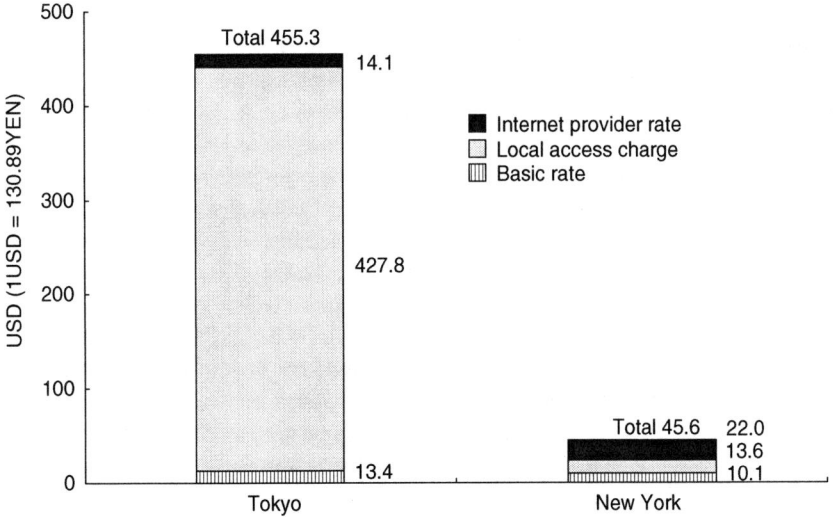

Figure 9.1 Rate for stay-online internet use as of 1999.

Source: Cabinet Office (2004) p. 3, figure I-2.

business from reaping the benefits of the information technology revolution, even though their strategies were surely appropriate for the business goals of NTT as a quasi-private company.

In the Internet-based information age, it is essential that network users be able to "stay online" and pay according to a "flat rate" formula, which is far from NTT's business strategies of the 1990s. Under NTT's business model, network users were charged in such a way that they had to pay the equivalent of a dime every three or five minutes for local access in addition to a monthly basic charge of approximately $13. As a result, network users were charged $455 a month if they stayed online all day (Figure 9.1). In Japan the use of the Internet was ten times as expensive as it was in the United States even though Japanese Internet providers offered lower rates than US providers.

Assuming "all-day" use may be extreme, but even the use of the Internet during business hours, from 9 a.m. to 5 p.m., was still too expensive. It was ten to fifteen dollars a day for local access charges only. The benefit of network externalities can be attained only if all users, from consumers to producers, from small firms to big ones, are able to access a network at a reasonable rate. Unlike large companies that could afford a leased line, small business proprietors, independent contractors, and individual consumers were able to access the network only via dial-up. Hence, it could be concluded that in the 1990s the Japanese telecommunications industry did not provide appropriate access service enabling every user to stay online and gain the benefit of network externalities. In Japan, there are still many small and medium-size businesses, so that it is important to consider small businesses rather than big names when we study the benefits of network externalities.[1]

Opportunities under the Koizumi reforms and e-Japan Strategy

The situation has changed somewhat since 2001 because the Japanese government's macroeconomic and industrial policies have changed from those of the 1990s. Over the last five years the Japanese government has put together aggressive policy packages that resulted in positive outcomes in industries related to information and communications technology. When Prime Minister Koizumi took office in 2001, fiscal expenditure cuts were the top priority in his policy agenda and he began structural reforms toward his policy goals of small government.

The Koizumi Administration also promoted investment in information technology under the "e-Japan Strategy" policy packages (IT Strategy Headquarters, 2001). As policy makers realized the importance of information technology and its dynamic potential, they had a sense of urgency that Japan was far behind, not only with respect to a leading country like the United States, but also with respect to several Asian countries, like Korea and Singapore. Hence the launch of the e-Japan Strategy in 2001 (see Box 9.1), setting aggressive goals for Japan to be a leading country within five years in the area of high speed network infrastructure and its effective use. This, in turn, would allow Japan to regain competitive edge in the global economy.

So far, this policy mix seems successful. Today, the highest levels of broadband and wireless communications infrastructures are available with the lowest service rate in the world (Figures 9.2 and 9.3).

Box 9.1 Japan's e-Japan Strategy

"To become the world's most advanced IT nation by 2005"—In order to achieve this goal set forth by the e-Japan Strategy in January 2001, the public and private sectors, with the IT Strategic Headquarters playing a central role, have been making an all-out effort for more than four years in implementing various measures such as the development of communications infrastructure and the e-commerce market. As a result, Japan has made significant progress in the area of IT and has realized remarkable achievements. For example, Internet service in Japan is now the fastest and cheapest in the world, and Japan's e-commerce market has grown to become the second largest in the world after the United States in terms of scale. On the other hand, where the use of IT in areas such as e-government, medical services, and education is concerned, there still remain issues that need to be addressed in order to ensure that people can safely and genuinely have a real sense of the convenience that IT offers.

(IT Strategic Headquarters, 2005)

The e-Japan Strategy is an industrial policy initiative involving public and private sector actions. The initial e-Japan Strategy that was intended to make Japan a "knowledge-emergent society" prioritized the creation of an ultra high speed network, on the side of physical infrastructure, and, on the softer side, policies that would encourage competition. These were thought to facilitate electronic commerce, the creation of e-government (and other e-services), and the nurturing of appropriate human resources. Specific targets in each area were established and a menu of government actions was proposed. In most cases, these suggested actions were not direct public expenditures but rather shifts in regulatory policy. For example, "the government should, based on the philosophies of 'maximizing the benefits of the users' and 'promoting fair competition,' shift its administrative attitude from prior regulations-oriented to [an] ex-post-facto check approach according to transparent rules" (IT Strategy Headquarters, 2001, p. 4). Similarly, promotion of e-commerce involves legal and regulatory changes that would facilitate paperless electronic transactions. The establishment of e-government also calls for investments in equipment and programming to make government services available on an electronic basis and for digitizing of information. Similar tasks are required to deal with medical information. Nurturing high quality human resources aims to improve information literacy and increases the Internet diffusion rate. It also seeks to provide IT-driven education systems at all levels of the educational system and to increase masters and doctoral graduates in IT-related fields Interestingly, it calls for receiving many foreign IT experts in Japan and for more English education, this "being the most important language in the Internet era" (IT Strategy Headquarters, 2001, p. 8).

The Japanese IT Policy Package-2005 recognizes that substantial progress has been made, and focuses on all kinds of government and consumer, taxpayer and business interactions that can be handled and automated through electronic connections. Similar initiatives are being promoted for handling of medical records and transactions including remote medical care. A broad range of initiatives in education and in the application of IT to improvement of numerous dimensions of lifestyle is proposed. There are proposals to further stimulate e-commerce to help revitalize small business. As in most countries, there is a need for measures to protect personal information.

It is apparent from this discussion that physical investments represent only the first step, and perhaps the most easily solved one, in promoting an e-Society. The challenges of developing IT applications to carry out business transactions, government functions, education, medical services, and so on remain substantial in Japan as in other countries.

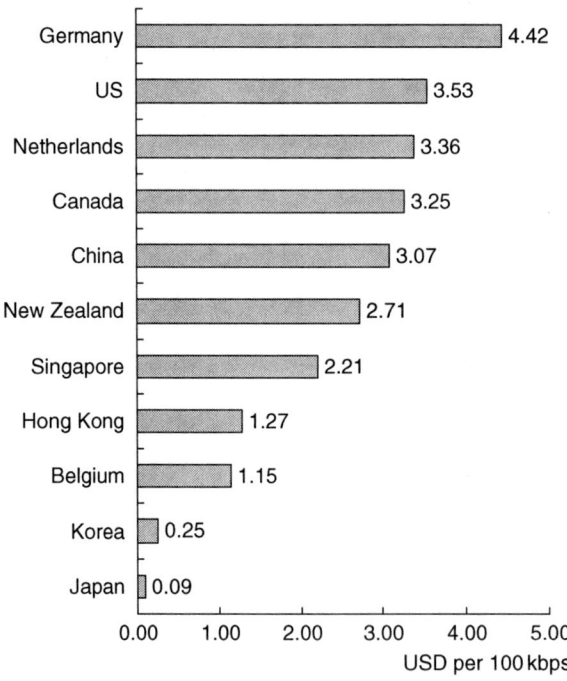

Figure 9.2 Broadband access rate per 100 kbps.

Source: Cabinet Office (2004) p. 5, figure 9-3.

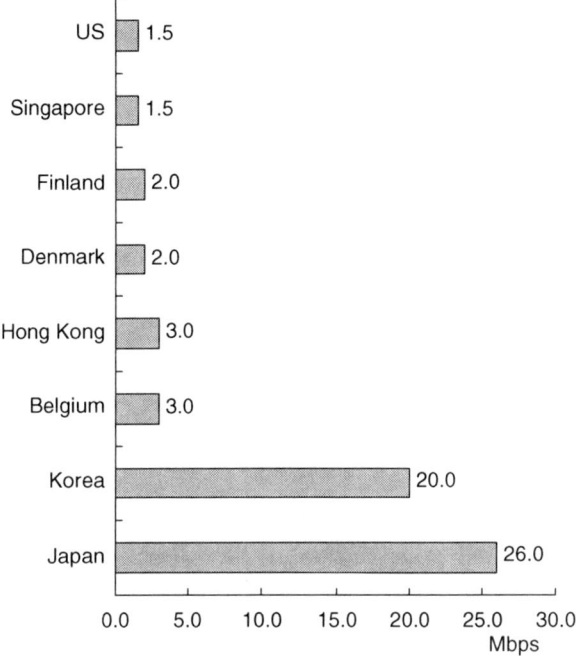

Figure 9.3 Broadband access speed.
Source: Cabinet Office (2004) p. 6, figure 1-5.

One of the important features of the Japanese IT market is that the Internet and cellular phone have been closely linked. Almost 90% of Japanese cellular phones have web access (Figure 9.4). The cellular-phone business is no longer a "telephone" industry but is a new "*keitai*" industry that combines mobile receivers with Internet access services. According to the Ministry of Internal Affairs and Communications (Figure 9.5), there are 85 million Internet users in Japan, or two third of the total population, of which 69 million users access via cellular phone while 66 million users access via PCs (dual users are 50 millions).

For the wired broadband market, the government strongly supported new business by enforcing a pro-competitive legal framework when several newcomers started up businesses and competed with NTT in the ADSL market. The Ministry of Posts and Telecommunications, a regulatory authority of the telecommunications industry, provided guidelines that put pressure on NTT to open its wired-access network to newcomers. In addition, the Fair Trade Commission strictly enforced the Anti-Trust Law in the ADSL market.

Unlike the wired network market that has a long history of government control, the wireless network market has been highly competitive because the history of cellular-phone service is relatively new and NTT DoCoMo, a cellular-phone service company and one of NTT's affiliates (spun-off in 1992), is a purely

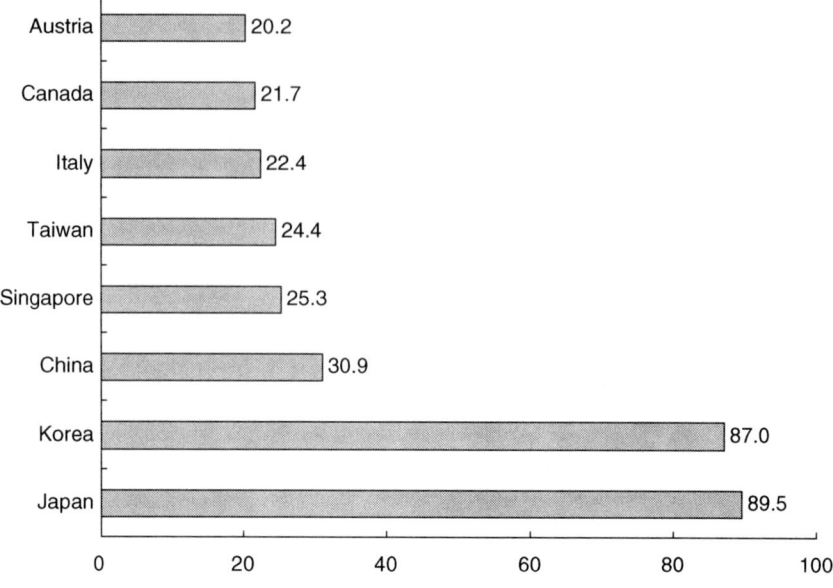

Figure 9.4 Internet access via cellular phone (% of total cellular users).
Source: Cabinet Office (2004) p. 7, figure I-8.

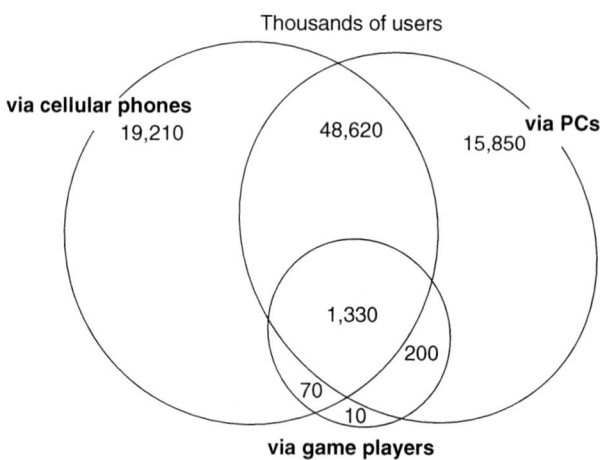

Figure 9.5 Number of internet access users in Japan.
Source: Ministry of Internal Affairs and Communications.

private company rather than a quasi-government company. Although analog wireless service started in 1979 by the former NTT as a government company, the market had been very small until 1994 when the market began expanding due to deregulation and the introduction of new digital technology. Competition really began in the mid-1990s. Since then, cellular-phone companies have invested intensively in enhanced wireless infrastructure and have provided a variety of new services such as Internet access service via cellular phones. As a result, the market is extremely competitive, compared to the wired network service market.

Although Japan failed to transform the telecommunications business from a switched network system to the Internet access system in the 1990s, Japan has leapfrogged into the broadband and mobile Internet access system in the 2000s. Today, Japan is ready to expand the new frontier of the ubiquitous computing information age. One should not be too pessimistic about the growth potential in Japanese telecommunications and related markets. We should instead ensure that Japan has an opportunity in the next-generation network of broadband, mobile, and omnipresent computing.

Opportunities and new challenges of continued technological change

The issue is whether the Japanese economy has the potential to achieve faster growth given continuous corporate reforms and the appropriate policy mix. The Japanese economy seems to have undergone several important reforms in both the private and government sectors since the 1990s. In this sense, the last decade enabled the economy to prepare for the transition into the Information Age.

As shown in Table 9.2, information technology kept changing. In the 1990s, there were changes in the form of significant transformations: from analog to digital; from a switched network system to a router (TCP/IP) network system; from charging according to access time and distance to charging a flat rate; and from intermittent access to staying online. Today's shifts are different: from narrowband to broadband, from fixed (wired) network to fixed mobile convergence or FMC, from copper cable line to optical fiber bundle; from low–medium volume data communications to extra-high volume data communications; and from business-oriented computing networks into ubiquitous computing networks such as home electronics computing networks.

However, there are some concerns in the industry. One is the slowing diffusion rate of both cellular phones and the Internet. These fields seem to be maturing and reaching ceilings. Another one is a small presence of Japanese IT businesses in the global market. Market shares of Japanese companies are small in most foreign IT markets even though their business in the domestic market has expanded vigorously. That is, these businesses have not been as successful on the global market as at home even though the foreign market has more opportunity to grow than the domestic one, especially in the emerging markets of the BRICs. A different market model may be required to give Japanese companies a competitive edge in the world market.

Today, technology and market conditions are changing further. The number of network users is expanding drastically. Varieties of electronic appliances are being networked such as music players, cellular-phone receivers, PDAs, and networking home electronics as well as personal computers. What is more, optical fiber bundles make it possible for a telecommunications network to carry movies and TV programs like broadcasting networks or CATV networks do. Volumes of data transactions, therefore, are mushrooming.

One of the resultant effects is that the wall separating the telecommunications business from the broadcasting business seems to be disappearing, at least in technological terms. Accordingly, wide ranges of related markets seem to be merging and integrating together. *Media convergence* arises from the recent spread of broadband networks. The number of users on broadband networks such as ADSL began exploding as the diffusion rate of cellular-phone users reached ceilings a few years ago. This new trend provides another business opportunity in the border area between broadcasting and the telecommunications industry: stress-free download and upload of rich content such as music or video at reasonable cost. Now, we have broadband networks as an alternative medium for rich content. A huge level market, rather than small fragmented markets, is emerging in the broadband and ubiquitous information age. The emerging market consists of the markets of broadcasting, telecommunications, content businesses such as animation production and movies, electronic appliance manufacturing such as home electronics as well as computers. In the trend to media convergence, they are going to come together and shape a single, information network industry, and become one of the strong engines of economic growth.

What is novel is that the electronic equipment, the iPod, for example, the network and the content are provided to users seamlessly, as if they were integrated into one service. The characteristics of mobile phone, broadband, and ubiquitous network are incorporated into "*ketai*" receivers in Japan. Activities ranging from business transactions, education, medical treatment, to entertainment can be digitized and put on networks as "rich" content.

These changes have implications for industry organization. In the early days of the "*ketai*" market, cellular-phone suppliers (electronics manufacturers) and network carriers had established close business relationships as if they were quasi-integral organizations. They created vertically integrated structures. Similar relationships had been built up between broadcasting firms and content providers (TV program production firms). In the coming media convergence age, we may need to reconsider whether vertical integration is an appropriate business model as it may have been in the early stages of the market. Modular alliances rather than vertical integration may be more appropriate in the expanding frontier of media convergence.

Another important dimension of IT-based progress is the increased applications of sophisticated IT technology in industries that are not, in themselves, highly techno-logical such as wholesale and retail distribution and finance. As we have observed, the logistical and inventory control techniques employed by large American enterprises have contributed greatly to productivity gains in the United States. In this direction, Japan has many unfulfilled possibilities. Given the organization of Japanese wholesale and retail distribution, these may also entail huge challenges.

Adam Smith, considered the founder of modern economics, pointed out that the size of the market determines the degree of the division of labor and the resultant productivity level. In this context, the expansion and integration of markets improve the potential for applying specialized technology. A large scale is required for effective use of IT technology and distribution operations. That may pose a challenge particularly to the smaller enterprises in the wholesale and retail distribution sectors of Japan.

Challenges for the Japanese economic policy in telecommunications

Although emerging new information technology paves the way for business opportunities and growth in Japanese telecommunications, these are not automatically realized without any effort. It is necessary for the telecommunications business sectors to make continuous efforts at business process reengineering and business unit restructuring, especially in those firms that have been less enthusiastic in the past about the effective use of the technology.

As for policies directed toward the telecommunication industries, some of the underlying regulations in broadcasting and telecommunications industries are no longer appropriate today. Most of these regulations were established decades ago when the state of technology was completely different from that of today and broadcasting and telecommunications were considered as having different businesses models. It is inevitable that regulations lag behind technical innovations. Thus, revisions of broadcasting laws, telecommunications business laws, copyright laws, and other related regulations are required in accordance with technological changes.

Take copyright law for example. The ministry's guidelines prohibit the dissemination of the contents of TV programs or movies via optical fibers in a telecommunications network to the home while doing so via a cable television network is allowed. From the consumer's viewpoint, however, it does not matter whether TV programs or movies are provided by a cable television network, telecommunications fiber to the home (FTTH) network, or a ground wave or satellite broadcasting network. Consumers just want to enjoy TV programs or movies on a clear, advanced screen and pay the lowest service charges.

Revisions of informal constraints are also required in several industries. The broadcast industry is known for exclusive and ambiguous business practices and conventions.[2]

As a result of restrictions on issuing licenses, existing licensees were able to obtain overwhelming advantages. They maintained high profit margins, a kind of monopoly rent. Broadcasting firms dominated the market and built business practices and conventions that were to their own advantage. For instance, content producers are at a disadvantage against broadcasting firms. In some cases, content producers have virtually no right of secondary distribution of their own content because broadcasting firms have exclusive bargaining power to put the content on their broadcasting network.

There are also regulations in the telecommunications industry that seem inappropriate for both NTT and its competitors. The formal roles of the Broadcasting Act or the Telecommunications Act were established when the mainstream businesses were radio broadcasting or telephony communications rather than digital broadcasting or digital data communications. These rules are no longer appropriate for new businesses in the media convergence age.

This situation of NTT may need to change further. It may be plausible that NTT be given a free hand as a purely private firm under the regulations of the Telecommunications Business Law in general and strict enforcement of the Anti Trust Law, rather than as a quasi-private (or quasi-government) firm controlled by specifically designed NTT Law. Otherwise, resources contained in the NTT group could never be used to their full potential in an emerging and huge integrated market of network service, nor in the global market. The application of fair trade rules and pro-competitive regulations is certainly important since huge gaps in market share or competitive advantage between NTT and other competitors exist in several parts of the telecommunication market due to incomplete liberalization and privatization over the past 20 years. One reasonable solution may be to break the quasi-private businesses of the existing NTT group into two categories of business and to operate them under completely different standards without any ownership ties: (1) quasi-governmental businesses that operate and maintain physical assets of legacy copper line access networks and rights of way or conduits as a provider of public goods and services; and (2) purely private network businesses that involve next-generation networks and value-added network services in the competitive market both domestically and globally. Thus, it is essential to examine the benefits of a free hand for NTT's business and reorganization of the NTT group in light of the prospects of the next generation of network systems.

Finally, it would be helpful to consider consolidation of some of the regulatory agencies. It might be possible for some authorities to commit to common policy goals, allowing each organization to cooperate in an effort to create a competitive telecommunications environment.

Conclusions

The telecommunications industry is a rather special extreme example. This is an industry where technological change has been extremely rapid, a case of disruptive innovation. It is also an example of a sector that started out under public ownership, that has been privatized in stages, and that still lacks a flat competitive setting particularly in the wired communication part of the business. Other parts of the Japanese economy differ considerably. Some of the advanced high-technology companies that operate in the international environment are leaders in their fields and have adapted their organizations and their technologies fully to the latest advancements. But other sectors, for example, wholesale and retail distribution, have yet to adopt many of the new technologies. These sectors where there is much room for productivity gains may require additional public financial and technical aid to make the transition into the new economy.

10 IT-related development and policy

Some examples from the United States with relevance to Japan

As a leader in some important IT sectors, like cell phone communications, Japan has set an example for many other countries. The United States also offers some good illustration of what can be accomplished when a country's industries adapt quickly to new technologies and these experiences may, in turn, be useful background for developing strategy accelerating Japanese growth. There is broad agreement among the many studies in this field that the improvement in the economic performance of the United States relates to the IT revolution and we have noted that in recent years much of the improvement in productivity has been in retail and wholesale trade and finance (Basu *et al.*, 2001). While much progress has been made, there remain large possibilities for further development in the United States and, also, in Japan.

In this Chapter, we consider some of the organizational forces and policy approaches that can be seen in the United States. Some of these offer examples for Japan; others may represent indications of what still needs to be done and, even, warnings of what to avoid. We will describe the setting in which growth in the United States is taking place and give some examples of developments in the commercial and government application of IT. We also consider the macro policy stance, public incentives for investment, modernization, and R&D, and the American dispute about industrial policy.

It is important to recognize, however, that success with new IT or e-business ventures in one country does not signal that the same efforts will be successful in another. Historical, sociological, and cultural considerations influence the path of economic development. Computerization is path dependent. In this respect the fact that American IT was initially largely land-based through broadband connections while in Japan cellphone connections predominated may make a difference in the ultimate outcome, but recent technological progress is bringing the two approaches closer together. Another example is that business communication and organization may require quite different technological structures in a country with integrated businesses and close personal communication like Japan than in a country with more modular organizational characteristics like the United States. Similarly, as we discuss later, the scale and logistical requirements of retail and wholesale business may be quite different in a densely populated country than in an environment of greater distances and greater reliance on private automobile transportation. Ultimately the social environment will influence how and with what effect IT programs will be introduced.

The economic setting and institutions in the United States

The principal forces supporting the development of the IT industries and their applications in the United States must be related to broad economic philosophy and competitive market policies going back for many years. This is not so much a matter of specific policy as a statement about the economic environment that has been established in United States. Note that there has not been an e-US initiative in the United States on the scale of e-Japan, though efforts to establish e-government are wide spread. The US market environment favors dynamic competition with little government intervention. An entrepreneurial tradition has been particularly beneficial to the creation and application of new IT industries. Innovators have been aided by venture capital firms that have made capital available to people with ideas, even young people without business experience. The cases of Stephen Jobs at Apple Computer and Bill Gates at Microsoft are good examples. The original developers of the new technology have frequently been smaller firms, newcomers, but ultimately some of these have become enormous enterprises or their inventions have been adopted by existing national and international firms.

The development of Silicon Valley is a classic example of the way in which high-level academic institutions, inventors and entrepreneurs, and venture capital interacted to produce a high-tech cluster (Wikipedia, 2006). Inspired by a Stanford University professor, Frederick Terman, in 1939 the University established an industrial research park which attracted such new high-tech firms as Hewlett-Packard, Varian Associates, and the Xerox PARC research center. These firms were among the initial developers not only of chips and other hardware but also of much of the critical software and operating systems of today's computers. Young people from the University and from high-tech companies established in the area went on to create many of the leading hardware and software companies in the region: Fairchild Semiconductor, National Semiconductor, Intel, AMD, Apple, 3Com, Adobe Systems, and Cisco. Coincidentally, the growth in the area was stimulated by the development of the venture capital industry beginning with Kleiner Perkins in 1972 and the successful IPOs of many companies in the region. Although semiconductors are still a large part of the region's industry, Silicon Valley has become most famous for innovations in software and Internet services. That the role of the University in this area remains important is confirmed by the fact that Sergey Brin and Larry Page, founders of Google, developed their basic search programming as graduate students at Stanford University. A *Wall Street Journal* story in 2006 reports that on the basis of patent counts ten of the twenty most inventive towns in America were in Silicon Valley. The region presents clear evidence of the power of close technical interaction and finance available in a highly specialized area. There are also other such specialized technology clusters in the United States, for example, around Seattle, Washington, Austin, Texas, and the biotechnology research center being established near MIT in Cambridge, Massachusetts.

While there is evidence of technical clustering and entrepreneurial initiative in many countries including Japan, the case of Silicon Valley is unique. Efforts to build technological centers are widespread, for example Tsukuba in Japan, but it would be difficult to use policy to produce the spontaneous developments that spawned the IT industry in California.

Sectors in United States IT development

IT development in the United States has expanded far beyond the technological developments originating in Silicon Valley. Large American enterprises in many fields of manufacturing and distribution have adopted sophisticated IT application systems to handle their business transactions, human resource management operations, accounting, logistics, and other "back office" functions. Computer automation has replaced paper shuffling, increasing productivity and reducing the need to employ office workers. The Internet has extended the network from the business directly to the consumer. Consumer purchases directly from the Internet are increasing rapidly. High speed communications has made it possible to offshore some tasks to office centers in South Asia and Africa where labor costs are much lower than in the United States. But, even, in the United States, the level of technological application is far from even, so that some businesses and, even, some sectors like health care lag behind.

Later, we summarize some illustrations of productivity improvement with IT in particular sectors. The sectoral case study view illustrates how uneven the development has been, even in the United States. It suggests some areas of potential growth and some areas of continued difficulty. The experience may offer some positive and some negative examples.

Retail distribution: Wal-Mart and Amazon

Important structural differences between retail and wholesale distribution in the United States and Japan account for differences in productivity. Japan has a more complicated distributional structure with numerous wholesalers and smaller retailers. (Table 10.1) There is less investment in information technology and

Table 10.1 Statistics on distribution: Japan and United States

	Japan	US
No. of retail stores per 10,000 population	91	55
Sales per store	0.9 (million $)	2.1 (million $)
Frequency of consumers' visits to retail stores	Every day (46%) 2–3 times a week (36%) Other (18%)	Once a week (42%) Twice a week (29%) 3 times a week (15%) Other (14%)
Labor productivity in commerce sector (USA = 100)	91	100
Value added per employee in 2000	76.4	100

Source: Ministry of Economics, Trade, and Industry. Computed from OECD data, PPP conversion.

there is less standardization, that is, firm-specific customized data processing systems. (According to the Ministry of Economics, Trade, and Industry (METI), 62% of retailers use their own customized information system.) It is not surprising, consequently, that Japanese productivity in distribution is lower than the United States, leaving substantial room for productivity improvement. But it is problematic how that productivity improvement can be achieved in a very different Japanese setting.

Wal-Mart and Amazon are classic examples of new economy wholesale and retail distribution in United States.

Wal-Mart, the world's largest retailer, is an exceptional case even in the United States. It boasts bigger sales than any other businesses in the world, operating at a far larger scale than comparable firms in Japan (Table 10.2). For the past 5–10 years, Wal-Mart has made great progress with a strategy of building enormous stores selling all varieties of consumer goods including foods in the outskirts of medium and small cities, leaving its competitors far behind. The success of Wal-Mart may be associated with savings associated with its large scale and effective use of IT. Much of its operation has involved computerized logistics for its many low-price products, mainly sourced in China. The low cost of goods sold by this company has often been referred to as an explanation for inflation control in the United States. Table 10.3 indicates the very large difference in cost structure with respect to operating expenses between Wal-Mart and major Japanese retailers.

Wal-Mart has applied IT to various business processes, from purchasing or logistics to in-store product inventory management and sales. One of the examples is the use of the barcode system. Wal-Mart was one of the first retailers to introduce the technology, benefiting the whole industry in improving efficiency. Now, the company is concentrating on introducing RFID[1] tags,

Table 10.2 Major retailers' sales ranking and performances (2002) (millions of $)

Rank	Company	Country	Sales	Earnings
1	Wal-Mart	USA	229,617	8,039
2	Carrefour	France	65,011	1,314
3	Home Depot	USA	58,247	3,664
4	Kroger	USA	51,760	1,205
5	Metro	Germany	48,349	475
6	Target	USA	42,722	1,654
7	Ahold	Netherlands	40,755	(1,143)
8	Tesco	UK	40,071	1,451
9	Costco	USA	37,993	700
10	Sears	USA	35,698	1,376
⋮	⋮	⋮	⋮	⋮
22	Itoh–Yokado	Japan	26,179	171
⋮	⋮	⋮	⋮	⋮
26	AEON	Japan	23,030	418

Source: Authors computation from data from the Ministry of Economics, Trade, and Industry.

Table 10.3 Financial statement analysis—US and Japanese retailers
(2003)

	Wal-Mart	Itoh–Yokado	AEON
	(% of total sales)		
Sales	100.0	100.0	100.0
Cost of goods sold	77.5	74.7	72.3
Gross margin	23.4	25.3	27.7
Other revenue	0.9	5.3	1.3
Operating expenses	17.5	29.2	27.3
Operating income	5.9	1.4	1.6

Source: Annual Reports.

a technology that is expected to replace the barcode. Following experimental introduction of RFIDs, the rate of product shortage was decreased significantly, and the speed of product replenishment was improved three times. Wal-Mart is now planning to begin the use of RFIDs widely throughout its system. They are planning to start off by attaching RFIDs to the product cases and pallets but, eventually, when the cost of the RFIDs comes down they will be incorporated into individual products.[2]

Wal-Mart's initiatives in this area will have a great positive impact on the market. Competitive pressures will force other US distributors like Costco, Home Depot, and the large department stores to take similar steps though some do not have the advantages of Wal-Mart's enormous scale. Japanese retail distributors are moving rapidly in the same direction but it is unclear that they can or would want to achieve the same scale and type of operation. Japanese consumers rely much more heavily on convenience stores, readily available in business and residential areas, and, being less reliant on automobiles, they are less able to buy in large volume at suburban warehouse stores. The prevalence of smaller stores means that IT logistical techniques will need adaptation, though it is possible that the advantages of computerization are even greater for complex small-scale operations than for huge enterprises the size of Wal-Mart.

Amazon represents the next stage of commerce in the United States, operating its B2C retailing entirely on the Internet. Originally a seller of books, Amazon now sells a wide variety of merchandise and makes its computer programs, warehouses, and shipping facilities available to other Internet-based retailers.

Commenting on possibilities for "pervasive" computing, Agoston *et al.* (2000) say "Worldwide, the United States is the leading market in terms of e-commerce adoption,... but Japan is ahead with devices and ubiquitous connectivity networks.... The growth in e-commerce is lagging in Japan because of cultural preference for face-to-face transactions, especially in the business to consumer market space." Expanding the use of e-commerce in Japan may require more effective links to the cellular phone system. Progress in this direction is quite rapid.

Express delivery: FedEx and logistics of delivery

Express delivery has been a growth area in the United States as an increasing volume of products purchased over the Internet and over the telephone requires delivery. FedEx, a leading express delivery company with extensive air and ground transport operations, is one of the outstanding examples of a firm that successfully introduced IT logistical support to most areas of its operation. FedEx's rapid growth is a remarkable achievement when we consider the fact that they achieved their record despite the recent wide spread of network tools such as e-mailing or instant-messaging (text conversation through the Internet) or groupware (co-working system within a group) that replace written messages on paper that would in the past have been carried by FedEx.

FedEx's success and that of competing delivery companies like UPS is largely due to their successful use of IT. Application of IT programs enable these firms to track all shipments in real time from origin to destination.

Financial industry: banking, security markets and Internet Loan Service

Banking and financial operations are fields where large IT investments have transformed relationships with customers in the United States over several decades. What began with back office operations on large mainframe computers was extended to relationships between banks and their customers on the ATM machine and has been extended further toward Internet-based banking systems. Many transactions today are being carried on through the customers' own computers and the Internet and much billing and depositing is being done automatically and electronically. Some payments are made directly through banks while others call for specialized services like PayPal. Salaries and retirement payments, including Social Security, are being made automatically into bank accounts and regular charges are also being withdrawn automatically. On the other hand, entirely Internet-based banks have not been very successful; computer-based bank transactions are typically offered as an ancillary service by ordinary banks. Commercial banks are still building buildings and serving many customers personally through their teller windows. Some banks, however, have begun to charge extra for personal service.

Securities brokers have been more successful in linking to their customers directly through the Internet. Huge brokerage companies like E*TRADE operate entirely on the Internet. Others, like Fidelity, operate a large part of their business through Internet accounts but retain some offices and account executives. Charges for making securities transactions through the Internet have been greatly reduced; recently Chase Manhattan Bank has offered to do securities transactions for large depositors at no cost. The actual trading of securities is increasingly being done electronically Even the New York Stock Exchange, "practically the last bastion of the centuries-old system of putting together investors through auctions on a hardwood trading floor" (*Wall Street Journal*, November 11, 2006), is closing one of its trading floors.

An interesting example of Internet-based financial transactions has been the development of Internet loans, a loan system in which customers can submit applications through the Internet without visiting financial institutions. Types of loans available vary widely, including housing loans, auto loans, educational loans and others. In 2005 the Internet accounted for approximately one third of total loans made. The use of the Internet to transmit full information check records has greatly reduced the time required to process loan applications.

Other IT success stories

A number of other fields have been highly successful in their use of the Internet to deal with their customers.

Airline ticketing is a striking example. A large share of airline tickets are being purchased on the web where consumers have direct access to airline websites or to ticketing organizations like Orbitz, Travelocity, Amadeus, and Expedia. Travel agents have had direct access to the airline ticketing systems for some time. The international airlines expect that all ticketing will be electronic by the end of 2007.

A great deal of educational and entertainment content as well as music, of course, is now being taken directly from the web. It is premature, however, to say that a majority of these materials will be transmitted electronically even looking far toward the future.

Advertising is another field undergoing rapid change. Traditional print advertising in newspapers is declining even as Internet advertising, for example as part of Google and Yahoo, is booming.

In these activities, patterns that have been developed in the United States and advanced countries of Europe and Japan are spreading worldwide. But as we shall see later, even in the United States some sectors continue to lag behind.

Medical insurance and records

In the medical insurance and medical records fields large investments in IT hardware and software are being made but, in the United States, there is still much room for development. Medical insurance organizations like Blue Cross/ Blue Shield (BC/BS) of many states have undertaken large-scale efforts to computerize operations. For businesses in any field, the use of the large-scale systems that connect basic operations and accounting operations is essential. Through back office systems, general operations data are passed to the accounting system, which enables accounting settlement or performance management to be carried out. What the BC/BS groups have attempted is to make the customer information in its back office system accessible to the medical customers, through the Internet.

In the past, when an inquiry was received by BC/BS from a customer, it was accepted through a customer service phone line and dealt with by a service operator, who would refer the query to the back office system for the specific information. The new systems will make it possible for customers to access relevant information in the computerized system of BC/BS through the Internet. With the new system, customers will be able to access a personalized web-site, in which they can select the insurance plans that meet their needs and their budget, or make an estimate of its cost, or learn about prescription medicine and medical treatment. It is also possible for them to search for the nearest affiliated hospitals or doctors, or to trace the status of insurance approval for a specific transaction. In short, the system will allow customers to fulfill most of their own needs at any time by accessing the Internet, without needing to talk to operators on the phone. The gains in company productivity are readily apparent though the increasing difficulty for the client, sometimes a serious challenge, is typically not measured.

For health information, the ultimate objective announced by President Bush in 2004 was to develop a nationwide health information technology infrastructure with the objective of reducing healthcare costs. However, a US national system does not yet exist and electronic health record systems (EHRs) are not yet widespread. In a study of the use of healthcare technology in the OECD, Anderson *et al.* (2006) concluded that "the United States lags as much as a dozen years behind other industrialized countries in HIT (health information technology) adoption—countries where national governments played major roles in establishing the rule and health insurers paid most of the costs." The difficulty lies not so much in the availability of technology as in fact that the US healthcare system is fragmented between public and private for-profit and not-for-profit systems operating at the state and local level. This will make it difficult technically and politically to establish a national information system. According to the national health care survey, EHRs were in use in only 17% of physicians' offices, 31% of emergency rooms, and 29% of hospital outpatient departments in 2003 (Sidorov, 2006).

The impact of EHR systems on the costs of medical care and on productivity is still being debated (Sidorov, 2006), systems are being installed by many health providers and new programs will be developed and installed. That, in turn, would increase productivity in many of the auxiliary operations of the healthcare field. The United States is still a long way from establishing a comprehensive system. The cost of further progress in applying IT to the medical care system in the United States is likely to be substantial, though the potential for improving efficiency also remains large. Other countries, like Japan, must seek to avoid the difficulties encountered with IT management, particularly its fragmentation, in the medical care field in the United States.

Government

In the United States, as in Japan, it is the government agencies that are most poorly provided with IT. The United States recognizes this as a serious issue and has been trying to establish electronic government. Some important operations have been computerized. Yet the task of applying IT to the full range of government activities, namely, to establish e-government, appears much more demanding compared to practices in private enterprises, and the United States is still in the process of trial and error. Indeed, $45 billion was invested in e-government projects in 2002, without seeing widespread results so far. The main obstacles to such a project in the United States is the horizontally segmented structure of state and local governments and of different departments in the Federal government. It is crucial to share information horizontally with the use of IT in order to realize "e-Government." However, the nature of the administration structures continues to be a major barrier. Government agencies tend to be reluctant to share information with each other and to regard IT from the perspective of benefits for their own specialized functions.

In the United States, the e-government project was launched at full-scale when the current Bush Administration appointed a task-force in 2001. The results of the task-force's activity (called "Quicksilver Task-Force") were put together in a report to the Office of Management and Budget in February, 2002. This is the so-called E-Government Strategy of the Bush Administration.

The main aims of the project are as follows:

- Share information horizontally through agencies and transform their vertical structure.
- Provide high-quality service to citizens, whether by phone or through the Internet or face to face.
- Reduce and simplify the financial transaction processing between the government and citizens.
- Reduce the federal management expenses.
- Provide easier access to the agencies' websites or e-government applications to citizens with disabilities.
- Increase transparency and strengthen accountability of the Federal Government.

The government set up 24 E-Government Initiatives. These range very widely from functions that relate government to citizens (G2C), like responses to inquiries, availability of forms, and submission of tax returns, to functions relating to business (G2B), licenses and other reports, as well as internal government functions (G2G) like budgets, personnel records, and cost reports. The objective is to computerize government operations on a standard basis everywhere.

While many steps forward are being made—a large share of individual income tax returns are now being made on line—progress reports suggest that much still needs to be accomplished (OMB, 2005). It will be some years before the United States will serve as an example of successful e-government. Other country governments are also making substantial efforts in this direction.

We note that since government output is measured on a cost basis in the national accounts, improvements in productivity associated with improved use of IT in government will not appear in the GDP productivity statistics.

Conclusions on IT applications in the United States and implications for Japan

The application of IT in industry business practice for financial transactions, trading, distribution, inventory control, e-business and so on has played an important role in recent years in promoting productivity in American business. These applications have been favored by large competitive firms able to take advantage of the latest logistical and inventory control procedures. As we have noted, significant productivity gains in finance and retail and wholesale distribution can be linked to IT applications.

While performance and prospects in the business fields in the United States have been very good, there is clearly much still to be done in other service entities like the medical fields and government. It is unlikely that US operations in these fields, which are organized very differently in Japan from their counterparts in the United States, will be a good example for Japan.

It would take an elaborate sector by sector study of IT and its application in the United States and a comparison to Japan to make detailed prescriptions on how to accelerate the development of IT-based industry. In some activities, wireless telephony for example, Japan has been in the forefront of development, while in others, like wholesale and retail distribution, Japan may be lagging behind. Some of the differences between the US and Japan may be related to cultural and organizational considerations, or simply to customary ways of making transactions, as we have noted in Chapter 8. The scale and form of Japanese retail trade may call for different, more flexible, IT systems. There is no doubt, however, that a dynamically competitive marketplace supported by high levels of education and venture capital financing favors the development of IT-related industries and applications in US business and that these contribute to the growth of productivity. We will consider the relationship of growth to economic policy in the next section.

Policy and the IT revolution in the United States

Some of the recent progress in the United States economy related to development and application of IT technology is policy-based. In this section, we will examine policies at various levels. We begin with the general policy and economic philosophy setting and then we examine policies—industrial policies providing incentives to particular industries, more general incentive policies fostering research, investment, and innovation, and macroeconomic policies.

Deregulation

Beginning in the early 1970s, the United States began a systematic policy of deregulation. In contrast to many other countries, very few businesses were under public ownership in the United States. On the other hand, large sectors of the economy including energy distribution, telephone communications, and air, rail, and truck transportation were highly regulated. Deregulation, and the breakup of some large monopolies, like AT&T, opened these fields to dynamic competition. Substantial changes in industrial structure and technology occurred. New firms entered the deregulated markets. There have been significant increases in competition and improvements in productivity and reductions in prices. It is not clear, however, that these changes always improve the quality of service provided. Today, there is again some tendency toward industrial concentration.

Some of the energy distribution companies remain regulated. But there is broad agreement that the deregulated industries in a competitive environment have been quicker to adapt to new technology than they would have under a continued regulatory regime.

Industrial policies

The American economic environment of dynamic markets has clearly been fostered by a non-interventionist market-based economic policy philosophy. There has been little formal industrial policy aimed at the development of IT industries or at the application of IT methodologies though many of these industries have benefited from government-sponsored basic research, investment tax credits, and accelerated depreciation.

The 1980s and 1990s were the period of Intel chips and of Microsoft operating systems. From a technical perspective, it was the time of the Internet and the age of cell phone communication. Some firms developed and sold hardware—chips, computers, routers and network components. Others provided software—operating systems and applications. Still others facilitated applications, like IT methods for trade and finance. More recently, we have seen the development of vast new enterprises using IT program applications, Google, Ebay, Orbitz, and Yahoo, for example. As we have noted, particularly important has been the use of new IT communications and logistical techniques by the express companies, FedEx, by large retail and wholesale merchandising companies, Wal-Mart, by Internet distributors, Amazon, and by banks and securities companies, Bank of America and Fidelity. This period was, of course, also the time of the dot.com boom and, more recently, the dot.com bust.

At an early stage of development, many of the new technologies were supported by government programs, like the Defense Department's DARPA for applied research and the NSF for basic research. In the early 1990s, US vice-president Al Gore was a strong advocate of an "information superhighway" but the public sector did not implement such a proposal and, unlike Japan, the United States has not had an official e-society strategy plan. Few e-business applications have antecedents that relied on public funds. More often, funding originated internally or from venture capital firms, and many enterprises rode successfully on the back of the Silicon Valley stock price boom.

In the late 1970s and early 1980s, industrial policy was a subject of political dispute in the United States (Adams and Klein (eds), 1983). Liberal economists were promoting targeted industrial policy to advance promising new industries, the so-called sunrise industries, and to phase out the losers. This policy position was similar to the support for critical industries provided by MITI in Japan during the 1950s and 1960s. On the other side were more conservative people who promoted free markets and who sought to avoid government intervention. They argued that government officials did not make good economic choices and that the industries chosen for promotion might not be economically viable. With the turn to political conservatism, the United States did not institute targeted industrial policies, not even ones favoring the IT industries, except in the energy and energy-related industries.

General tax cuts and incentive policies

On the other hand, there has been an abundance of general incentive and tax cut policies, favoring investment and modernization without targeting on specific sectors or industries. The Reagan Administration's "Supply Side" policies, cutting personal and corporate income taxes by approximately one third are a classic example, although today most observers believe that these policies had their impact not so much through improved work and saving/investment incentives as through increased consumer spending. There have also been in the United States policy measures with more specific targets to stimulate investment such as investment tax credits and accelerated depreciation. While these tax measures are generally not targeted on specific industries like information technology, they favor business investment in hardware and software and consequently provide incentives for investment in the IT fields. It is widely thought that these measures stimulated corporate hardware spending and also account for increase of spending in business management software (Busom, 1999; Shoch, 1999; No author, *The Big Picture*, 2004, p. 1).

Education and university R&D

The American educational system and the research that is performed there have made a significant contribution to the technological revolution that lies behind the new economy. The United States has been a leader in advanced technical education, though most recently there have been serious concerns that educational performance is slipping and that not enough young engineers and scientists are being produced. (Committee, 2005). In the United States, higher education is a mixture between public and private. Significant public money from the states and the federal government contributes to the support of university education and research. Some of the critical basic developments relating to computers and the Internet are a consequence of publicly funded research many years ago. But, in recent years, public support of universities has been a diminishing share of total expenditures and declining public R&D support has increasingly focused on health sciences and defense rather than IT. While government policies have made an important contribution, it would not be realistic to argue that recent developments in the IT revolution are the result of a conscious US government policy to develop and/or to commercialize the applications of IT technology.

Another dimension of education may also be relevant. The American educational system has put heavy emphasis in business programs and particularly on the MBA degree. The MBA is different from other university programs in its emphasis on small group teamwork and application. Today, almost all American business executives have at least the equivalent of an MBA degree. It would be difficult to determine how much influence MBA education has had on the organization and practice of American business. Many people, particularly in the MBA establishment, would argue that MBA training is a major conditioning factor in the interpersonal relationships of American business people. It is noteworthy that, by and large, Japanese management lacks such training, since MBA programs are a much more recent and limited phenomenon in Japan than in the United States. On the other hand, as we have noted, Japanese management also places a heavy emphasis on team relationships. One can only speculate whether formal training at the university level is a consideration in the difference between integrated and modular organization of management that we note in Chapter 8.

Financial system and venture capital

The financial system for business is another major difference between the United States and Japan. In the past, Japanese businesses have been largely bank financed. Even though the traditional "main bank" system in the *keiretsu* has faded, bank financing is still prevalent. The failure until the 2000s to consolidate Japanese banks and to fix the difficult non-performing loan (NPL) situation increased the difficulty of financing new business ventures through the banking system in Japan. In the United States, until the stock market crashed in 2001, plentiful financing was available on securities markets. Moreover the United States has an institution, the venture capital firm, that is unique as a provider of capital to high-tech ventures. These firms supplement the capital resources they provide to new firms with management supervision and training that help inexperienced new entrepreneurs get started.

Macroeconomic environment and policy considerations

The macroeconomic setting, whether a country is booming or in recession, greatly influences the rate of capital accumulation and modernization and affects the growth of productivity.[3] Jorgenson *et al.* (2005) conclude that a surge in IT investment after 1995 in all the G-7 economies accounts for a large portion of the growth in United States, and also in Europe and Japan. They also note that "For Japan the dramatic upward leap in the impact of IT investment was *insufficient* to overcome downward pressure from deficient growth of aggregate demand" (p. 84, our italics). The implication is that the United States IT industries gained from rapid economic expansion in the second half of the 1990s, and that Japan lacked this upward pressure.

It is not clear, of course, that the expansion in United States in the late 1990s and again more recently was a result of policy. But appropriate fiscal and monetary stimuli were in place. The IT revolution and introduction of IT capital goods may have a basis in a broadbased expansion that had macro policy support. This was a situation that prevailed in the United States in contrast to the deflation that prevailed so long in Japan. An economy that is operating at high levels of demand pressure is considerably more receptive to the introduction of new technology and the development of new industries than one that is in stagnation or deflation. On the other hand, the direction of causation is not entirely clear, since rapid growth does, itself, reflect the influence of the introduction of new technology.

Our point here, important for the thesis of this volume, is that a high level of demand is favorable to the introduction of new technologies and for rapid growth. A low growth target may create an environment that makes technical progress and innovation difficult.

Conclusion

The United States experience offers some important lessons for the linkages between economic policy and economic performance:

- Perhaps most importantly, a healthy and growing, economic setting provides maximum opportunity for creating and introducing new technology. Investment and productivity growth are closely linked to rapid economic growth.
- A large part of the gains in productivity are the result of applying IT techniques in services like wholesale and retail distribution and finance. In other fields, particularly ones like health care and government, that are not exposed to competition, performance in the United States has been less satisfactory.
- Incentives and public support for research and development can have important impacts on basic knowledge but sometimes with very long time lags until the new information is widely disseminated and applied to yield productivity gains.
- An educated labor force and relationships between universities and business facilitate the application of the technology into the business world.
- Availability of funding is an important contributor to the development and application of new high-technology. Venture capital firms make an important contribution by providing capital and guidance to upstart new high-tech firms.

Some of these factors may be transferable to policy in Japan and other countries but others represent cultural and social phenomena that are difficult to transfer.

11 Estimating a new economy production function for Japan

This chapter summarizes our empirical work on estimating a production function for Japan suitable for the new economy. This production function allows for increasing returns and technical change associated with the IT economy.

Re-estimating the Japanese aggregate production function

Our empirical studies are intended to explore whether it is realistic to assume a 3% economic growth rate even though conventional computations might suggest a growth rate of at most 2%. When economic policies are planned for the next decade, a difference of 1% in economic growth can give a very different picture of the future Japanese economy.

The first step in making these calculations is to introduce the following characteristics of the impact of the IT revolution on the production function into the economic analysis:

1 Changes in the quality of labor—The IT revolution requires continuous improvement of worker education and training.
2 The distinction between IT and non-IT capital—IT investments may have very different impacts from non-IT investments.
3 Economies of scale—Network effects may produce increasing returns as Metcalfe's Law suggests.
4 Embodied technical progress—technical change can be embodied in capital stock.
5 Variable elasticity between output and IT capital stock—The effect of the investment in computers and network systems in 2005 on output may be much bigger than that in 1995.

In order to consider these elements, a generalized Cobb–Douglas production function is useful (Kumasaka and Tange, 2004). We will compare the estimates and the implications for potential GDP growth of this new production function with the more traditional Cobb–Douglas function that has been used for Japanese growth estimates.

A new (IT) type Cobb–Douglas production function

$$Y_t = A_t\{(1 + \rho)^{t*}L_t\}^\alpha(KO_t)^\beta(KI_t)^\gamma \tag{1}$$

where
Y: Real GDP
A: Total factor productivity
ρ: labor-augmenting rate
L: the employment
KO: Real net non-IT capital stock, and
KI: real net IT capital stock

In the actual estimation of Eqn (1), labor input is presented as average man-hours multiplied by labor force by $L*WH$ and capital inputs are multiplied by capacity utilization by $KO*CU$, $KI*CU$ or $(KO+KI)*CU$ where

WH: Average working hours for employed
CU: Capacity utilization.

Equation (1) is transformed into Eqn (2) which shows the relationship among the growth rates of both output and inputs. Subscript t of each variable in Eqn (2) is omitted.

For example, $d\log(Y)$ is the growth rate of Y, $(Y / Y_{-1})-1$.

$$d\log(Y) = d\log(A) + \alpha\log(1 + \rho) + \alpha d\log(L) + \beta d\log(KO) + \gamma d\log(KI) \tag{2}$$

Before we estimate Eqn (1), we need to determine the labor augmentation rate.

Figure 11.1 illustrates the average education years for the employed workers. It shows an increasing trend from 11.7 years in 1986 to 12.9 years in 2005.

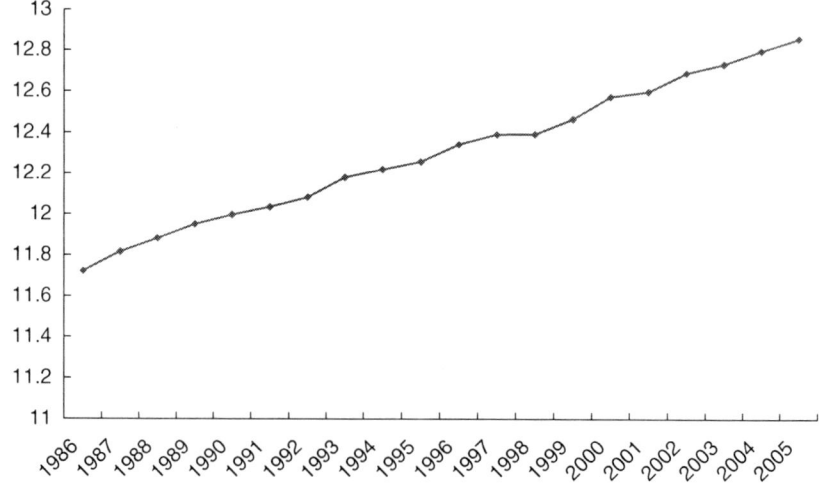

Figure 11.1 Average education years of employed.

Source: Authors' calculation from "Labor Force Survey" published by Ministry of Internal Affairs and Communications.

$$L1_t = (1 + \rho)^t L_t \tag{3}$$
$$X_t = (1 + \rho)^t \tag{4}$$

where X_t: Average education years for employed.

    t: time.

We can obtain ρ by estimating Eqn (5) which is transformed from Eqn (4).

$$\log(X_t) = c(1) + c(2)*t \tag{5}$$

Then,

$$c(2) = \log(1 + \rho) \tag{6}$$
$$\rho = \exp(c(2)) - 1 \tag{7}$$

The statistical estimates of this rate of labor augmentation are summarized in Table 11.1.

We use $\rho = 0.004675$ as the labor augmentation rate. Labor quality is improving by about 0.5% every year.

The estimation result of Eqn (1) is shown in Table 11.2.

According to Table 11.2, Eqn (2) is written as Eqn (8) on an annual basis,

$$\begin{aligned} d\log(Y) = {} & d\log(A) + 0.80*\log(1 + 0.004675) + 0.80*d\log(L) \\ & + 0.22*d\log(KO) + 0.13*d\log(KI) \end{aligned} \tag{8}$$

Table 11.1 Estimation result of labor-augmenting rate

Dependent Variable: LOG(X)
Method: Least Squares
Date: May 16, 2006   Time: 15:00
Sample: 1986–2005
Included observations: 20
LOG(X) = C(1) + C(2)*T

	Coefficient	Std. error	t-statistic	Prob.
C(1)	2.436692	0.001116	2184.110	0.0000
C(2)	0.004675	6.75E–05	69.30746	0.0000
R-squared	0.996267	Mean dependent variable		2.509162
Adjusted R-squared	0.996059	S.D. dependent variable		0.027712
S.E. of regression	0.001740	Akaike info criterion		−9.775643
Sum squared residual	5.45E–05	Schwarz criterion		−9.676070
Log likelihood	99.75643	Durbin–Watson statistic		1.691256

Source: Authors' calculation.

Table 11.2 Estimation result of the new (IT) Type Cobb–Douglas production function
Eqn (1)

Dependent Variable: LOG(*Y*)
Method: Least Squares
Date: May 16, 2006   Time: 15:35
Sample: 1994Q4 2005Q4
Included observations: 45
Convergence achieved after 4 iterations
LOG(*Y*) = C(1) + C(2)*LOG(*L*1*WH) + C(3)*LOG(KO*CU) + (1.15 − C(2) − C(3))
*LOG(KI*CU) + [AR(1) = C(9)]

	Coefficient	Std. error	t-statistic	Prob.
C(1)	−4.990477	0.295085	−16.91201	0.0000
C(2)	0.797886	0.059482	13.41383	0.0000
C(3)	0.222763	0.099334	2.242562	0.0304
C(90)	0.728409	0.109864	6.630096	0.0000
R-squared	0.947439	Mean dependent variable		13.12594
Adjusted R-squared	0.943593	S.D. dependent variable		0.035844
S.E. of regression	0.008513	Akaike info criterion		−6.609745
Sum squared residual	0.002971	Schwarz criterion		−6.449153
Log likelihood	152.7193	Durbin–Watson statistic		2.069189
Inverted AR Roots	0.73			

Source: Authors' calculation.

We discover the following from our statistical estimate of Eqn (8):

1   Labor quality improves by 0.5% per year. Even if the number of employed workers declines by 0.5% every year, the improvement in labor quality offsets the decline in the number of workers as labor input. This implies that education, probably IT education and training for workers, will play an important role in the New Economy.

2   We determine economies of scale using $\alpha + \beta + \gamma = 1.15$.

3   Output elasticities with respect to labor, non-IT capital stock and IT capital stock are 0.80, 0.22, and 0.13, respectively.

4   As for the output elasticity with respect to IT capital stock, we should consider 0.13 as the average of the output elasticity with respect to IT capital stock during the sample period of 1994–2005. In the case of IT investment, it is reasonable to assume that the elasticity in 2005 is much larger than that in 1995. IT infrastructure has been developing quickly. For example, when a generalized Cobb–Douglas production function was applied to the Japanese macroeconomy during the period of 1972–99, the output elasticity with respect to IT capital stock increased from 0.12 in 1995 to 0.31 in 1999, as Table 11.3 shows.[1] Based on this finding, it seems reasonable that the output elasticity of IT capital stock has increased from 0.13 as the average elasticity during the sample period 1994–2005 to 0.30 in 2005 and after.

Table 11.3 Output elasticity with respect to IT capital stock estimated by the Cobb–Douglas
production function

IT Stock (trillion yen)	Elasticity in 1985	Elasticity in 1995	Elasticity in 1999
10	0.0088	0.0216	0.0340
20	0.0165	0.0428	0.0678
30	0.0245	0.0641	0.1018
40	0.0325	0.0855	0.1359
50	0.0406	0.1069	0.1702
60	0.0486	0.1284	0.2045
70	0.0567	0.1500	0.2390
80	0.0648	0.1716	0.2736
90	0.0729	0.1932	0.3083
100	0.0810	0.2149	0.3432

Source: Authors' calculation.

Note: IT capital stock is 21.5 trillion yen in 1985. 56.7 trillion yen in 1995 and 89.9 trillion yen in
89.9 trillion yen.

The traditional (Non-IT) type Cobb–Douglas production function

$$Y_t = A_t(L_t)^\sigma \{(KO_t + KI_t)\}^\tau e^{\lambda t} \tag{9}$$

The traditional version of the Cobb–Douglas function was used by the Japanese
Cabinet Office, to support its low growth estimates for Japanese growth. Labor
input is measured by man-hours without considering labor quality improvement,
and capital stock is not separated into IT and non-IT capital stocks. Disembodied
technical progress is assumed a function of Time. This technical progress applies
equally and alike to all resources of workers and machines in current use. In
addition, constant returns to scale ($\sigma + \tau = 1$) is assumed in Eqn (9) λ denotes
technical progress.

We can estimate Eqn (9) after taking logarithms of both sides. The estimates
are summarized in Table 11.4.

When we estimated alternative versions of this function separating ($KO + KI$)
into KO and KI in Eqn (9) with t (time) and without t under the assumption of
constant returns to scale, we could not obtain statistically significant estimation
results. This implies that when IT capital stock is explicitly introduced in a
production function, economies of scale or embodied technical progress should
be considered.

Eqn (9) is expressed as Eqn (10) in the form of growth rates

$$\mathrm{dlog}(Y) = \mathrm{dlog}(A) + 0.68*\mathrm{dlog}(L) + 0.32*\mathrm{dlog}(KO + KI) + 0.002 \tag{10}$$

We can calculate the possible growth rate of the real GDP by using Eqn (8) and
Eqn (10). As a result, the "high growth" and the "low growth" groups in the
Japanese government can project their estimates of the possible economic growth
rate on the basis of Eqn (8) and Eqn (10), respectively.

Table 11.4 The estimation result of old (non-IT) type Cobb–Douglas production function Eqn (9)

Dependent Variable: LOG(Y)
Method: Least Squares
Date: May 16, 2006   Time: 15:35
Sample: 1994Q4 2005Q4
Included observations: 45
Convergence achieved after 3 iterations
LOG(Y) = C(1) + C(2)*LOG(L*WH) + (1 − C(2))*LOG((KO + KI)*CU)
   + C(3) + [AR(1) = C(90)]

	Coefficient	Std. error	t-statistic	Prob.
C(1)	−3.108808	0.159158	−19.53280	0.0000
C(2)	0.681540	0.058574	11.63553	0.0000
C(3)	0.002075	0.000622	3.333972	0.0018
C(90)	0.722802	0.113024	6.395115	0.0000
R-squared	0.953794	Mean dependent variable		13.12594
Adjusted R-squared	0.950413	S.D. dependent variable		0.035844
S.E. of regression	0.007982	Akaike info criterion		−6.738593
Sum squared residual	0.002612	Schwarz criterion		−6.578000
Log likelihood	155.6183	Durbin–Watson statistic		1.979471
Inverted AR Roots	0.72			

Source: Authors' calculation.

Table 11.5 summarizes alternative results as follows:

1   The dark gray section in Table 11.5 shows the average growth rate of input factors during the periods of 1981–2005 (after the second oil crisis), 1991–2005 (after bubble burst), and 1994–2005 (sample period). For example, the growth rate of employed is 0.58%, 0.22%, and −0.14% respectively for the periods of 1981–2005, 1991–2005, and 1994–2005.

2   The elasticity row in Table 11.5 shows the output elasticities with respect to input factors estimated in Eqns (see Tables 11.2 and 11.4). The 0.3 elasticity is assumed for the output elasticity with respect to IT capital stock after 2005. This seems to be reasonable as shown in the result estimated by a generalized Cobb–Douglas production function (see Table 11.3).

3   As for TFP, we assumed 0% as the worst case and 0.5% as the normal case.

4   When we use the conventional (non-IT) type of Cobb–Douglas production function (second half of Table 11.5), we have to conclude that it is not likely for Japan to achieve a 3% rate of economic growth. Under any conditions, the calculated economic growth rate is below 3%. The highest growth rate is 2.7% when we use the average growth rate of input factors during the period of 1981–2005 and assume 0.5% for TFP.

Table 11.5 Possible economic growth rates calculated by the new (IT) type and the old (non-IT) type Cobb–Douglas production functions

	Real GDP (%)	TFP (%)	Improvement of quality of labor (%)	Employed (%)	Non-IT capital stock (%)	IT capital stock (%)	Technical progress time (%)
New (IT) type equation							
(1) Average: 1981–2005			0.8*log(1+0.004675)*100	0.58	4.71	9.42	
(2) Average: 1991–2005			0.8*log(1+0.004675)*100	0.22	3.34	7.52	
(3) Average: 1994–2005			0.8*log(1+0.004675)*100	−0.14	2.53	6.85	
Elasticity				**0.8**	**0.22**	**0.13**	
Real GDP (%)							
(1)	3.11	0.0	0.38	0.47	1.04	1.23	
(2)	2.27	0.0	0.38	0.18	0.73	0.98	
(3)	1.72	0.0	0.38	−0.11	0.56	0.89	
(1)	3.61	0.5	0.38	0.47	1.04	1.23	
(2)	2.77	0.5	0.38	0.18	0.73	0.98	
(3)	2.22	0.5	0.38	−0.11	0.56	0.89	
Elasticity			0.8*log(1+0.004675)*100	**0.8**	**0.22**	**0.30**	
Real GDP (%)							
(1)	4.71	0.0	0.38	0.47	1.04	2.83	
(2)	3.55	0.0	0.38	0.18	0.73	2.26	
(3)	2.88	0.0	0.38	−0.11	0.56	2.05	
(1)	5.21	0.5	0.38	0.47	1.04	2.83	
(2)	4.05	0.5	0.38	0.18	0.73	2.26	
(3)	3.38	0.5	0.38	−0.11	0.56	2.05	

(Table 11.5 continued)

Table 11.5 Continued

	TFP (%)	Improvement of quality of labor (%)	Employed (%)	Non-IT capital stock (%)	IT capital stock (%)	Technical progress time (%)
Old (Non-IT) type equation						
(1) Average: 1981–2005	0.0	0.0	0.58	4.96		
(2) Average: 1991–2005	0.0	0.0	0.22	3.61		
(3) Average: 1994–2005	0.0	0.0	−0.14	2.83		
Elasticity			**0.68**	**0.32**		
Real GDP (%)						
(1) 2.19	0.0	0.0	0.40	1.59		0.21
(2) 1.52	0.0	0.0	0.15	1.16		0.21
(3) 1.02	0.0	0.0	−0.09	0.90		0.21
(1) 2.69	0.5	0.0	0.40	1.59		0.21
(2) 2.02	0.5	0.0	0.15	1.16		0.21
(3) 1.52	0.5	0.0	−0.09	0.90		0.21

Source: Authors' calculation.

Notes
(1), (2) and (3) use the average growth rate of inputs during the periods of 1981–2005, 1991–2005, and 1994–2005 respectively. The first three simulations assume TFP = 0.0, the second three assume TFP = 0.5.

Alternatively, results for the generalized production function (first part of Table 11.5) are as follows:

1   When we use a new (IT) type Cobb–Douglas production function, the improvement of labor quality contributes 0.5% to economic growth, which offsets the decline in employment for the 1994–2005 period.

2   In the case of the output elasticity with respect to IT capital stock of 0.13, the growth rate of real GDP exceeds 3% for the cases using the average growth rates of factor inputs during the 1981–2005 period.

3   If we assume 0.5% for TFP, the growth rate of the real GDP is calculated to be 2.2% and 2.8% for the periods of 1994–2005 and 1994–2005, respectively.

4   When we assume the higher output elasticity with respect to IT capital stock, the growth rate of real GDP exceeds 3% in all cases. This seems to be realistic.

12 Simulation studies for accelerating Japanese economic growth

The second phase of our empirical work carries on model simulations testing the impact of alternative policies aimed at achieving a higher rate of growth. This step is a way to validate the potentials for more rapid Japanese growth in a comprehensive empirical framework.

The simulation study made use of a Japanese macroeconomic model originally developed by Prof. Y. Inada of Konan University.[1] The Inada model is a typical example of a modern quarterly macro model. It is a highly aggregated system intended primarily for forecasting applications. With some modifications which we have carried out, it makes an excellent tool to test out whether more rapid growth is feasible and how the economy would be affected by alternative policies. It emphasizes the demand side with clear effects of the consumption tax on consumer expenditures. Other demand components are also treated as broad aggregates. During the period of low interest rates, when Japan can be said to be in a liquidity trap, money supply does not affect interest rates, though presumably at other times changes in monetary policy would ultimately influence investment and output. On the supply side, in the original version of the model, potential output is estimated by a conventional Cobb–Douglas production function under the assumption of constant returns to scale. Since the model does not differentiate between different types of investment, it was necessary to disaggregate IT and non-IT investment and capital stock in order to analyze the effect of the IT revolution on the economy. The specific changes made in the model are as follows:

1   We introduced the quality of labor input into the production function, since education and training will play increasingly important roles in the new economy.
2   We separated private investment into IT investment and non-IT investment. IT investment is treated as an exogenous variable.
3   The potential output function now explicitly includes IT capital stock, non-IT capital stock and labor input in terms of efficiency. This function shows economies of scale.

Operation of the model for forecasting and simulation under new economy conditions requires comparison between a baseline forecast and a number of alternatives.

We first set up the baseline simulation aimed at a 3% economic growth scenario. This calculation assumes that there will not be an increase in the consumption tax rate. Then, to illustrate the impact of the consumption tax rate, we examine the effect of an increase in the consumption tax rate from 5% to 10% in April 2007. A 10% consumption tax rate may be possible as that is not high compared to the consumption tax rates in other developed countries. Second, we make a simulation that assumes considerably more rapid growth of IT investment. We then test the impacts of a change in the interest rate, imposition of an investment tax credit, and a revaluation of the exchange rate of the Japanese yen (with and without a macro policy response).

Baseline projection

The Japanese economy grew at an annual rate of 1.8% in 2003, 2.3% in 2004, and 2.8% in 2005. It has been recovering after the many slow years since the bubble burst in 1991. It is important for Japan to maintain this momentum. The tentative baseline is set up for the economic growth rate to be between 2.6% and 3% for 2006–11 (see Tables 12.1 and 12.2). Importantly, we assume that the consumption tax rate will not be changed. We assume that real IT investment will grow at an annual rate of about 6% for the period of 2006–11, as it grew in 2005.

This is neither a projection of past trends nor a forecast. This is a baseline simulation making appropriate assumptions to test whether a 3% growth rate was an achievable consistent objective. The Baseline Simulation shows an economy growing near 3% per year over the 2005–11 period. The inflation rate shows modest increase to between 2% and 3%, a little lower for the GDP deflator and little higher for the CPI. The unemployment rate declines gradually to 3.1% in 2011. Potential GDP increases slowly at the beginning of the forecast period but reaches a growth rate of 3.6% in 2011.

In other words, this simulation shows a moderate expansion, healthy by Japanese standards. Fortunately, this scenario also improves the government's budgetary situation. Despite the fact that no increase in the consumption tax rate has been assumed, there are substantial increases in revenues, in line with the growth of nominal GDP of approximately 5% annually. The increases in tax receipts more than offset substantial increases in expenditures.

As long as the Japanese economy returns to close to 3% economic growth at a modest rate of inflation, the Japanese government budget deficit will be improving. The general government deficit to nominal GDP ratio would decline from 11% in 2003 to 6.3% in 2011 (see Figure 12.2).

Japanese economists and politicians have recently focused on the primary budget balance, government revenue excluding revenue from issuing bonds to government outlays excluding debt service outlay (Table 12.3). When the primary balance deficit is reduced to zero, general outlays are covered by tax revenue and other revenues including revenue of government enterprises, transfer of the Bank of Japan's profits, sales of government property, and surplus from the previous year's budget. The Baseline Solution (without the consumption tax increase)

Table 12.1 Economic forecast: summary Table 1 (Baseline), Unit: Billion yen (or 2000 year base)

	Actual			Forecast					
	2003	2004	2005	2006	2007	2008	2009	2010	2011
Real GDP	513,602.0	525,240.0	539,862.0	556,077.0	570,692.0	586,139.0	602,565.0	619,777.0	638,200.0
% change	1.8	2.3	2.8	3.0	2.6	2.7	2.8	2.9	3.0
Personal consumption exp.	291,937.0	297,598.0	303,937.0	310,254.0	316,964.0	324,113.0	332,116.0	341,006.0	350,537.0
% change	0.6	1.9	2.1	2.1	2.2	2.3	2.5	2.7	2.8
Government consumption exp.	91,549.0	93,385.0	95,013.0	95,850.0	97,725.0	100,100.0	102,425.0	104,425.0	106,550.0
% change	2.3	2.0	1.7	0.9	2.0	2.4	2.3	2.0	2.0
Gross capital formation	120,188.0	120,311.0	126,091.0	131,825.0	136,342.0	141,813.0	147,809.0	154,078.0	160,676.0
% change	2.0	0.1	4.8	4.6	3.4	4.0	4.2	4.2	4.3
Fixed capital formation	119,738.0	120,999.0	125,963.0	129,887.0	134,132.0	139,353.0	145,066.0	151,031.0	157,280.0
% change	0.5	1.1	4.1	3.1	3.3	3.9	4.1	4.1	4.1
Private sector	91,384.0	95,138.0	101,540.0	107,312.0	111,407.0	115,853.0	120,766.0	125,931.0	131,530.0
% change	4.7	4.1	6.7	5.7	3.8	4.0	4.2	4.3	4.5
Dwellings	18,294.0	18,656.0	18,512.0	19,000.0	19,376.0	19,879.0	20,540.0	21,117.0	21,814.0
% change	-0.9	2.0	-0.8	2.6	2.0	2.6	3.3	2.8	3.3
Plant and equipment	73,090.0	76,482.0	83,029.0	88,312.0	92,031.0	95,975.0	100,226.0	104,814.0	109,715.0
% change	6.2	4.6	8.6	6.4	4.2	4.3	4.4	4.6	4.7
IT	19,900.0	20,855.0	22,100.0	23,389.0	24,824.0	26,347.0	27,964.0	29,680.0	31,501.0
% change	0.4	4.8	6.0	5.8	6.1	6.1	6.1	6.1	6.1
Other	53,190.0	55,627.0	60,929.0	64,923.0	67,207.0	69,627.0	72,262.0	75,134.0	78,214.0
% change	8.5	4.6	9.5	6.6	3.5	3.6	3.8	4.0	4.1
Public sector	28,354.0	25,861.0	24,423.0	22,575.0	22,725.0	23,500.0	24,300.0	25,100.0	25,750.0
% change	-10.8	-8.8	-5.6	-7.6	0.7	3.4	3.4	3.3	2.6
Changes in inventories	450.0	-688.5	128.4	1,938.5	2,210.8	2,459.4	2,742.9	3,047.0	3,396.1
Private sector	286.1	-913.2	-186.1	1,624.1	1,896.4	2,145.0	2,428.5	2,732.6	3,081.7
Public sector	163.9	224.7	314.4	314.4	314.4	314.4	314.4	314.4	314.4
Net exports of Goods and Services	9,714.0	13,836.0	15,107.0	18,468.0	19,982.0	20,435.0	20,537.0	20,590.0	20,759.0

Exports of Goods and Services	60,410.0	68,825.0	73,454.0	79,160.0	83,187.0	86,320.0	89,538.0	93,245.0	97,167.0
% change	9.0	13.9	6.7	7.8	5.1	3.8	3.7	4.1	4.2
Imports of Goods and Services	50,696.0	54,989.0	58,347.0	60,691.0	63,205.0	65,885.0	69,001.0	72,655.0	76,409.0
% change	4.0	8.5	6.1	4.0	4.1	4.2	4.7	5.3	5.2
Mineral fuel	2,093.6	2,149.2	2,115.5	2,162.8	2,225.1	2,299.6	2,380.0	2,466.7	2,559.9
% change	7.2	2.7	−1.6	2.2	2.9	3.4	3.5	3.6	3.8
Other	48,602.0	52,840.0	56,232.0	58,528.0	60,980.0	63,585.0	66,622.0	70,188.0	73,849.0
% change	3.8	8.7	6.4	4.1	4.2	4.3	4.8	5.4	5.2
Nominal GDP	490,732.0	496,062.0	503,268.0	522,054.0	545,182.0	571,572.0	601,874.0	634,980.0	672,257.0
% change	0.2	1.1	1.5	3.7	4.4	4.8	5.3	5.5	5.9
GDP price deflator	95.6	94.4	93.2	93.9	95.5	97.5	99.9	102.4	105.3
% change	−1.6	−1.2	−1.3	0.7	1.8	2.1	2.4	2.6	2.8
Pri. con. exp. price deflator	96.4	95.8	95.0	95.4	96.5	98.3	100.6	103.2	106.0
% change	−0.9	−0.7	−0.8	0.4	1.2	1.8	2.4	2.5	2.8
Exports of Goods and Services price deflator	97.4	96.2	97.5	105.7	112.3	117.6	122.9	128.7	135.3
% change	−3.3	−1.3	1.3	8.5	6.2	4.8	4.5	4.7	5.1
Imports of Goods and Services price deflator	100.4	102.9	111.0	121.2	125.5	129.2	132.9	137.0	141.4
% change	−0.9	2.5	7.8	9.2	3.6	3.0	2.9	3.0	3.3
Import P. deflator for mineral fuel	111.6	124.0	172.1	182.9	172.3	165.2	155.7	146.2	138.0
% change	6.7	11.2	38.8	6.3	−5.8	−4.1	−5.8	−6.1	−5.7
Consumer price index	98.1	98.1	97.8	98.6	100.3	102.8	105.9	109.3	113.1
% change	−0.3	0.0	−0.3	0.8	1.8	2.4	3.0	3.3	3.5
Domestic firms' price index (PPI)	94.9	96.1	97.7	99.4	100.6	102.1	104.0	106.1	108.6
% change	−0.8	1.2	1.7	1.8	1.2	1.5	1.8	2.1	2.4

Source: Authors' calculation.

Table 12.2 Economic forecast: summary Table 2 (Baseline), Unit: Billion yen (or 2000 year base)

	Actual			Forecast					
	2003	2004	2005	2006	2007	2008	2009	2010	2011
Labor force	6,687.3	6,666.3	6,643.1	6,614.6	6,618.6	6,658.5	6,722.0	6,816.9	6,933.4
% change	−1.0	−0.3	−0.4	−0.4	0.1	0.6	1.0	1.4	1.7
Employed	6,328.9	6,316.1	6,329.6	6,322.1	6,344.6	6,402.8	6,481.7	6,593.0	6,726.0
% change	−1.3	−0.2	0.2	−0.1	0.4	0.9	1.2	1.7	2.0
Employees	5,329.7	5,335.1	5,355.7	5,350.3	5,364.6	5,396.3	5,448.3	5,528.8	5,631.9
% change	−0.7	0.1	0.4	−0.1	0.3	0.6	1.0	1.5	1.9
Unemployment rate	5.4	5.3	4.7	4.4	4.2	3.9	3.6	3.4	3.1
Labor productivity growth	3.2	2.5	2.6	3.1	2.3	1.8	1.6	1.1	0.9
Unit labor cost (% change)	−3.2	−3.5	−1.5	0.5	1.7	2.3	2.6	2.9	3.3
Per capita wage and salary	4,196.5	4,132.4	4,167.2	4,314.9	4,501.0	4,715.2	4,943.8	5,173.8	5,419.6
% change	0.1	−1.5	0.8	3.5	4.3	4.8	4.9	4.7	4.8
Potential GDP	581,260.0	583,909.0	589,783.0	598,070.0	614,187.0	633,069.0	654,428.0	678,182.0	702,802.0
% change	0.8	0.5	1.0	1.4	2.7	3.1	3.4	3.6	3.6
CD Rate	0.0	0.0	0.0	0.3	1.1	2.3	3.7	5.0	5.9
Long-term bond yield	1.0	1.5	1.4	1.3	2.0	3.1	4.4	5.6	6.6
Household disposable income	297,713.0	295,666.0	293,641.0	305,565.0	318,269.0	333,881.0	352,454.0	372,899.0	396,178.0
% change	−0.3	−0.7	−0.7	4.1	4.2	4.9	5.6	5.8	6.2
Wage and salary	223,656.0	220,469.0	223,179.0	230,860.0	241,465.0	254,456.0	269,365.0	286,063.0	305,251.0
% change	−0.7	−1.4	1.2	3.4	4.6	5.4	5.9	6.2	6.7
Compensation of employees	258,692.0	255,250.0	258,388.0	267,554.0	279,293.0	293,396.0	309,581.0	327,700.0	348,445.0
% change	−1.5	−1.3	1.2	3.6	4.4	5.1	5.5	5.9	6.3
Corporate income	48,646.0	71,795.0	79,174.0	92,927.0	100,560.0	107,732.0	115,186.0	122,128.0	129,469.0
% change	8.4	47.6	10.3	17.4	17.4	7.1	6.9	6.0	6.0
Corporate income after tax	35,676.0	52,902.0	58,458.0	68,614.0	74,249.0	79,545.0	85,048.0	90,174.0	95,595.0
% change	10.1	48.3	10.5	17.4	8.2	7.1	6.9	6.0	6.0

General government fiscal balance	−54,151.0	−49,284.0	−45,984.0	−40,088.0	−39,761.0	−40,976.0	−42,495.0	−42,939.0	−42,673.0
% change	−3.8	−9.0	−6.7	−12.8	−0.8	3.1	3.7	1.0	−0.6
GDP ratio (%)	−11.0	−9.9	−9.1	−7.7	−7.3	−7.2	−7.1	−6.8	−6.3
Direct tax revenue	37,338.0	42,102.0	44,545.0	49,882.0	53,899.0	58,083.0	62,609.0	67,256.0	72,366.0
% change	−4.0	12.8	5.8	12.0	8.1	7.8	7.8	7.4	7.6
Individual income tax revenue	23,753.0	22,822.0	23,232.0	24,899.0	26,865.0	29,117.0	31,632.0	34,399.0	37,520.0
% change	−5.3	−3.9	1.8	7.2	7.9	8.4	8.6	8.8	9.1
Private sector corporate tax revenue	12,970.0	18,893.0	20,715.0	24,314.0	26,311.0	28,187.0	30,137.0	31,954.0	33,874.0
% change	4.0	45.7	9.6	17.4	8.2	7.1	6.9	6.0	6.0
Indirect tax revenue	40,961.0	41,182.0	41,933.0	43,121.0	44,668.0	46,617.0	48,991.0	51,645.0	54,609.0
% change	−1.2	0.5	1.8	2.8	3.6	4.4	5.1	5.4	5.7
Consumption tax revenue	12,256.0	12,113.0	12,375.0	12,710.0	13,180.0	13,788.0	14,510.0	15,291.0	16,158.0
% change	1.0	−1.2	2.2	2.7	3.7	4.6	5.2	5.4	5.7
Social security benefits	71,272.0	70,676.0	71,574.0	73,318.0	76,608.0	80,327.0	84,222.0	87,567.0	90,628.0
% change	−0.4	−0.8	1.3	2.4	4.5	4.9	4.9	4.0	3.5
Social security contribution	70,973.0	67,064.0	68,894.0	69,842.0	71,928.0	75,305.0	79,221.0	83,623.0	88,449.0
% change	1.3	−5.5	2.7	1.4	3.0	4.7	5.2	5.6	5.8
Central government primary balance	−20,156.0	−18,853.0	−17,004.0	−16,071.0	−15,585.0	−15,963.0	−16,219.0	−16,530.0	−16,092.0
% change	13.4	−6.5	−9.8	−5.5	−3.0	2.4	1.6	1.9	−2.7
GDP ratio	−3.9	−3.6	−3.2	−2.9	−2.7	−2.7	−2.7	−2.7	−2.5
Central government revenue	85,849.0	88,432.0	84,798.0	78,109.0	79,792.0	87,109.0	97,895.0	111,534.0	121,733.0
% change	−1.4	3.0	−4.1	−7.9	2.2	9.2	12.4	13.9	9.1
Tax revenue	43,125.0	45,113.0	44,767.0	46,104.0	48,862.0	51,902.0	55,323.0	58,942.0	62,945.0
% change	−3.6	4.6	−0.8	3.0	6.0	6.2	6.6	6.5	6.8
Central government outlays	82,422.0	86,040.0	84,215.0	85,241.0	87,794.0	92,758.0	99,560.0	107,031.0	116,314.0
% change	−1.7	4.4	−2.1	1.2	3.0	5.7	7.3	7.5	8.7

Source: Authors' calculation.

Table 12.3 Primary budget balance

Revenue	Outlays
Tax revenue, and so on	General outlays
	Deficit of Primary Balance
Issuing bonds	Interest Payments
	Amortization

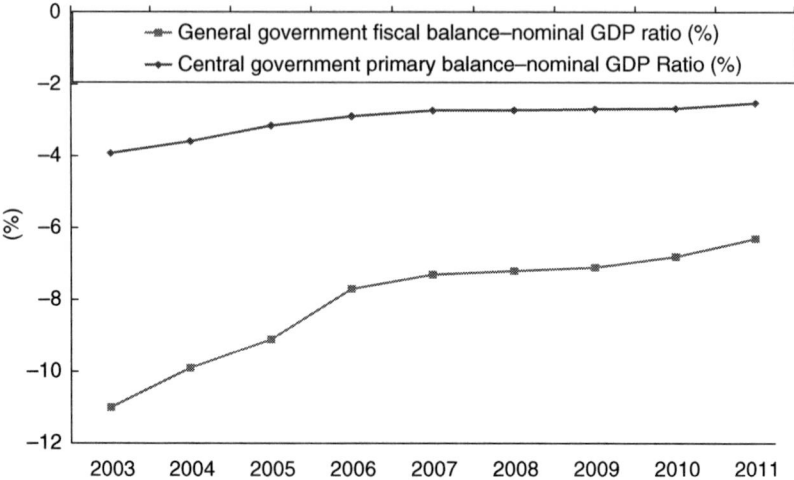

Figure 12.1 Government deficit to nominal GDP ratio.

Notes
Deficit as a percentage of GDP is shown as a negative number. Improvements take the form of an upward slope in the lines.

shows that the Central government primary balance deficit will decline steadily from 3.9% of nominal GDP in 2003 to 2.5% in 2011 (Figure 12.1).

Alternative simulation: increase consumption tax rate to 10% in 2007Q2

Whether the consumption tax rate should be increased and when the increase should be introduced is a politically sensitive issue. Despite the disastrous 1997 experience, there has been significant pressure for a return to a higher consumption tax rate. Mr Tanigaki, Minister of Finance, has proposed to introduce the higher consumption tax rate in 2007Q2. We present this alternative simulation in Tables 12.4 and 12.5.

An increase in the consumption tax rate in the second quarter of 2007 would sharply reduce the economy's growth rate during 2007–8.

Personal consumption expenditures

When the consumption tax rate was increased from 3% to 5% in 1997Q2, the growth rate of real personal consumption expenditure fell from 2.3% in 1996 to 0.8% in 1997 and −0.8% in 1998 (Figure 12.2). Since then, the growth of personal consumption expenditures was very slow until 2004 when they grew at an annual rate of almost 2%. In this simulation study, the growth rate of real personal consumption expenditures drops from 2.1% in 2006 to −1.4% in 2007 and −0.5% in 2008. Although Figure 12.2 shows that the growth rate of real personal consumption expenditures will return to 2.5% in 2009, we cannot exclude the possibility that it may slow for a longer period, as it did during the period of 1997–2003.

Gross domestic product

When the consumption tax rate was increased from 3% to 5% in 1997Q2, the growth rate of the real GDP slowed down from 2.6% in 1996 to 1.4% in 1997, −1.9% in 1998 and −0.1% in 1999, a recession dip, and finally recovered to 2.9% in 2000 (Figure 12.3). Due to the increase in the consumption tax rate from 5% to 10% in 2007Q2, the growth rate would decline to 0.9% in 2007 and 1.8% in 2008, compared to 2.6% and 2.7%, respectively, in the baseline. As a result, the level of the real GDP during the period of 2007–11 would be lower by 2–2.5%, compared to that in the baseline. A small downward impact on the growth of potential GDP is apparent only during the early years of the simulation, 2006–8.

Tax revenues

Tax revenues are substantially increased by raising the consumption tax rate from 5% to 10% (Figure 12.4). But some of the increases in tax revenue are offset by the slowdown in economic activity. Consumption tax revenue would increase by 73% from 13.2 trillion yen in 2007 in the baseline to 22.0 trillion yen in the alternative simulation study (Figure 12.4). Although the government fiscal deficit would be reduced due to the higher consumption tax, the government fiscal deficit to nominal GDP ratio would not be improved greatly. The general government deficit to nominal GDP ratio declined from 7.7% in 1996 to 6.9% in 1998, but increased to 8.5% in 1999. In the simulation study, the ratio would decline by about 0.5% during the simulation period of 2006–11. The central government primary balance deficit to the nominal GDP ratio would not improve at all for the simulation period.

Thus, much caution should be exercised when raising the consumption tax rate from 5% to 10%. It is not clear that the gains from the tax increase outweigh its costs.

Table 12.4 Economic forecast: summary Table 1 (10% consumption tax rate from 2007Q2), Unit: Billion yen (or 2000 year base)

	Actual			Forecast					
	2003	2004	2005	2006	2007	2008	2009	2010	2011
Real GDP	513,602.0	525,240.0	539,862.0	556,077.0	561,271.0	571,349.0	587,774.0	604,914.0	623,296.0
% change	1.8	2.3	2.8	3.0	0.9	1.8	2.9	2.9	3.0
Personal consumption exp.	291,937.0	297,598.0	303,937.0	310,254.0	305,810.0	304,218.0	311,775.0	320,197.0	329,324.0
% change	0.6	1.9	2.1	2.1	−1.4	−0.5	2.5	2.7	2.9
Government consumption exp.	91,549.0	93,385.0	95,013.0	95,850.0	97,725.0	100,100.0	102,425.0	104,425.0	106,550.0
% change	2.3	2.0	1.7	0.9	2.0	2.4	2.3	2.0	2.0
Gross capital formation	120,188.0	120,311.0	126,091.0	131,825.0	135,615.0	140,718.0	146,723.0	152,922.0	159,415.0
% change	2.0	0.1	4.8	4.6	2.9	3.8	4.3	4.2	4.3
Fixed capital formation	119,738.0	120,999.0	125,963.0	129,887.0	133,591.0	138,692.0	144,429.0	150,340.0	156,504.0
% change	0.5	1.1	4.1	3.1	2.9	3.8	4.1	4.1	4.1
Private sector	91,384.0	95,138.0	101,540.0	107,312.0	110,866.0	115,192.0	120,129.0	125,240.0	130,754.0
% change	4.7	4.1	6.7	5.7	3.3	3.9	4.3	4.3	4.4
Dwellings	18,294.0	18,656.0	18,512.0	19,000.0	19,375.0	19,856.0	20,440.0	20,893.0	21,444.0
% change	−0.9	2.0	−0.8	2.6	2.0	2.5	2.9	2.2	2.6
Plant and equipment	73,090.0	76,482.0	83,029.0	88,312.0	91,492.0	95,337.0	99,689.0	104,347.0	109,310.0
% change	6.2	4.6	8.6	6.4	3.6	4.2	4.6	4.7	4.8
IT	19,900.0	20,855.0	22,100.0	23,389.0	24,824.0	26,347.0	27,964.0	29,680.0	31,501.0
% change	0.4	4.8	6.0	5.8	6.1	6.1	6.1	6.1	6.1
Other	53,190.0	55,627.0	60,929.0	64,923.0	66,667.0	68,989.0	71,725.0	74,667.0	77,809.0
% change	8.5	4.6	9.5	6.6	2.7	3.5	4.0	4.1	4.2
Public sector	28,354.0	25,861.0	24,423.0	22,575.0	22,725.0	23,500.0	24,300.0	25,100.0	25,750.0
% change	−10.8	−8.8	−5.6	−7.6	0.7	3.4	3.4	3.3	2.6
Changes in inventories	450.0	−688.5	128.4	1,938.5	2,023.1	2,025.5	2,293.9	2,581.7	2,911.5
Private sector	286.1	−913.2	−186.1	1,624.1	1,708.7	1,711.1	1,979.5	2,267.3	2,597.1
Public sector	163.9	224.7	314.4	314.4	314.4	314.4	314.4	314.4	314.4
Net exports of Goods and Services	9,714.0	13,836.0	15,107.0	18,468.0	22,444.0	26,635.0	27,173.0	27,692.0	28,328.0

Exports of Goods and Services	60,410.0	68,825.0	73,454.0	79,160.0	83,184.0	86,304.0	89,514.0	93,225.0	97,158.0
% change	9.0	13.9	6.7	7.8	5.1	3.8	3.7	4.1	4.2
Imports of Goods and Services	50,696.0	54,989.0	58,347.0	60,691.0	60,740.0	59,669.0	62,341.0	65,534.0	68,830.0
% change	4.0	8.5	6.1	4.0	0.1	-1.8	4.5	5.1	5.0
Mineral fuel	2,093.6	2,149.2	2,115.5	2,162.8	2,185.8	2,237.8	2,317.9	2,403.9	2,496.4
% change	7.2	2.7	-1.6	2.2	1.1	2.4	3.6	3.7	3.9
Other	48,602.0	52,840.0	56,232.0	58,528.0	58,554.0	57,431.0	60,023.0	63,130.0	66,334.0
% change	3.8	8.7	6.4	4.1	0.0	-1.9	4.5	5.2	5.1
Nominal GDP	490,732.0	496,062.0	503,268.0	522,054.0	536,825.0	558,866.0	588,845.0	621,568.0	658,502.0
% change	0.2	1.1	1.5	3.7	2.8	4.1	5.4	5.6	5.9
GDP price deflator	95.6	94.4	93.2	93.9	95.6	97.8	100.2	102.7	105.6
% change	-1.6	-1.2	-1.3	0.7	1.9	2.3	2.4	2.6	2.8
Private consumption exp. price deflator	96.4	95.8	95.0	95.4	96.5	98.3	100.6	103.2	106.0
% change	-0.9	-0.7	-0.8	0.4	1.2	1.8	2.4	2.5	2.8
Exports of Goods and Services price deflator	97.4	96.2	97.5	105.7	112.3	117.7	123.0	128.8	135.3
% change	-3.3	-1.3	1.3	8.5	6.2	4.8	4.5	4.7	5.0
Imports of Goods and Services price deflator	100.4	102.9	111.0	121.2	125.5	129.3	133.0	137.0	141.4
% change	-0.9	2.5	7.8	9.2	3.6	3.0	2.8	3.0	3.2
Import P. deflator for mineral fuel	111.6	124.0	172.1	182.9	172.3	165.2	155.7	146.2	138.0
% change	6.7	11.2	38.8	6.3	-5.8	-4.1	-5.8	-6.1	-5.7
Consumer price index	98.1	98.1	97.8	98.6	100.4	102.8	105.8	109.3	113.1
% change	-0.3	0.0	-0.3	0.8	1.8	2.4	3.0	3.3	3.5
Domestic firms' price index (PPI)	94.9	96.1	97.7	99.4	100.7	102.2	104.0	106.1	108.6
% change	-0.8	1.2	1.7	1.8	1.2	1.5	1.8	2.0	2.3

Source: Authors' calculation.

Table 12.5 Economic forecast: summary Table 2 (10% consumption tax rate from 2007Q2), Unit: Billion yen (or 2000 year base)

	Actual			Forecast					
	2003	2004	2005	2006	2007	2008	2009	2010	2011
Labor force	6,687.3	6,666.3	6,643.1	6,614.6	6,618.5	6,656.8	6,716.1	6,805.1	6,915.0
% change	−1.0	−0.3	−0.4	−0.4	0.1	0.6	0.9	1.3	1.6
Employed	6,328.9	6,316.1	6,329.6	6,322.1	6,343.2	6,394.2	6,463.2	6,563.8	6,685.9
% change	−1.3	−0.2	0.2	−0.1	0.3	0.8	1.1	1.6	1.9
Employees	5,329.7	5,335.1	5,355.7	5,350.3	5,363.4	5,389.1	5,432.8	5,504.2	5,598.4
% change	−0.7	0.1	0.4	−0.1	0.3	0.5	0.8	1.3	1.7
Unemployment rate	5.4	5.3	4.7	4.4	4.2	4.0	3.8	3.6	3.4
Labor productivity growth	3.2	2.5	2.6	3.1	0.6	1.0	1.8	1.3	1.2
Unit labor cost (% change)	−3.2	−3.5	−1.5	0.5	3.4	2.9	2.3	2.6	3.0
Per capita wage and salary	4,196.5	4,132.4	4,167.2	4,314.9	4,498.3	4,700.8	4,920.0	5,143.8	5,385.5
% change	0.1	−1.5	0.8	3.5	4.3	4.5	4.7	4.6	4.7
Potential GDP	581,260.0	583,909.0	589,783.0	598,070.0	613,127.0	630,699.0	652,255.0	676,189.0	700,977.0
% change	0.8	0.5	1.0	1.4	2.5	2.9	3.4	3.7	3.7
CD rate	0.0	0.0	0.0	0.3	1.0	2.1	3.5	4.7	5.6
Long-term bond yield	1.0	1.5	1.4	1.3	2.0	3.0	4.2	5.4	6.5
Household disposable income	297,713.0	295,666.0	293,641.0	305,565.0	318,158.0	333,226.0	351,254.0	371,264.0	394,205.0
% change	−0.3	−0.7	−0.7	4.1	4.1	4.7	5.4	5.7	6.2
Wage and salary	223,656.0	220,469.0	223,179.0	230,860.0	241,265.0	253,337.0	267,304.0	283,143.0	301,523.0
% change	−0.7	−1.4	1.2	3.4	4.5	5.0	5.5	5.9	6.5
Compensation of employees	258,692.0	255,250.0	258,388.0	267,554.0	279,091.0	292,251.0	307,445.0	324,649.0	344,531.0
% change	−1.5	−1.3	1.2	3.6	4.3	4.7	5.2	5.6	6.1
Corporate income	48,646.0	71,795.0	79,174.0	92,927.0	84,796.0	86,945.0	95,397.0	103,386.0	112,122.0
% change	8.4	47.6	10.3	17.4	−8.7	2.5	9.7	8.4	8.5
Corporate income after tax	35,676.0	52,902.0	58,458.0	68,614.0	62,610.0	64,196.0	70,437.0	76,336.0	82,786.0
% change	10.1	48.3	10.5	17.4	−8.7	2.5	9.7	8.4	8.5

General government fiscal balance	−54,151.0	−49,284.0	−45,984.0	−40,088.0	−36,308.0	−37,072.0	−38,387.0	−38,572.0	−37,946.0
% change	−3.8	−9.0	−6.7	−12.8	−9.4	2.1	3.5	0.5	−1.6
GDP Ratio (%)	−11.0	−9.9	−9.1	−7.7	−6.8	−6.6	−6.5	−6.2	−5.8
Direct tax revenue	37,338.0	42,102.0	44,545.0	49,882.0	49,703.0	52,468.0	57,153.0	61,974.0	67,353.0
% change	−4.0	12.8	5.8	−12.0	−0.4	5.6	8.9	8.4	8.7
Individual income tax revenue	23,753.0	22,822.0	23,232.0	24,899.0	26,849.0	29,015.0	31,426.0	34,092.0	37,113.0
% change	−5.3	−3.9	1.8	7.2	7.8	8.1	8.3	8.5	8.9
Private sector corporate tax revenue	12,970.0	18,893.0	20,715.0	24,314.0	22,186.0	22,748.0	24,960.0	27,050.0	29,336.0
% change	4.0	45.7	9.6	17.4	−8.7	2.5	9.7	8.4	8.5
Indirect tax revenue	40,961.0	41,182.0	41,933.0	43,121.0	52,370.0	56,487.0	59,336.0	62,507.0	66,061.0
% change	−1.2	0.5	1.8	2.8	21.4	7.9	5.0	5.3	5.7
Consumption tax revenue	12,256.0	12,113.0	12,375.0	12,710.0	21,994.0	25,717.0	27,024.0	28,440.0	30,017.0
% change	0.9	−1.2	2.2	2.7	73.0	16.9	5.1	5.2	5.5
Social security benefits	71,272.0	70,676.0	71,574.0	73,318.0	76,629.0	80,484.0	84,612.0	88,254.0	91,671.0
% change	−0.4	−0.8	1.3	2.4	4.5	5.0	5.1	4.3	3.9
Social security contribution	70,973.0	67,064.0	68,894.0	69,842.0	71,911.0	75,164.0	78,902.0	83,129.0	87,792.0
% change	1.3	−5.5	2.7	1.4	3.0	4.5	5.0	5.4	5.6
Central government primary balance	−20,156.0	−18,853.0	−17,004.0	−16,071.0	−15,465.0	−16,060.0	−16,206.0	−16,397.0	−15,798.0
% change	13.4	−6.5	−9.8	−5.5	−3.8	3.8	0.9	1.2	−3.7
GDP ratio	−3.9	−3.6	−3.2	−2.9	−2.8	−2.8	−2.8	−2.7	−2.5
Central govt. revenue	85,849.0	88,432.0	84,798.0	78,109.0	81,512.0	89,038.0	100,214.0	114,597.0	125,761.0
% change	−1.4	3.0	−4.1	−7.9	4.4	9.2	12.6	14.4	9.7
Tax revenue	43,125.0	45,113.0	44,767.0	46,104.0	50,600.0	54,011.0	57,747.0	61,708.0	66,137.0
% change	−3.6	4.6	−0.8	3.0	9.8	6.7	6.9	6.9	7.2
Central government outlays	82,422.0	86,040.0	84,215.0	85,241.0	89,385.0	94,808.0	101,660.0	109,207.0	118,608.0
% change	−1.7	4.4	−2.1	1.2	4.9	6.1	7.2	7.4	8.6

Source: Authors' calculation.

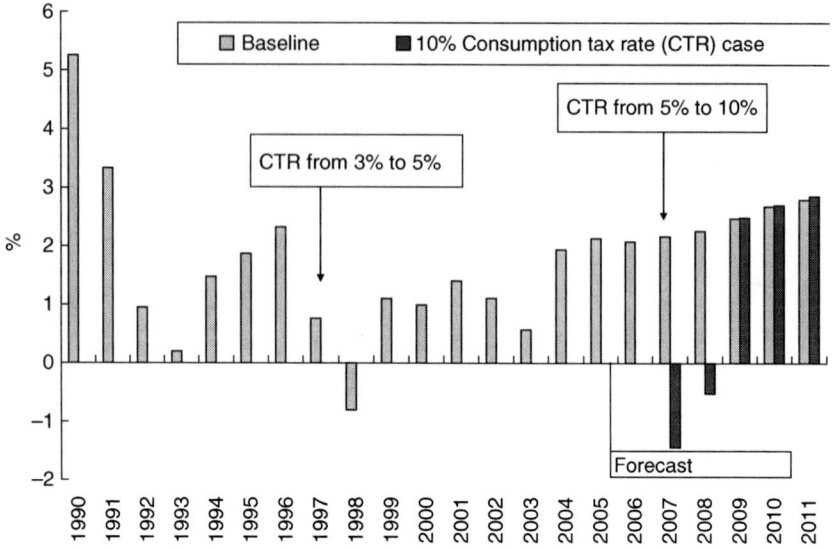

Figure 12.2 The effect of 10% consumption tax rate on real personal consumption expenditure (%).

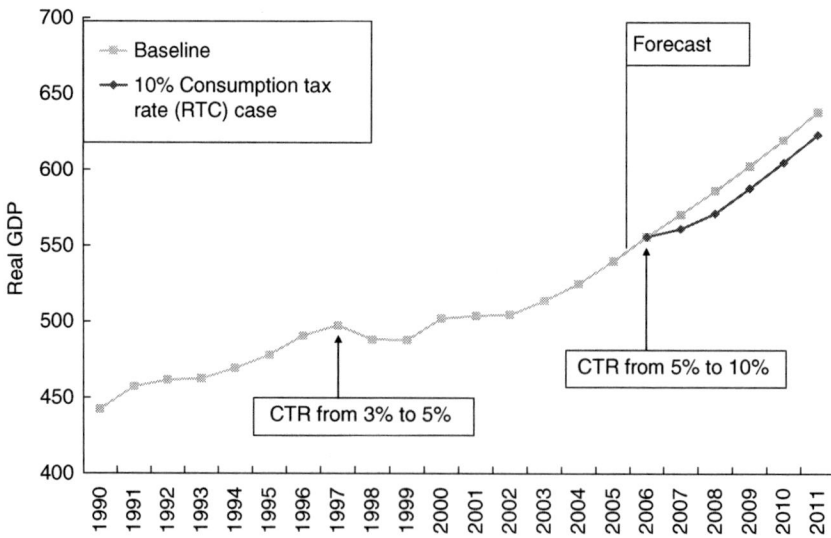

Figure 12.3 The effect of 10% consumption tax rate on real GDP (trillion yen in prices of 2000).

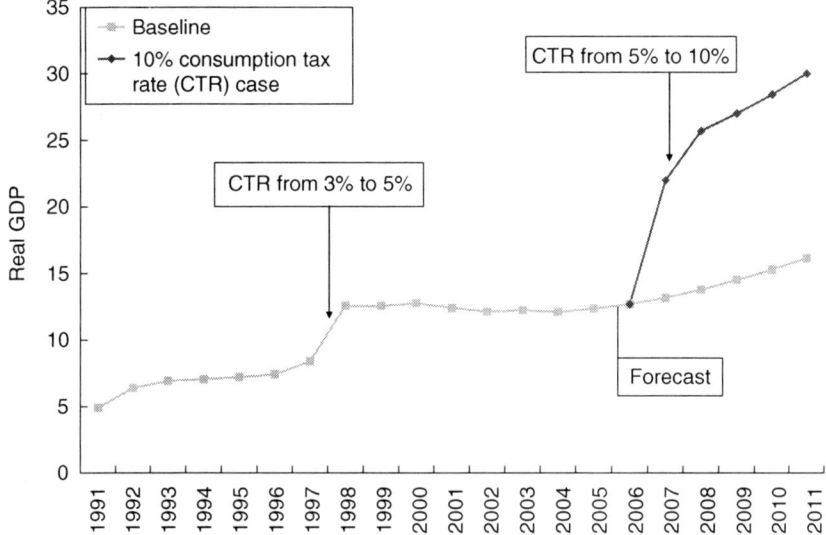

Figure 12.4 The effect of 10% consumption tax rate on consumption tax revenue (trillion yen).

Alternative simulation: increase IT investment at annual rate of 15% from 2006

Real IT investment increased at an annual rate of 19.3% on average from 1981 to 1991 when the bubble burst, as seen in Figure 12.5. On the other hand, real IT investment increased at an annual rate of only 5.2% between 1992 and 2005.

Since the IT revolution began to develop rapidly in the past 20 years, there have been many potential areas for IT investment. The more the IT revolution spread, the harder it was for firms to survive without keeping their investment in IT current. There is still a lot of room for investment in IT infrastructure. Software and content will also play an increasingly important role going forward. It would be helpful to provide additional government support for IT investment.

There are a number of possible ways for the Japanese government to stimulate IT investment. While some of this investment could take the form of direct government expenditures to develop e-government and similar activities, much of it would involve indirect support through subsidies or tax benefits. It is beyond the scope of this volume to carry out detailed empirical studies of alternative schemes for stimulating IT investments. We will be discussing some of the options in Chapter 13.

For purposes of a simulation exercise, it is not unrealistic to assume that with public support real IT investment will grow at an annual rate of 15%, approximately as it did during the 1980s. Tables 12.6 and 12.7 show the simulation results when real IT investment is assumed to grow 15% every year after 2006. This is 9 percentage points per year higher growth rate than in the baseline solution—15% as compared to 6%.

The growth rate of the real GDP would then be between 3.0% and 3.4%, some 0.3–0.4% higher every year, compared to that in the Baseline Solution

Table 12.6 Economic forecast: summary Table 1 (15% IT investment increase from 2006), Unit: Billion yen (or 2000 year base)

	Actual			Forecast					
	2003	2004	2005	2006	2007	2008	2009	2010	2011
Real GDP	513,602.0	525,240.0	539,862.0	557,601.0	574,079.0	591,683.0	610,604.0	630,687.0	652,403.0
% change	1.8	2.3	2.8	3.3	3.0	3.1	3.2	3.3	3.4
Personal consumption expenditure	291,937.0	297,598.0	303,937.0	310,290.0	317,055.0	324,292.0	332,356.0	341,281.0	350,810.0
% change	0.6	1.9	2.1	2.1	2.2	2.3	2.5	2.7	2.8
Government consumption expenditure	91,549.0	93,385.0	95,013.0	95,850.0	97,725.0	100,100.0	102,425.0	104,425.0	106,550.0
% change	2.3	2.0	1.7	0.9	2.0	2.4	2.3	2.0	2.0
Gross capital formation	120,188.0	120,311.0	126,091.0	133,728.0	140,739.0	149,181.0	158,726.0	169,219.0	180,827.0
% change	2.0	0.1	4.8	6.1	5.2	6.0	6.4	6.6	6.9
Fixed capital formation	119,738.0	120,999.0	125,963.0	131,760.0	138,460.0	146,615.0	155,833.0	165,973.0	177,170.0
% change	0.5	1.1	4.1	4.6	5.1	5.9	6.3	6.5	6.8
Private sector	91,384.0	95,138.0	101,540.0	109,185.0	115,735.0	123,115.0	131,533.0	140,873.0	151,420.0
% change	4.7	4.1	6.7	7.5	6.0	6.4	6.8	7.1	7.5
Dwellings	18,294.0	18,656.0	18,512.0	19,000.0	19,379.0	19,891.0	20,569.0	21,171.0	21,901.0
% change	−0.9	2.0	−0.8	2.6	2.0	2.6	3.4	2.9	3.5
Plant and equipment	73,090.0	76,482.0	83,029.0	90,184.0	96,356.0	103,224.0	110,964.0	119,702.0	129,519.0
% change	6.2	4.6	8.6	8.6	6.8	7.1	7.5	7.9	8.2
IT	19,900.0	20,855.0	22,100.0	25,415.0	29,227.0	33,611.0	38,653.0	44,451.0	51,119.0
% change	0.4	4.8	6.0	15.0	15.0	15.0	15.0	15.0	15.0
Other	53,190.0	55,627.0	60,929.0	64,769.0	67,129.0	69,612.0	72,311.0	75,251.0	78,400.0
% change	8.5	4.6	9.5	6.3	3.6	3.7	3.9	4.1	4.2
Public sector	28,354.0	25,861.0	24,423.0	22,575.0	22,725.0	23,500.0	24,300.0	25,100.0	25,750.0
% change	−10.8	−8.8	−5.6	−7.6	0.7	3.4	3.4	3.3	2.6
Changes in inventories	450.0	−688.5	128.4	1,968.4	2,278.7	2,566.3	2,892.7	3,246.8	3,656.6
Private sector	286.1	−913.2	−186.1	1,654.0	1,964.3	2,251.9	2,578.3	2,932.4	3,342.2
Public sector	163.9	224.7	314.4	314.4	314.4	314.4	314.4	314.4	314.4
Net exports of Goods and Services	9,714.0	13,836.0	15,107.0	18,054.0	18,882.0	18,432.0	17,419.0	16,083.0	14,538.0

Exports of Goods and Services	60,410.0	68,825.0	73,454.0	79,160.0	83,191.0	86,330.0	89,556.0	93,272.0	97,205.0
% change	9.0	13.9	6.7	7.8	5.1	3.8	3.7	4.1	4.2
Imports of Goods and Services	50,696.0	54,989.0	58,347.0	61,107.0	64,309.0	67,898.0	72,136.0	77,189.0	82,667.0
% change	4.0	8.5	6.1	4.7	5.2	5.6	6.2	7.0	7.1
Mineral fuel	2,093.6	2,149.2	2,115.5	2,169.1	2,239.0	2,322.4	2,413.1	2,511.8	2,618.9
% change	7.2	2.7	-1.6	2.5	3.2	3.7	3.9	4.1	4.3
Other	48,602.0	52,840.0	56,232.0	58,938.0	62,070.0	65,576.0	69,723.0	74,677.0	80,048.0
% change	3.8	8.7	6.4	4.8	5.3	5.7	6.3	7.1	7.2
Nominal GDP	490,732.0	496,062.0	503,268.0	522,970.0	547,088.0	574,449.0	605,676.0	639,583.0	677,458.0
% change	0.2	1.1	1.5	3.9	4.6	5.0	5.4	5.6	5.9
GDP price deflator	95.6	94.4	93.2	93.8	95.3	97.1	99.2	101.4	103.8
% change	-1.6	-1.2	-1.3	0.6	1.6	1.9	2.2	2.2	2.4
Private consumption expenditure price deflator	96.4	95.8	95.0	95.4	96.5	98.3	100.6	103.2	106.0
% change	-0.9	-0.7	-0.8	0.4	1.2	1.8	2.4	2.5	2.8
Exports of Goods and Services price deflator	97.4	96.2	97.5	105.7	112.2	117.6	122.9	128.6	135.1
% change	-3.3	-1.3	1.3	8.5	6.1	4.8	4.5	4.7	5.0
Imports of Goods and Services price deflator	100.4	102.9	111.0	121.2	125.5	129.2	132.9	136.9	141.4
% change	-0.9	2.5	7.8	9.2	3.6	3.0	2.9	3.1	3.3
Import price deflator for mineral fuel	111.6	124.0	172.1	182.9	172.3	165.2	155.7	146.2	138.0
% change	6.7	11.2	38.8	6.3	-5.8	-4.1	-5.8	-6.1	-5.7
Consumer price index	98.1	98.1	97.8	98.6	100.3	102.8	105.8	109.3	113.1
% change	-0.3	0.0	-0.3	0.8	1.8	2.4	3.0	3.3	3.5
Domestic firms' price index (PPI)	94.9	96.1	97.7	99.4	100.6	102.0	103.9	106.0	108.5
% change	-0.8	1.2	1.7	1.8	1.2	1.5	1.8	2.0	2.3

Source: Authors' calculation.

Table 12.7 Economic forecast: summary Table 2 (15% IT investment increase from 2006), Unit: Billion yen (or 2000 year base)

	Actual			Forecast					
	2003	2004	2005	2006	2007	2008	2009	2010	2011
Labor force	6,687.3	6,666.3	6,643.1	6,614.6	6,618.9	6,659.6	6,724.3	6,821.0	6,939.7
% change	-1.0	-0.3	-0.4	-0.4	0.1	0.6	1.0	1.4	1.7
Employed	6,328.9	6,316.1	6,329.6	6,322.4	6,345.9	6,406.1	6,487.9	6,603.0	6,740.9
% change	-1.3	-0.2	0.2	-0.1	0.4	1.0	1.3	1.8	2.1
Employees	5,329.7	5,335.1	5,355.7	5,350.6	5,365.7	5,399.1	5,453.5	5,537.2	5,644.4
% change	-0.7	0.1	0.4	-0.1	0.3	0.6	1.0	1.5	1.9
Unemployment rate	5.4	5.3	4.7	4.4	4.2	3.9	3.6	3.3	3.0
Labor productivity growth	3.2	2.5	2.6	3.4	2.6	2.1	1.9	1.5	1.3
Unit labor cost (% change)	-3.2	-3.5	-1.5	0.3	1.4	2.0	2.3	2.6	2.9
Per capita wage and salary	4,196.5	4,132.4	4,167.2	4,315.4	4,503.0	4,719.2	4,950.2	5,182.9	5,431.9
% change	0.1	-1.5	0.8	3.6	4.4	4.8	4.9	4.7	4.8
Potential GDP	581,260.0	583,909.0	589,783.0	599,091.0	617,462.0	639,655.0	665,253.0	694,079.0	724,518.0
% change	0.8	0.5	1.0	1.6	3.1	3.6	4.0	4.3	4.4
CD rate	0.0	0.0	0.0	0.3	1.2	2.4	3.8	5.1	6.0
Long-term bond yield	1.0	1.5	1.4	1.3	2.1	3.2	4.4	5.6	6.7
Household disposable income	297,713.0	295,666.0	293,641.0	305,588.0	318,362.0	334,078.0	352,778.0	373,366.0	396,800.0
% change	-0.3	-0.7	-0.7	4.1	4.2	4.9	5.6	5.8	6.3
Wage and salary	223,656.0	220,469.0	223,179.0	230,900.0	241,625.0	254,805.0	269,972.0	287,004.0	306,620.0
% change	-0.7	-1.4	1.2	3.5	4.6	5.5	6.0	6.3	6.8
Compensation of employees	258,692.0	255,250.0	258,388.0	267,595.0	279,457.0	293,757.0	310,212.0	328,682.0	349,876.0
% change	-1.5	-1.3	1.2	3.6	4.4	5.1	5.6	6.0	6.5
Corporate income	48,646.0	71,795.0	79,174.0	93,743.0	102,038.0	109,603.0	117,118.0	123,605.0	129,729.0
% change	8.4	47.6	10.3	18.4	8.8	7.4	6.9	5.5	5.0
Corporate income after tax	35,676.0	52,902.0	58,458.0	69,216.0	75,340.0	80,926.0	86,475.0	91,265.0	95,787.0
% change	10.1	48.3	10.5	18.4	8.8	7.4	6.9	5.5	5.0

General government fiscal balance	−54,151.0	−49,284.0	−45,984.0	−39,847.0	−39,273.0	−40,255.0	−41,578.0	−41,899.0	−41,625.0
% change	−3.8	−9.0	−6.7	−13.3	−1.4	2.5	3.3	0.8	−0.7
GDP ratio (%)	−11.0	−9.9	−9.1	−7.6	−7.2	−7.0	−6.9	−6.6	−6.1
Direct tax revenue	37,338.0	42,102.0	44,545.0	50,101.0	54,305.0	58,613.0	63,183.0	67,747.0	72,584.0
% change	−4.0	12.8	5.8	12.5	8.4	7.9	7.8	7.2	7.1
Individual income tax revenue	23,753.0	22,822.0	23,232.0	24,902.0	26,879.0	29,150.0	31,693.0	34,497.0	37,667.0
% change	−5.3	−3.9	1.8	7.2	7.9	8.5	8.7	8.9	9.2
Private sector corporate tax revenue	12,970.0	18,893.0	20,715.0	24,527.0	26,697.0	28,677.0	30,643.0	32,340.0	33,942.0
% change	4.0	45.7	9.6	18.4	8.8	7.4	6.9	5.5	5.0
Indirect tax revenue	40,961.0	41,182.0	41,933.0	43,133.0	44,700.0	46,681.0	49,089.0	51,784.0	54,794.0
% change	−1.2	0.5	1.8	2.9	3.6	4.4	5.2	5.5	5.8
Consumption tax revenue	12,256.0	12,113.0	12,375.0	12,711.0	13,183.0	13,794.0	14,520.0	15,304.0	16,173.0
% change	1.0	−1.2	2.2	2.7	3.7	4.6	5.3	5.4	5.7
Social security benefits	71,272.0	70,676.0	71,574.0	73,314.0	76,585.0	80,260.0	84,075.0	87,292.0	90,158.0
% change	−0.4	−0.8	1.3	2.4	4.5	4.8	4.8	3.8	3.3
Social security contribution	70,973.0	67,064.0	68,894.0	69,846.0	71,949.0	75,356.0	79,317.0	83,777.0	88,677.0
% change	1.3	−5.5	2.7	1.4	3.0	4.7	5.3	5.6	5.9
Central government primary balance	−20,156.0	−18,853.0	−17,004.0	−16,004.0	−15,456.0	−15,785.0	−16,012.0	−16,326.0	−15,940.0
% change	13.4	−6.5	−9.8	−5.9	−3.4	2.1	1.4	2.0	−2.4
GDP ratio	−3.9	−3.6	−3.2	−2.9	−2.7	−2.7	−2.6	−2.6	−2.4
Central government revenue	85,849.0	88,432.0	84,798.0	78,255.0	80,128.0	87,597.0	98,447.0	112,013.0	121,937.0
% change	−1.4	3.0	−4.1	−7.7	2.4	9.3	12.4	13.8	8.9
Tax revenue	43,125.0	45,113.0	44,767.0	46,219.0	49,080.0	52,197.0	55,657.0	59,255.0	63,144.0
% change	−3.6	4.6	−0.8	3.2	6.2	6.4	6.6	6.5	6.6
Central government outlays	82,422.0	86,040.0	84,215.0	85,293.0	87,905.0	92,929.0	99,791.0	107,311.0	116,624.0
% change	−1.7	4.4	−2.1	1.3	3.1	5.7	7.4	7.5	8.7

Source: Authors' calculation.

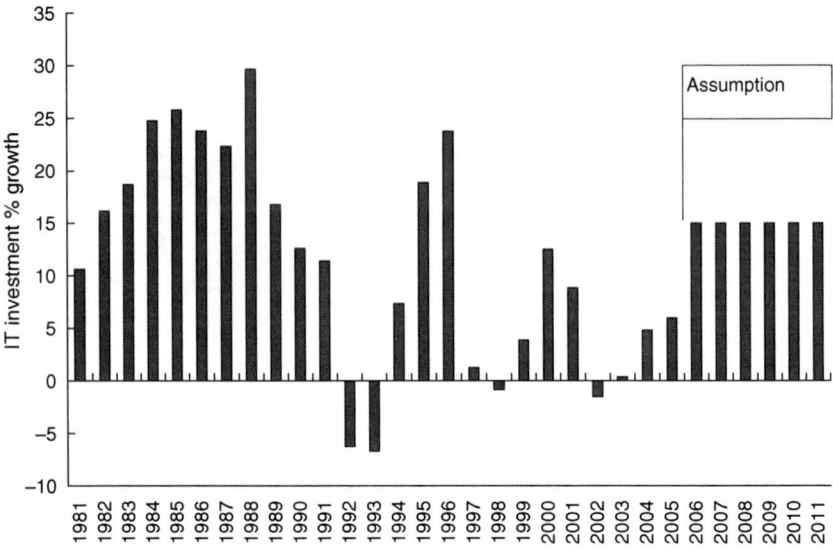

Figure 12.5 The growth rate of real IT investment (%).

(Figure 12.6). Alternative simulations with 5% and 10% growth of IT investments show that an increase in the growth of IT investment of 5% accounts for an increase in the real GDP growth rate of approximately 0.2% annually above its underlying path.

The growth rate of potential GDP associated with 15% annual growth of IT is increased significantly by 0.2–6% per year above the baseline so that in 2011 potential GDP is 3% higher than in the Baseline Simulation. Importantly, inflation as measured by the GDP deflator would show a small decline below the baseline and the government deficit to nominal GDP ratio would improve slightly.

Monetary policy simulation

In order to test the possibilities for monetary policy, we present a simulation with a 0.5% increase in the CD interest rate.[2] The effects of such an adjustment, shown in Tables 12.8 and 12.9, are quite small, but note that the changes assumed are themselves also of very small magnitude. An increase in the CD rate of 0.5% results in an increase in the long-term interest rates of 0.2% and ultimately results in a change in the growth of gross capital formation of 0.6% and a change in growth rate GDP of 0.1%. This suggests that moderation of monetary policy would have a small but perceptible impact on the growth of the economy. There was no discernible effect on potential GDP.

Investment tax credit

The imposition of an investment tax credit is another way to provide stimulus to the economy. The simulation assumes that from 2006 there would be an investment

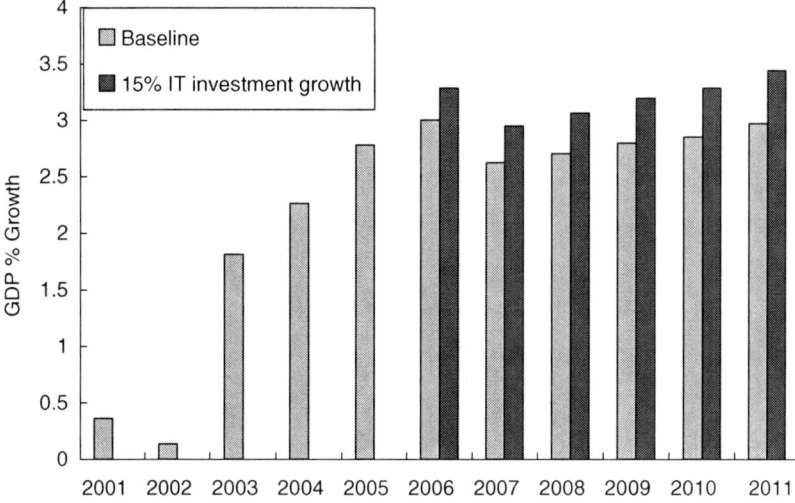

Figure 12.6 The effect of 15% IT investment growth on real GDP growth (%).

tax credit amounting to 50% of the user cost of capital.[3] In view of the limitations of the model, it was possible only to test the impact of a general investment tax credit. The calculation was done in two stages. First we imposed the investment tax credit on all non-IT investment by reducing the user cost of capital by 50% and then we added separately the impact of the investment tax credit on investment in IT, assuming the impact would be similar to that observed for non-IT products. The results obtained are summarized in Tables 12.10 and 12.11.

The results obtained from a general tax credit are quite small and effect growth only in a transitory way. The level of plant and equipment investment expenditure is 2.0% higher in 2006 than in the Baseline solution. GDP growth is 0.3% higher in 2006 and 0.1% higher at 2007 and approximately the same as in the Baseline Solution throughout the remainder of the forecast period. This result is disappointing, but the estimate is perhaps too low. An investment tax credit of substantial magnitude focused on IT hardware and software or an accelerated depreciation rule, like that now available in the United States, might have more substantial impact.

Trade/exchange rate simulation

Direct intervention in trade through changes in import restrictions or through export subsidies is not likely to be a feasible option for Japanese policy makers. The role of Japan in world trade, and in the trade of East Asian region, is likely to be affected by changes in the exchange rate of the Japanese yen. In this simulation, we assume that, given the continued balance of trade surplus, the Japanese yen would be allowed to appreciate by 10% beginning in 2006. The results are presented in Tables 12.12 and 12.13.

Table 12.8 Economic forecast: summary Table 1 (Increase in short term interest rate of 0.5% from 2006), Unit: Billion yen (or 2000 year base)

	Actual			Forecast					
	2003	2004	2005	2006	2007	2008	2009	2010	2011
Real GDP	513,602.0	525,240.0	539,862.0	555,235.0	569,143.0	584,514.0	600,923.0	618,149.0	636,606.0
% change	1.8	2.3	2.8	2.9	2.5	2.7	2.8	2.9	3.0
Personal consumption expenditure	291,937.0	297,598.0	303,937.0	309,395.0	315,227.0	322,259.0	330,235.0	339,118.0	348,650.0
% change	0.6	1.9	2.1	1.8	1.9	2.2	2.5	2.7	2.8
Government consumption expenditure	91,549.0	93,385.0	95,013.0	95,850.0	97,725.0	100,100.0	102,425.0	104,425.0	106,550.0
% change	2.3	2.0	1.7	0.9	2.0	2.4	2.3	2.0	2.0
Gross capital formation	120,188.0	120,311.0	126,091.0	131,246.0	134,977.0	139,593.0	144,664.0	149,930.0	155,443.0
% change	2.0	0.1	4.8	4.1	2.8	3.4	3.6	3.6	3.7
Fixed capital formation	119,738.0	120,999.0	125,963.0	129,316.0	132,787.0	137,165.0	141,963.0	146,933.0	152,105.0
% change	0.5	1.1	4.1	2.7	2.7	3.3	3.5	3.5	3.5
Private sector	91,384.0	95,138.0	101,540.0	106,741.0	110,062.0	113,665.0	117,663.0	121,833.0	126,355.0
% change	4.7	4.1	6.7	5.1	3.1	3.3	3.5	3.5	3.7
Dwellings	18,294.0	18,656.0	18,512.0	18,963.0	19,241.0	19,656.0	20,252.0	20,787.0	21,469.0
% change	−0.9	2.0	−0.8	2.4	1.5	2.2	3.0	2.6	3.3
Plant and equipment	73,090.0	76,482.0	83,029.0	88,176.0	91,818.0	95,788.0	100,062.0	104,670.0	109,588.0
% change	6.2	4.6	8.6	6.2	4.1	4.3	4.5	4.6	4.7
IT	19,900.0	20,855.0	22,100.0	23,389.0	24,824.0	26,347.0	27,964.0	29,680.0	31,501.0
% change	0.4	4.8	6.0	5.8	6.1	6.1	6.1	6.1	6.1
Other	53,190.0	55,627.0	60,929.0	64,788.0	66,994.0	69,441.0	72,098.0	74,990.0	78,086.0
% change	8.5	4.6	9.5	6.3	3.4	3.7	3.8	4.0	4.1
Public sector	28,354.0	25,861.0	24,423.0	22,575.0	22,725.0	23,500.0	24,300.0	25,100.0	25,750.0
% change	−10.8	−8.8	−5.6	−7.6	0.7	3.4	3.4	3.3	2.6
Changes in inventories	450.0	−688.5	128.4	1,921.8	2,167.7	2,411.1	2,692.5	2,995.1	3,342.9
Private sector	286.1	−913.2	−186.1	1,607.4	1,853.3	2,096.7	2,378.1	2,680.7	3,028.5
Public sector	163.9	224.7	314.4	314.4	314.4	314.4	314.4	314.4	314.4
Net exports of Goods and Services	9,714.0	13,836.0	15,107.0	18,676.0	20,561.0	21,120.0	21,277.0	21,375.0	21,579.0

Exports of Goods and Services	60,410.0	68,825.0	73,454.0	79,159.0	83,185.0	86,318.0	89,536.0	93,243.0	97,167.0
% change	9.0	13.9	6.7	7.8	5.1	3.8	3.7	4.1	4.2
Imports of Goods and Services	50,696.0	54,989.0	58,347.0	60,484.0	62,625.0	65,197.0	68,259.0	71,868.0	75,589.0
% change	4.0	8.5	6.1	3.7	3.5	4.1	4.7	5.3	5.2
Mineral fuel	2,093.6	2,149.2	2,115.5	2,159.3	2,218.7	2,292.8	2,373.1	2,459.8	2,553.1
% change	7.2	2.7	-1.6	2.1	2.8	3.3	3.5	3.7	3.8
Other	48,602.0	52,840.0	56,232.0	58,324.0	60,406.0	62,905.0	65,886.0	69,409.0	73,035.0
% change	3.8	8.7	6.4	3.7	3.6	4.1	4.7	5.4	5.2
Nominal GDP	490,732.0	496,062.0	503,268.0	521,304.0	543,842.0	570,152.0	600,410.0	633,501.0	670,783.0
% change	0.2	1.1	1.5	3.6	4.3	4.8	5.3	5.5	5.9
GDP price deflator	95.6	94.4	93.2	93.9	95.6	97.5	99.9	102.5	105.4
% change	-1.6	-1.2	-1.3	0.7	1.8	2.1	2.4	2.6	2.8
Private consumption expenditure price deflator	96.4	95.8	95.0	95.4	96.5	98.3	100.6	103.2	106.0
% change	-0.9	-0.7	-0.8	0.4	1.2	1.8	2.4	2.5	2.8
Exports of Goods and Services price deflator	97.4	96.2	97.5	105.7	112.3	117.6	123.0	128.7	135.3
% change	-3.3	-1.3	1.3	8.5	6.2	4.8	4.5	4.7	5.1
Imports of Goods and Services price deflator	100.4	102.9	111.0	121.2	125.5	129.2	132.9	137.0	141.4
% change	-0.9	2.5	7.8	9.2	3.6	3.0	2.9	3.0	3.3
Import P. deflator for mineral fuel	111.6	124.0	172.1	182.9	172.3	165.2	155.7	146.2	138.0
% change	6.7	11.2	38.8	6.3	-5.8	-4.1	-5.8	-6.1	-5.7
Consumer price index	98.1	98.1	97.8	98.6	100.3	102.8	105.9	109.3	113.1
% change	-0.3	0.0	-0.3	0.8	1.8	2.4	3.0	3.3	3.5
Domestic firms' price index (PPI)	94.9	96.1	97.7	99.4	100.6	102.1	104.0	106.1	108.6
% change	-0.8	1.2	1.7	1.8	1.2	1.5	1.8	2.1	2.4

Source: Authors' calculation.

Table 12.9 Economic forecast: summary Table 2 (Increase in short term interest rate of 0.5% from 2006), Unit: Billion yen (or 2000 year base)

	Actual			Forecast					
	2003	2004	2005	2006	2007	2008	2009	2010	2011
Labor force	6,687.3	6,666.3	6,643.1	6,614.6	6,618.4	6,658.0	6,720.8	6,815.0	6,930.8
% change	−1.0	−0.3	−0.4	−0.4	0.1	0.6	0.9	1.4	1.7
Employed	6,328.9	6,316.1	6,329.6	6,321.9	6,343.7	6,400.9	6,478.7	6,588.8	6,720.7
% change	−1.3	−0.2	0.2	−0.1	0.3	0.9	1.2	1.7	2.0
Employees	5,329.7	5,335.1	5,355.7	5,350.2	5,363.9	5,394.8	5,445.8	5,525.3	5,627.5
% change	−0.7	0.1	0.4	−0.1	0.3	0.6	1.0	1.5	1.9
Unemployment rate	5.4	5.3	4.7	4.4	4.2	3.9	3.7	3.4	3.1
Labor productivity growth	3.2	2.5	2.6	3.0	2.2	1.8	1.6	1.2	1.0
Unit labor cost (% change)	−3.2	−3.5	−1.5	0.7	1.8	2.3	2.6	2.9	3.2
Per capita wage and salary	4,196.5	4,132.4	4,167.2	4,314.6	4,499.7	4,712.9	4,940.7	5,170.2	5,415.7
% change	0.1	−1.5	0.8	3.5	4.3	4.7	4.8	4.6	4.8
Potential GDP	581,260.0	583,909.0	589,783.0	597,970.0	613,928.0	632,793.0	654,158.0	677,923.0	702,557.0
% change	0.8	0.5	1.0	1.4	2.7	3.1	3.4	3.6	3.6
CD rate	0.0	0.0	0.0	0.8	1.6	2.8	4.2	5.5	6.4
Long-term bond yield	1.0	1.5	1.4	1.5	2.3	3.3	4.6	5.8	6.9
Household disposable income	297,713.0	295,666.0	293,641.0	305,288.0	317,807.0	333,337.0	351,858.0	372,267.0	395,521.0
% change	−0.3	−0.7	−0.7	4.0	4.1	4.9	5.6	5.8	6.3
Wage and salary	223,656.0	220,469.0	223,179.0	230,841.0	241,363.0	254,254.0	269,071.0	285,683.0	304,792.0
% change	−0.7	−1.4	1.2	3.4	4.6	5.3	5.8	6.2	6.7
Compensation of employees	258,692.0	255,250.0	258,388.0	267,536.0	279,188.0	293,187.0	309,274.0	327,302.0	347,962.0
% change	−1.5	−1.3	1.2	3.5	4.4	5.0	5.5	5.8	6.3
Corporate income	48,646.0	71,795.0	79,174.0	92,337.0	99,369.0	106,436.0	113,901.0	120,878.0	128,278.0
% change	8.4	47.6	10.3	16.6	7.6	7.1	7.0	6.1	6.1
Corporate income after tax	35,676.0	52,902.0	58,458.0	68,178.0	73,370.0	78,588.0	84,100.0	89,251.0	94,715.0
% change	10.1	48.3	10.5	16.6	7.6	7.1	7.0	6.1	6.1

General government fiscal balance	−54,151.0	−49,284.0	−45,984.0	−40,297.0	−40,065.0	−41,224.0	−42,778.0	−43,260.0	−43,031.0
% change	−3.8	−9.0	−6.7	−12.4	−0.6	2.9	3.8	1.1	−0.5
GDP ratio (%)	−11.0	−9.9	−9.1	−7.3	−7.0	−7.1	−7.1	−7.0	−6.8
Direct tax revenue	37,338.0	42,102.0	44,545.0	49,697.0	53,531.0	57,673.0	62,190.0	66,834.0	71,948.0
% change	−4.0	12.8	5.8	11.6	7.7	7.7	7.8	7.5	7.7
Individual income tax revenue	23,753.0	22,822.0	23,232.0	24,870.0	26,814.0	29,051.0	31,554.0	34,310.0	37,420.0
% change	−5.3	−3.9	1.8	7.1	7.8	8.3	8.6	8.7	9.1
Private sector corporate tax revenue	12,970.0	18,893.0	20,715.0	24,159.0	25,999.0	27,848.0	29,801.0	31,627.0	33,563.0
% change	4.0	45.7	9.6	16.6	7.6	7.1	7.0	6.1	6.1
Indirect tax revenue	40,961.0	41,182.0	41,933.0	43,010.0	44,434.0	46,358.0	48,718.0	51,361.0	54,316.0
% change	−1.2	0.5	1.8	2.6	3.3	4.3	5.1	5.4	5.8
Consumption tax revenue	12,256.0	12,113.0	12,375.0	12,683.0	13,123.0	13,724.0	14,441.0	15,219.0	16,082.0
% change	1.0	−1.2	2.2	2.5	3.5	4.6	5.2	5.4	5.7
Social security benefits	71,272.0	70,676.0	71,574.0	73,319.0	76,620.0	80,361.0	84,286.0	87,667.0	90,770.0
% change	−0.4	−0.8	1.3	2.4	4.5	4.9	4.9	4.0	3.5
Social security contribution	70,973.0	67,064.0	68,894.0	69,841.0	71,916.0	75,274.0	79,172.0	83,556.0	88,366.0
% change	1.3	−5.5	2.7	1.4	3.0	4.7	5.2	5.5	5.8
Central government primary balance	−20,156.0	−18,853.0	−17,004.0	−16,170.0	−15,788.0	−16,189.0	−16,453.0	−16,769.0	−16,334.0
% change	13.4	−6.5	−9.8	−4.9	−2.4	2.5	1.6	1.9	−2.6
GDP ratio	−3.9	−3.6	−3.2	−2.9	−2.7	−2.7	−2.7	−2.7	−2.5
Central government revenue	85,849.0	88,432.0	84,798.0	77,920.0	79,035.0	85,760.0	95,961.0	109,000.0	118,564.0
% change	−1.4	3.0	−4.1	−8.1	1.4	8.5	11.9	13.6	8.8
Tax revenue	43,125.0	45,113.0	44,767.0	45,957.0	48,564.0	51,571.0	54,980.0	58,592.0	62,592.0
% change	−3.6	4.6	−0.8	2.7	5.7	6.2	6.6	6.6	6.8
Central government outlays	82,422.0	86,040.0	84,215.0	85,269.0	87,964.0	93,130.0	100,164.0	107,880.0	117,447.0
% change	−1.7	4.4	−2.1	1.3	3.2	5.9	7.6	7.7	8.9

Source: Authors' calculation.

Table 12.10 Simulation study: summary Table 1 (Investment tax credit from 2006), Unit: Billion yen (or 2000 year base)

	Actual			Forecast					
	2003	2004	2005	2006	2007	2008	2009	2010	2011
Real GDP	513,602.0	525,240.0	539,862.0	557,438.0	572,257.0	587,709.0	604,207.0	621,494.0	639,962.0
% change	1.8	2.3	2.8	3.3	2.7	2.7	2.8	2.9	3.0
Personal consumption expenditure	291,937.0	297,598.0	303,937.0	310,275.0	316,969.0	324,109.0	332,089.0	340,941.0	350,422.0
% change	0.6	1.9	2.1	2.1	2.2	2.3	2.5	2.7	2.8
Government consumption expenditure	91,549.0	93,385.0	95,013.0	95,850.0	97,725.0	100,100.0	102,425.0	104,425.0	106,550.0
% change	2.3	2.0	1.7	0.9	2.0	2.4	2.3	2.0	2.0
Gross capital formation	120,188.0	120,311.0	126,091.0	131,825.0	135,615.0	140,718.0	146,723.0	152,922.0	159,415.0
% change	2.0	0.1	4.8	4.6	2.9	3.8	4.3	4.2	4.3
Fixed capital formation	119,738.0	120,999.0	125,963.0	129,887.0	133,591.0	138,692.0	144,429.0	150,340.0	156,504.0
% change	0.5	1.1	4.1	3.1	2.9	3.8	4.1	4.1	4.1
Private sector	91,384.0	95,138.0	101,540.0	107,312.0	110,866.0	115,192.0	120,129.0	125,240.0	130,754.0
% change	4.7	4.1	6.7	5.7	3.3	3.9	4.3	4.3	4.4
Dwellings	18,294.0	18,656.0	18,512.0	19,000.0	19,378.0	19,888.0	20,558.0	21,143.0	21,847.0
% change	−0.9	2.0	−0.8	2.6	2.0	2.6	3.4	2.9	3.3
Plant and equipment	73,090.0	76,482.0	83,029.0	89,986.0	94,155.0	98,124.0	102,513.0	107,263.0	112,300.0
% change	6.2	4.6	8.6	8.4	4.6	4.2	4.5	4.6	4.7
IT	19,900.0	20,855.0	22,100.0	23,826.0	25,390.0	26,932.0	28,597.0	30,369.0	32,239.0
% change	0.4	4.8	6.0	7.8	6.6	6.1	6.2	6.2	6.2
Other	53,190.0	55,627.0	60,929.0	64,923.0	66,667.0	68,989.0	71,725.0	74,667.0	77,809.0
% change	8.5	4.6	9.5	6.6	2.7	3.5	4.0	4.1	4.2
Public sector	28,354.0	25,861.0	24,423.0	22,575.0	22,725.0	23,500.0	24,300.0	25,100.0	25,750.0
% change	−10.8	−8.8	−5.6	−7.6	0.7	3.4	3.4	3.3	2.6
Changes in inventories	450.0	−688.5	128.4	1,966.6	2,252.2	2,497.4	2,780.6	3,085.4	3,435.0
Private sector	286.1	−913.2	−186.1	1,652.2	1,937.8	2,183.0	2,466.2	2,771.0	3,120.6
Public sector	163.9	224.7	314.4	314.4	314.4	314.4	314.4	314.4	314.4
Net exports of Goods and Services	9,714.0	13,836.0	15,107.0	18,106.0	19,374.0	19,812.0	19,863.0	19,858.0	19,980.0

Exports of Goods and Services	60,410.0	68,825.0	73,454.0	79,160.0	83,189.0	86,324.0	89,542.0	93,248.0	97,171.0
% change	9.0	13.9	6.7	7.8	5.1	3.8	3.7	4.1	4.2
Imports of Goods and Services	50,696.0	54,989.0	58,347.0	61,054.0	63,815.0	66,512.0	69,679.0	73,391.0	77,191.0
% change	4.0	8.5	6.1	4.6	4.5	4.2	4.8	5.3	5.2
Mineral fuel	2,093.6	2,149.2	2,115.5	2,168.4	2,231.6	2,306.1	2,386.8	2,473.9	2,567.3
% change	7.2	2.7	−1.6	2.5	2.9	3.3	3.5	3.7	3.8
Other	48,602.0	52,840.0	56,232.0	58,885.0	61,584.0	64,206.0	67,292.0	70,917.0	74,624.0
% change	3.8	8.7	6.4	4.7	4.6	4.3	4.8	5.4	5.2
Nominal GDP	490,732.0	496,062.0	503,268.0	523,174.0	546,408.0	572,798.0	603,147.0	636,292.0	673,584.0
% change	0.2	1.1	1.5	4.0	4.4	4.8	5.3	5.5	5.9
GDP price deflator	95.6	94.4	93.2	93.8	95.5	97.5	99.8	102.4	105.2
% change	−1.6	−1.2	−1.3	0.7	1.7	2.1	2.4	2.6	2.8
Private consumption expenditure price deflator	96.4	95.8	95.0	95.4	96.5	98.3	100.6	103.2	106.0
% change	−0.9	−0.7	−0.8	0.4	1.2	1.8	2.4	2.5	2.8
Exports of Goods and Services price deflator	97.4	96.2	97.5	105.7	112.2	117.6	122.9	128.7	135.2
% change	−3.3	−1.3	1.3	8.5	6.2	4.8	4.5	4.7	5.1
Imports of Goods and Services price deflator	100.4	102.9	111.0	121.2	125.5	129.2	132.9	137.0	141.4
% change	−0.9	2.5	7.8	9.2	3.6	3.0	2.9	3.1	3.3
Import price deflator for mineral fuel	111.6	124.0	172.1	182.9	172.3	165.2	155.7	146.2	138.0
% change	6.7	11.2	38.8	6.3	−5.8	−4.1	−5.8	−6.1	−5.7
Consumer price index	98.1	98.1	97.8	98.6	100.3	102.8	105.9	109.3	113.2
% change	−0.3	0.0	−0.3	0.8	1.8	2.4	3.0	3.3	3.5
Domestic firms' price index (PPI)	94.9	96.1	97.7	99.4	100.6	102.1	104.0	106.1	108.6
% change	−0.8	1.2	1.7	1.8	1.2	1.5	1.8	2.1	2.4

Source: Authors' calculation.

Table 12.11 Simulation study: summary Table 2 (Investment tax credit from 2006), Unit: Billion yen (or 2000 year base)

	Actual			Forecast					
	2003	2004	2005	2006	2007	2008	2009	2010	2011
Labor force	6,687.3	6,666.3	6,643.1	6,614.6	6,618.8	6,659.3	6,723.3	6,818.7	6,935.7
% change	−1.0	−0.3	−0.4	−0.4	0.1	0.6	1.0	1.4	1.7
Employed	6,328.9	6,316.1	6,329.6	6,322.3	6,345.6	6,404.8	6,484.6	6,596.8	6,730.5
% change	−1.3	−0.2	0.2	−0.1	0.4	0.9	1.3	1.7	2.0
Employees	5,329.7	5,335.1	5,355.7	5,350.5	5,365.5	5,398.0	5,450.7	5,531.9	5,635.7
% change	−0.7	0.1	0.4	−0.1	0.3	0.6	1.0	1.5	1.9
Unemployment rate	5.4	5.3	4.7	4.4	4.2	3.9	3.6	3.3	3.1
Labor productivity growth	3.2	2.5	2.6	3.4	2.3	1.8	1.5	1.1	0.9
Unit labor cost (% change)	−3.2	−3.5	−1.5	0.3	1.7	2.3	2.7	2.9	3.3
Per capita wage and salary	4,196.5	4,132.4	4,167.2	4,315.4	4,502.6	4,717.4	4,946.3	5,176.4	5,422.3
% change	0.1	−1.5	0.8	3.6	4.3	4.8	4.9	4.7	4.8
Potential GDP	581,260.0	583,909.0	589,783.0	598,475.0	615,154.0	634,422.0	656,146.0	680,248.0	705,194.0
% change	0.8	0.5	1.0	1.5	2.8	3.1	3.4	3.7	3.7
CD rate	0.0	0.0	0.0	0.3	1.1	2.3	3.7	5.0	5.9
Long-term bond yield	1.0	1.5	1.4	1.3	2.1	3.1	4.4	5.6	6.7
Household disposable income	297,713.0	295,666.0	293,641.0	305,585.0	318,345.0	333,999.0	352,598.0	373,061.0	396,350.0
% change	−0.3	−0.7	−0.7	4.1	4.2	4.9	5.6	5.8	6.2
Wage and salary	223,656.0	220,469.0	223,179.0	230,894.0	241,591.0	254,654.0	269,623.0	286,374.0	305,610.0
% change	−0.7	−1.4	1.2	3.5	4.6	5.4	5.9	6.2	6.7
Compensation of employees	258,692.0	255,250.0	258,388.0	267,589.0	279,422.0	293,602.0	309,852.0	328,028.0	348,825.0
% change	−1.5	−1.3	1.2	3.6	4.4	5.1	5.5	5.9	6.3
Corporate income	48,646.0	71,795.0	79,174.0	93,980.0	101,540.0	108,543.0	115,878.0	122,665.0	129,779.0
% change	8.4	47.6	10.3	18.7	8.0	6.9	6.8	5.9	5.8
Corporate income after tax	35,676.0	52,902.0	58,458.0	69,391.0	74,973.0	80,144.0	85,559.0	90,571.0	95,824.0
% change	10.1	48.3	10.5	18.7	8.0	6.9	6.8	5.9	5.8

General government fiscal balance	−54,151.0	−49,284.0	−45,984.0	−39,788.0	−39,436.0	−40,651.0	−42,166.0	−42,616.0	−42,377.0
% change	−3.8	−9.0	−6.7	−13.5	−0.9	3.1	3.7	1.1	−0.6
GDP ratio (%)	−11.0	−9.9	−9.1	−7.1	−6.9	−6.9	−7.0	−6.9	−6.6
Direct tax revenue	37,338.0	42,102.0	44,545.0	50,164.0	54,171.0	58,318.0	62,820.0	67,432.0	72,488.0
% change	−4.0	12.8	5.8	12.6	8.0	7.7	7.7	7.3	7.5
Individual income tax revenue	23,753.0	22,822.0	23,232.0	24,902.0	26,876.0	29,136.0	31,659.0	34,433.0	37,560.0
% change	−5.3	−3.9	1.8	7.2	7.9	8.4	8.7	8.8	9.1
Private sector corporate tax revenue	12,970.0	18,893.0	20,715.0	24,589.0	26,567.0	28,399.0	30,318.0	32,094.0	33,956.0
% change	4.0	45.7	9.6	18.7	8.0	6.9	6.8	5.9	5.8
Indirect tax revenue	40,961.0	41,182.0	41,933.0	43,130.0	44,681.0	46,631.0	49,004.0	51,656.0	54,614.0
% change	−1.2	0.5	1.8	2.9	3.6	4.4	5.1	5.4	5.7
Consumption tax revenue	12,256.0	12,113.0	12,375.0	12,710.0	13,181.0	13,789.0	14,511.0	15,292.0	16,156.0
% change	1.0	−1.2	2.2	2.7	3.7	4.6	5.2	5.4	5.7
Social security benefits	71,272.0	70,676.0	71,574.0	73,314.0	76,591.0	80,290.0	84,160.0	87,476.0	90,504.0
% change	−0.4	−0.8	1.3	2.4	4.5	4.8	4.8	3.9	3.5
Social security contribution	70,973.0	67,064.0	68,894.0	69,846.0	71,945.0	75,337.0	79,266.0	83,680.0	88,515.0
% change	1.3	−5.5	2.7	1.4	3.0	4.7	5.2	5.6	5.8
Central government primary balance	−20,156.0	−18,853.0	−17,004.0	−15,988.0	−15,503.0	−15,891.0	−16,154.0	−16,475.0	−16,054.0
% change	13.4	−6.5	−9.8	−6.0	−3.0	2.5	1.7	2.0	−2.6
GDP ratio	−3.9	−3.6	−3.2	−2.9	−2.8	−2.8	−2.8	−2.7	−2.5
Central govt. revenue	85,849.0	88,432.0	84,798.0	78,282.0	80,052.0	87,340.0	98,071.0	111,637.0	121,737.0
% change	−1.4	3.0	−4.1	−7.7	2.3	9.1	12.3	13.8	9.0
Tax revenue	43,125.0	45,113.0	44,767.0	46,248.0	49,003.0	52,026.0	55,434.0	59,035.0	63,008.0
% change	−3.6	4.6	−0.8	3.3	6.0	6.2	6.6	6.5	6.7
Central government outlays	82,422.0	86,040.0	84,215.0	85,307.0	87,872.0	92,846.0	99,660.0	107,142.0	116,434.0
% change	−1.7	4.4	−2.1	1.3	3.0	5.7	7.3	7.5	8.7

Source: Authors' calculation.

Table 12.12 Simulation study: summary Table 1 (10% appreciation of the Yen from 2006), Unit: Billion yen (or 2000 year base)

	Actual			Forecast					
	2003	*2004*	*2005*	*2006*	*2007*	*2008*	*2009*	*2010*	*2011*
Real GDP	513,602.0	525,240.0	539,862.0	550,110.0	556,598.0	563,854.0	571,314.0	579,871.0	589,503.0
% change	1.8	2.3	2.8	1.9	1.2	1.3	1.3	1.5	1.7
Personal consumption expenditure	291,937.0	297,598.0	303,937.0	315,819.0	323,856.0	329,734.0	333,508.0	337,896.0	342,902.0
% change	0.6	1.9	2.1	3.9	2.5	1.8	1.1	1.3	1.5
Government consumption expenditure	91,549.0	93,385.0	95,013.0	95,850.0	97,725.0	100,100.0	102,425.0	104,425.0	106,550.0
% change	2.3	2.0	1.7	0.9	2.0	2.4	2.3	2.0	2.0
Gross capital formation	120,188.0	120,311.0	126,091.0	132,691.0	138,257.0	144,922.0	152,291.0	160,131.0	168,523.0
% change	2.0	0.1	4.8	5.2	4.2	4.8	5.1	5.2	5.2
Fixed capital formation	119,738.0	120,999.0	125,963.0	130,739.0	136,016.0	142,419.0	149,488.0	157,007.0	165,031.0
% change	0.5	1.1	4.1	3.8	4.0	4.7	5.0	5.0	5.1
Private sector	91,384.0	95,138.0	101,540.0	108,164.0	113,291.0	118,919.0	125,188.0	131,907.0	139,281.0
% change	4.7	4.1	6.7	6.5	4.7	5.0	5.3	5.4	5.6
Dwellings	18,294.0	18,656.0	18,512.0	19,130.0	19,765.0	20,268.0	20,523.0	20,605.0	20,632.0
% change	-0.9	2.0	-0.8	3.3	3.3	2.6	1.3	0.4	0.1
Plant and equipment	73,090.0	76,482.0	83,029.0	81,338.0	78,969.0	77,562.0	76,798.0	76,604.0	76,860.0
% change	6.2	4.6	8.6	-2.0	-2.9	-1.8	-1.0	-0.3	0.3
IT	19,900.0	20,855.0	22,100.0	23,389.0	24,824.0	26,347.0	27,964.0	29,680.0	31,501.0
% change	0.4	4.8	6.0	5.8	6.1	6.1	6.1	6.1	6.1
Other	53,190.0	55,627.0	60,929.0	57,949.0	54,145.0	51,214.0	48,834.0	46,924.0	45,359.0
% change	8.5	4.6	9.5	-4.9	-6.6	-5.4	-4.7	-3.9	-3.3
Public sector	28,354.0	25,861.0	24,423.0	22,575.0	22,725.0	23,500.0	24,300.0	25,100.0	25,750.0
% change	-10.8	-8.8	-5.6	-7.6	0.7	3.4	3.4	3.3	2.6
Changes in inventories	450.0	-688.5	128.4	2,004.0	2,169.6	2,266.5	2,393.7	2,562.1	2,777.7
Private sector	286.1	-913.2	-186.1	1,689.6	1,855.2	1,952.1	2,079.3	2,247.7	2,463.3
Public sector	163.9	224.7	314.4	314.4	314.4	314.4	314.4	314.4	314.4
Net exports of Goods and Services	9,714.0	13,836.0	15,107.0	13,715.0	11,710.0	10,745.0	11,688.0	13,000.0	14,353.0

Exports of Goods and Services	60,410.0	68,825.0	73,454.0	74,928.0	76,529.0	79,751.0	83,764.0	88,407.0	93,463.0
% change	9.0	13.9	6.7	2.0	2.1	4.2	5.0	5.5	5.7
Imports of Goods and Services	50,696.0	54,989.0	58,347.0	61,213.0	64,819.0	69,006.0	72,076.0	75,407.0	79,110.0
% change	4.0	8.5	6.1	4.9	5.9	6.5	4.5	4.6	4.9
Mineral fuel	2,093.6	2,149.2	2,115.5	2,144.6	2,179.0	2,218.6	2,257.7	2,303.0	2,353.1
% change	7.2	2.7	−1.6	1.4	1.6	1.8	1.8	2.0	2.2
Other	48,602.0	52,840.0	56,232.0	59,068.0	62,640.0	66,788.0	69,819.0	73,104.0	76,757.0
% change	3.8	8.7	6.4	5.0	6.1	6.6	4.5	4.7	5.0
Nominal GDP	490,732.0	496,062.0	503,268.0	515,816.0	524,562.0	531,963.0	538,958.0	546,370.0	554,275.0
% change	0.2	1.1	1.5	2.5	1.7	1.4	1.3	1.4	1.5
GDP price deflator	95.6	94.4	93.2	93.8	94.2	94.3	94.3	94.2	94.0
% change	−1.6	−1.2	−1.3	0.6	0.5	0.1	0.0	−0.1	−0.2
Private consumption expenditure price deflator	96.4	95.8	95.0	95.0	95.4	95.8	96.2	96.5	96.7
% change	−0.9	−0.7	−0.8	−0.1	0.5	0.4	0.4	0.3	0.3
Exports of Goods and Services price deflator	97.4	96.2	97.5	103.4	106.7	109.2	111.2	113.2	115.3
% change	−3.3	−1.3	1.3	6.0	3.3	2.3	1.9	1.8	1.8
Imports of Goods and Services price deflator	100.4	102.9	111.0	114.6	116.9	120.2	123.7	127.5	131.8
% change	−0.9	2.5	7.8	3.2	2.0	2.9	2.9	3.1	3.3
Import price deflator for mineral fuel	111.6	124.0	172.1	164.6	155.1	148.7	140.1	131.6	124.2
% change	6.7	11.2	38.8	−4.4	−5.8	−4.1	−5.8	−6.1	−5.7
Consumer price index	98.1	98.1	97.8	98.1	98.4	98.6	98.8	99.0	99.2
% change	−0.3	0.0	−0.3	0.3	0.3	0.3	0.2	0.2	0.2
Domestic firms' price index (PPI)	94.9	96.1	97.7	98.3	98.0	97.7	97.3	97.0	96.8
% change	−0.8	1.2	1.7	0.6	−0.3	−0.3	−0.3	−0.3	−0.3

Source: Authors' calculation.

Table 12.13 Economic forecast: summary Table 2 (10% appreciation of Yen/$ from 2006), Unit: Billion yen (or 2000 year base)

	Actual			Forecast					
	2003	2004	2005	2006	2007	2008	2009	2010	2011
Labor force	6,687.3	6,666.3	6,643.1	6,612.0	6,594.5	6,583.4	6,570.4	6,571.5	6,582.5
% change	−1.0	−0.4	−0.4	−0.5	−0.3	−0.2	−0.2	0.0	0.2
Employed	6,328.9	6,316.1	6,329.6	6,320.4	6,323.0	6,331.2	6,334.2	6,351.9	6,379.6
% change	−1.3	−0.2	0.2	−0.2	0.0	0.1	0.1	0.3	0.4
Employees	5,329.7	5,335.1	5,355.7	5,348.9	5,346.3	5,336.0	5,324.4	5,326.6	5,341.9
% change	−0.7	0.1	0.4	−0.1	−0.1	−0.2	−0.2	0.0	0.3
Unemployment rate	5.4	5.3	4.7	4.4	4.1	3.9	3.7	3.4	3.2
Labor productivity growth	3.2	2.5	2.6	2.1	1.1	1.2	1.3	1.2	1.2
Unit labor cost (% change)	−3.2	−3.5	−1.5	0.1	0.0	−0.5	−0.6	−0.7	−0.6
Per capita wage and salary	4,196.5	4,132.4	4,167.2	4,244.7	4,287.3	4,325.2	4,359.0	4,390.2	4,420.0
% change	0.1	−1.5	0.8	1.9	1.0	0.9	0.8	0.7	0.7
Potential GDP	581,260.0	583,909.0	589,783.0	597,996.0	611,590.0	626,717.0	643,670.0	662,647.0	682,045.0
% change	0.8	0.5	1.0	1.4	2.3	2.5	2.7	2.9	2.9
CD rate	0.0	0.0	0.0	0.1	0.1	0.1	0.1	0.1	0.1
Long-term bond yield	1.0	1.5	1.4	1.1	1.0	0.9	0.8	0.7	0.7
Household disposable income	297,713.0	295,666.0	293,641.0	304,921.0	307,877.0	308,533.0	309,143.0	310,009.0	311,532.0
% change	−0.3	−0.7	−0.7	3.8	1.0	0.2	0.2	0.3	0.5
Wage and salary	223,656.0	220,469.0	223,179.0	227,040.0	229,215.0	230,793.0	232,091.0	233,849.0	236,109.0
% change	−0.7	−1.4	1.2	1.7	1.0	0.7	0.6	0.8	1.0
Compensation of employees	258,692.0	255,250.0	258,388.0	263,677.0	266,696.0	268,840.0	270,654.0	272,921.0	275,713.0
% change	−1.5	−1.3	1.2	2.1	1.1	0.8	0.7	0.8	1.0
Corporate income	48,646.0	71,795.0	79,174.0	86,705.0	91,401.0	96,909.0	102,247.0	106,982.0	111,026.0
% change	8.4	47.6	10.3	9.5	5.4	6.0	5.5	4.6	3.8
Corporate income after tax	35,676.0	52,902.0	58,458.0	64,019.0	67,487.0	71,553.0	75,495.0	78,991.0	81,977.0
% change	10.1	48.3	10.5	9.5	5.4	6.0	5.5	4.6	3.8

General government fiscal balance	−54,151.0	−49,284.0	−45,984.0	−40,507.0	−40,379.0	−40,757.0	−41,307.0	−40,897.0	−40,022.0
% change	−3.8	−9.0	−6.7	−11.9	−0.3	0.9	1.3	−1.0	−2.1
GDP ratio (%)	−11.0	−9.9	−9.1	−7.9	−7.7	−7.7	−7.7	−7.5	−7.2
Direct tax revenue	37,338.0	42,102.0	44,545.0	48,240.0	50,560.0	52,759.0	54,768.0	56,598.0	58,279.0
% change	−4.0	12.8	5.8	8.3	4.8	4.4	3.8	3.3	3.0
Individual income tax revenue	23,753.0	22,822.0	23,232.0	24,907.0	25,967.0	26,696.0	27,281.0	27,847.0	28,448.0
% change	−5.3	−3.9	1.8	7.2	4.3	2.8	2.2	2.1	2.2
Private sector corporate tax revenue	12,970.0	18,893.0	20,715.0	22,686.0	23,914.0	25,355.0	26,752.0	27,991.0	29,049.0
% change	4.0	45.7	9.6	9.5	5.4	6.0	5.5	4.6	3.8
Indirect tax revenue	40,961.0	41,182.0	41,933.0	43,562.0	44,954.0	46,104.0	46,939.0	47,830.0	48,800.0
% change	−1.2	0.5	1.8	3.9	3.2	2.6	1.8	1.9	2.0
Consumption tax revenue	12,256.0	12,113.0	12,375.0	12,817.0	13,212.0	13,558.0	13,825.0	14,089.0	14,365.0
% change	1.0	−1.2	2.2	3.6	3.1	2.6	2.0	1.9	2.0
Social security benefits	71,272.0	70,676.0	71,574.0	72,249.0	73,353.0	74,400.0	75,357.0	75,780.0	75,781.0
% change	−0.4	−0.8	1.3	0.9	1.5	1.4	1.3	0.6	0.0
Social security contribution	70,973.0	67,064.0	68,894.0	69,455.0	−,248.0	71,625.0	72,983.0	74,446.0	75,969.0
% change	1.3	−5.5	2.7	0.8	1.1	2.0	1.9	2.0	2.1
Central government primary balance	−20,156.0	−18,853.0	−17,004.0	−16,270.0	−16,266.0	−16,871.0	−17,505.0	−18,801.0	−19,655.0
% change	13.4	−6.5	−9.8	−4.3	0.0	3.7	3.8	7.4	4.5
GDP ratio	−4.1	−3.8	−3.4	−3.2	−3.1	−3.2	−3.3	−3.4	−3.6
Central government revenue	85,849.0	88,432.0	84,798.0	77,576.0	78,167.0	85,211.0	97,738.0	115,610.0	132,400.0
% change	−1.4	3.0	−4.1	−8.5	0.8	9.0	14.7	18.3	14.5
Tax revenue	43,125.0	45,113.0	44,767.0	45,509.0	47,348.0	49,009.0	50,419.0	51,768.0	53,082.0
% change	−3.6	4.6	−0.8	1.7	4.0	3.5	2.9	2.7	2.5
Central government outlays	82,422.0	86,040.0	84,215.0	84,764.0	86,267.0	88,402.0	90,483.0	92,073.0	93,645.0
% change	−1.7	4.4	−2.1	0.7	1.8	2.5	2.4	1.8	1.7

Source: Authors' calculation.

Appreciation of the Japanese yen has the anticipated consequences. The effect on trade and on the trade balance is as expected. There is a moderate reduction in growth of real exports of goods and services and an increase in growth of real imports but these changes are only temporary (Figures 12.7 and 12.8). GDP growth is sharply reduced to less than 2% per year (Figure 12.9). This result suggests the need either to stabilize the current exchange rate or to offset the appreciation of the exchange rate with macroeconomic stimulus policy.

An alternative simulation, advancing public sector investment expenditures by 10% over the base level each year from 2006 *in addition* to the 10% yen appreciation (Tables 12.14 and 12.15), demonstrates the short-run effect of such

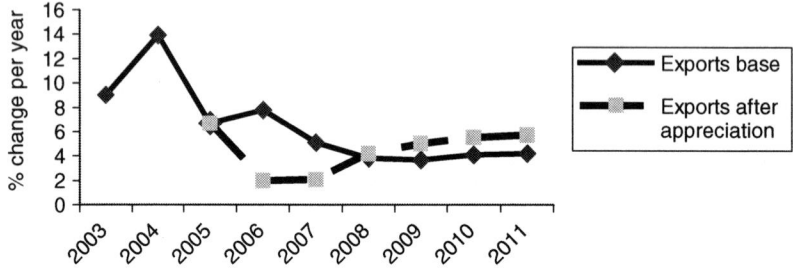

Figure 12.7 Real exports and Yen appreciation.

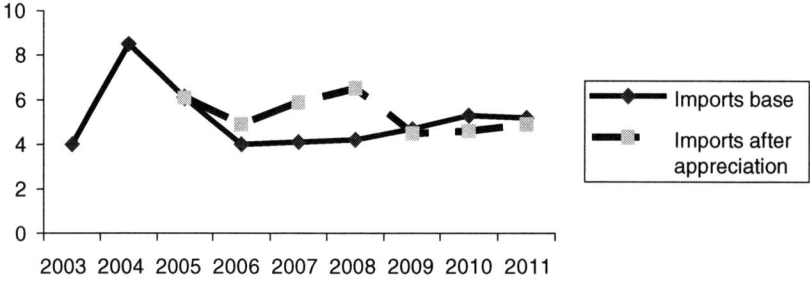

Figure 12.8 Real imports and Yen appreciation.

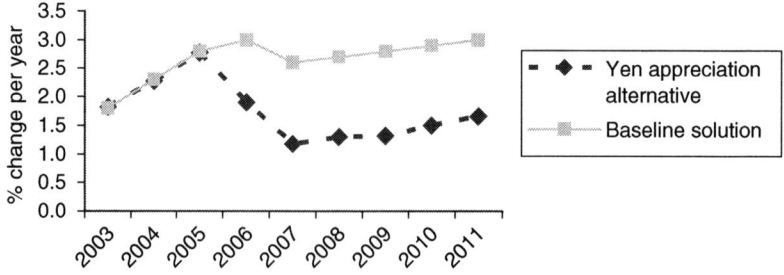

Figure 12.9 Effect of Yen appreciation on GDP growth.

Table 12.14 Economic forecast: summary Table 1 (10% appreciation of Yen/$ + IG 10% increase from 2006), Unit: Billion yen (or 2000 year base)

	Actual			Forecast					
	2003	2004	2005	2006	2007	2008	2009	2010	2011
Real GDP	513,602.0	525,240.0	539,862.0	551,702.0	556,675.0	562,506.0	568,519.0	575,379.0	583,087.0
% change	1.8	2.3	2.8	2.2	0.9	1.1	1.1	1.2	1.3
Personal consumption exp.	291,937.0	297,598.0	303,937.0	315,751.0	322,392.0	326,695.0	328,912.0	331,426.0	334,221.0
% change	0.6	1.9	2.1	3.9	2.1	1.3	0.7	0.8	0.8
Government consumption expenditure	91,549.0	93,385.0	95,013.0	95,850.0	97,725.0	100,100.0	102,425.0	104,425.0	106,550.0
% change	2.3	2.0	1.7	0.9	2.0	2.4	2.3	2.0	2.0
Gross capital formation	120,188.0	120,311.0	126,091.0	127,212.0	125,345.0	124,844.0	124,737.0	125,021.0	125,558.0
% change	2.0	0.1	4.8	0.9	−1.5	−0.4	−0.1	0.2	0.4
Fixed capital formation	119,738.0	120,999.0	125,963.0	125,354.0	123,467.0	122,986.0	122,886.0	123,165.0	123,670.0
% change	0.5	1.1	4.1	−0.5	−1.5	−0.4	−0.1	0.2	0.4
Private sector	91,384.0	95,138.0	101,540.0	100,522.0	98,470.0	97,136.0	96,156.0	95,555.0	95,345.0
% change	4.7	4.1	6.7	−1.0	−2.0	−1.4	−1.0	−0.6	−0.2
Dwellings	18,294.0	18,656.0	18,512.0	19,089.0	19,482.0	19,597.0	19,418.0	19,051.0	18,622.0
% change	−0.9	2.0	−0.8	3.1	2.1	0.6	−0.9	−1.9	−2.3
Plant and equipment	73,090.0	76,482.0	83,029.0	81,432.0	78,988.0	77,539.0	76,738.0	76,505.0	76,723.0
% change	6.2	4.6	8.6	−1.9	−3.0	−1.8	−1.0	−0.3	0.3
IT	19,900.0	20,855.0	22,100.0	23,389.0	24,824.0	26,347.0	27,964.0	29,680.0	31,501.0
% change	0.4	4.8	6.0	5.8	6.1	6.1	6.1	6.1	6.1
Other	53,190.0	55,627.0	60,929.0	58,043.0	54,164.0	51,191.0	48,774.0	46,825.0	45,221.0
% change	8.5	4.6	9.5	−4.7	−6.7	−5.5	−4.7	−4.0	−3.4
Public sector	28,354.0	25,861.0	24,423.0	24,833.0	24,998.0	25,850.0	26,730.0	27,610.0	28,325.0
% change	−10.8	−8.8	−5.6	1.7	0.7	3.4	3.4	3.3	2.6
Changes in inventories	450.0	−688.5	128.4	1,858.0	1,877.5	1,857.6	1,851.0	1,855.5	1,888.6
Private sector	286.1	−913.2	−186.1	1,543.6	1,563.1	1,543.2	1,536.6	1,541.1	1,574.2
Public sector	163.9	224.7	314.4	314.4	314.4	314.4	314.4	314.4	314.4
Net exports of Goods and Services	9,714.0	13,836.0	15,107.0	13,210.0	11,535.0	11,189.0	12,766.0	14,829.0	17,080.0
Exports of Goods and Services	60,410.0	68,825.0	73,454.0	74,937.0	76,561.0	79,810.0	83,850.0	88,526.0	93,623.0
% change	9.0	13.9	6.7	2.0	2.2	4.2	5.1	5.6	5.8

(Table 12.14 continued)

Table 12.14 Continued

	Actual			Forecast					
	2003	2004	2005	2006	2007	2008	2009	2010	2011
Imports of Goods and Services	50,696.0	54,989.0	58,347.0	61,726.0	65,026.0	68,621.0	71,084.0	73,697.0	76,543.0
% change	4.0	8.5	6.1	5.8	5.3	5.5	3.6	3.7	3.9
Mineral fuel	2,093.6	2,149.2	2,115.5	2,151.2	2,179.2	2,212.8	2,245.6	2,283.7	2,325.4
% change	7.2	2.7	−1.6	1.7	1.3	1.5	1.5	1.7	1.8
Other	48,602.0	52,840.0	56,232.0	59,575.0	62,846.0	66,408.0	68,839.0	71,413.0	74,217.0
% change	3.8	8.7	6.4	6.0	5.5	5.7	3.7	3.7	3.9
Nominal GDP	490,732.0	496,062.0	503,268.0	517,103.0	524,167.0	529,997.0	535,391.0	540,976.0	546,879.0
% change	0.2	1.1	1.5	2.8	1.4	1.1	1.0	1.0	1.1
GDP price deflator	95.6	94.4	93.2	93.7	94.2	94.2	94.2	94.0	93.8
% change	−1.6	−1.2	−1.3	0.5	0.5	0.1	−0.1	−0.2	−0.2
Private consumption expenditure price deflator	96.4	95.8	95.0	94.9	95.4	95.8	96.1	96.3	96.5
% change	−0.9	−0.7	−0.8	−0.1	0.5	0.4	0.3	0.3	0.2
Exports of Goods and Services price deflator	97.4	96.2	97.5	103.3	106.6	108.9	110.9	112.8	114.7
% change	−3.3	−1.3	1.3	5.9	3.2	2.2	1.8	1.7	1.7
Imports of Goods and Services price deflator	100.4	102.9	111.0	114.6	116.9	120.2	123.7	127.5	131.7
% change	−0.9	2.5	7.8	3.2	2.0	2.9	2.9	3.1	3.3
Import price deflator for mineral fuel	111.6	124.0	172.1	164.6	155.1	148.7	140.1	131.6	124.2
% change	6.7	11.2	38.8	−4.4	−5.8	−4.1	−5.8	−6.1	−5.7
Consumer price index	98.1	98.1	97.8	98.0	98.3	98.5	98.7	98.8	98.9
% change	−0.3	0.0	−0.3	0.2	0.3	0.2	0.2	0.1	0.1
Domestic firms' price index (PPI)	94.9	96.1	97.7	98.1	97.8	97.4	97.1	96.7	96.3
% change	−0.8	1.2	1.7	0.5	−0.4	−0.4	−0.4	−0.4	−0.4

Source: Authors' calculation.

Table 12.15 Economic forecast: summary Table 2 (10% appreciation of Yen/$ +IG 10% up from 2006), Unit: Billion yen (or 2000 year base)

	Actual			Forecast					
	2003	2004	2005	2006	2007	2008	2009	2010	2011
Labor force	6,687.3	6,666.3	6,643.1	6,611.9	6,593.3	6,579.0	6,560.5	6,554.0	6,555.2
% change	-1.0	-0.3	-0.4	-0.5	-0.3	-0.2	-0.3	-0.1	0.0
Employed	6,328.9	6,316.1	6,329.6	6,319.1	6,317.0	6,317.3	6,309.3	6,312.7	6,322.7
% change	-1.3	-0.2	0.2	-0.2	0.0	0.0	-0.1	0.1	0.2
Employees	5,329.7	5,335.1	5,355.7	5,347.7	5,341.3	5,324.3	5,303.4	5,293.7	5,294.2
% change	-0.7	0.1	0.4	-0.2	-0.1	-0.3	-0.4	-0.2	0.0
Unemployment rate	5.4	5.3	4.7	4.4	4.2	4.0	3.9	3.8	3.7
Labor productivity growth	3.2	2.5	2.6	2.4	0.9	1.0	1.2	1.2	1.2
Unit labor cost (% change)	-3.5	-3.5	-1.5	-0.2	0.0	-0.6	-0.8	-0.8	-0.8
Per capita wage and salary	4,196.5	4,132.4	4,167.2	4,241.1	4,275.1	4,303.3	4,326.8	4,346.4	4,363.3
% change	0.1	-1.5	0.8	1.8	0.8	0.7	0.6	0.5	0.4
Potential GDP	581,260.0	583,909.0	589,783.0	597,074.0	609,927.0	624,566.0	640,987.0	659,328.0	678,083.0
% change	0.8	0.5	1.0	1.2	2.2	2.4	2.6	2.9	2.8
CD rate	0.0	0.0	0.0	0.0	-0.1	-0.2	-0.3	-0.4	-0.4
Long-term bond yield	1.0	1.5	1.4	1.1	0.9	0.7	0.6	0.5	0.4
Household disposable income	297,713.0	295,666.0	293,641.0	304,163.0	304,974.0	303,688.0	302,253.0	300,653.0	299,385.0
% change	-0.3	-0.7	-0.7	3.6	0.3	-0.4	-0.5	-0.5	-0.4
Wage and salary	223,656.0	220,469.0	223,179.0	226,802.0	228,345.0	229,121.0	229,469.0	230,084.0	231,004.0
% change	-0.7	-1.4	1.2	1.6	0.7	0.3	0.2	0.3	0.4
Compensation of employees	258,692.0	255,250.0	258,388.0	263,436.0	265,801.0	267,103.0	267,911.0	268,964.0	270,330.0
% change	-1.5	-1.3	1.2	2.0	0.9	0.5	0.3	0.4	0.5
Corporate income	48,646.0	71,795.0	79,174.0	88,838.0	94,687.0	101,453.0	108,289.0	114,994.0	121,459.0
% change	8.4	47.6	10.3	12.2	6.6	7.1	6.7	6.2	5.6
Corporate income after tax	35,676.0	52,902.0	58,458.0	65,594.0	69,913.0	74,909.0	79,956.0	84,907.0	89,680.0
% change	10.1	48.3	10.5	12.2	6.6	7.1	6.7	6.2	5.6
General govt. fiscal balance	-54,151.0	-49,284.0	-45,984.0	-42,220.0	-42,338.0	-43,143.0	-44,181.0	-44,354.0	-44,165.0
% change	-3.8	-9.0	-6.7	-8.19	0.28	1.9	2.41	0.4	-0.43

(Table 12.15 continued)

Table 12.15 Continued

	Actual			Forecast					
	2003	2004	2005	2006	2007	2008	2009	2010	2011
GDP ratio (%)	−11.0	−9.9	−9.1	−7.7	−7.6	−7.7	−7.8	−7.7	−7.6
Direct tax revenue	37,338.0	42,102.0	44,545.0	48,724.0	51,105.0	53,394.0	55,526.0	57,538.0	59,466.0
% change	−4.0	12.8	5.8	9.4	4.9	4.5	4.0	3.6	3.4
Individual income tax rev.	23,753.0	22,822.0	23,232.0	24,827.0	25,645.0	26,133.0	26,448.0	26,679.0	26,889.0
% change	−5.3	−3.9	1.8	6.9	3.3	1.9	1.2	0.9	0.8
Private sector corporate tax revenue	12,970.0	18,893.0	20,715.0	23,244.0	24,774.0	26,544.0	28,333.0	30,087.0	31,779.0
% change	4.0	45.7	9.6	12.2	6.6	7.1	6.7	6.2	5.6
Indirect tax revenue	40,961.0	41,182.0	41,933.0	43,616.0	44,810.0	45,728.0	46,328.0	46,936.0	47,573.0
% change	−1.2	0.5	1.8	4.0	2.7	2.1	1.3	1.3	1.4
Consumption tax revenue	12,256.0	12,113.0	12,375.0	12,879.0	13,220.0	13,503.0	13,704.0	13,890.0	14,077.0
% change	1.0	−1.2	2.2	4.1	2.7	2.1	1.5	1.4	1.4
Social security benefits	71,272.0	70,676.0	71,574.0	72,250.0	73,397.0	74,550.0	75,680.0	76,353.0	76,696.0
% change	−0.4	−0.8	1.3	1.0	1.6	1.6	1.5	0.9	0.5
Social security contribution	70,973.0	67,064.0	68,894.0	69,431.0	70,130.0	71,360.0	72,532.0	73,766.0	75,013.0
% change	1.3	−5.5	2.7	0.8	1.0	1.8	1.6	1.7	1.7
Central government primary balance	−20,156.0	−18,853.0	−17,004.0	−16,826.0	−16,851.0	−17,497.0	−18,160.0	−19,478.0	−20,346.0
% change	13.4	−6.5	−9.8	−5.5	−3.8	3.8	0.9	1.2	−3.7
GDP ratio	−3.9	−3.6	−3.2	−2.9	−2.8	−2.8	−2.8	−2.7	−2.5
Central government revenue	85,849.0	88,432.0	84,798.0	77,484.0	77,346.0	84,159.0	96,732.0	114,869.0	132,141.0
% change	−1.4	3.0	−4.1	−8.6	−0.2	8.8	14.9	18.7	15.0
Tax revenue	43,125.0	45,113.0	44,767.0	45,776.0	47,548.0	49,137.0	50,492.0	51,791.0	53,062.0
% change	−3.6	4.6	−0.8	2.3	3.9	3.3	2.8	2.6	2.5
Central government outlays	82,422.0	86,040.0	84,215.0	85,575.0	86,985.0	88,984.0	90,869.0	92,193.0	93,399.0
% change	−1.7	4.4	−2.1	1.6	1.7	2.3	2.1	1.5	1.3

Source: Authors' calculation.

an outlay. In 2006, GDP growth is 2.3% as compared to 1.9% without the expenditure adjustment, but in subsequent years, GDP growth remains depressed between 1.2% and 1.4%. There is no impact on inflation. If public expenditure were further expanded and if it were directed to IT investment, perhaps toward infrastructure or e-government, it is probable that more sustained gains in output would result.

Conclusion

To fully show in simulation exercises of this kind the impact of productivity gains associated with new IT technologies is a difficult challenge. While it is possible to make adjustments on the supply-side, increasing potential output to allow for new economy gains, it is difficult for a demand-based model, like our system, to translate productivity impacts to GDP growth. Simulations which have been carried out with increases in potential output call for adjustments on the demand side to accelerate the aggregate growth rate. When such adjustments are made, it is possible to produce reasonable consistent simulations with GDP growth rates near 3% or year. The most likely basis for such simulations lies in rapid increase in IT investment.

We conclude that expansion of the Japanese economy at 3% per year or even a little higher appears to be feasible. This is not only a question of increasing potential output but of finding the mix of policies that will drive the actual output of the economy to an improved growth path. We will consider the policy options in Chapter 13.

13 Policies to achieve faster economic growth in Japan

The Japanese economy has the potential to achieve faster growth. Our production function calculations and model simulations indicate the possibilities. But whether these changes can be achieved depends greatly on continued reorganization of the business environment and on the handling of monetary, fiscal, trade, and industrial policy.

Japan needs to deal with low economic growth and fiscal imbalance simultaneously. Japan must achieve high economic growth and restoration of sound fiscal balance. Both the private business sector and the government should make continuous efforts to produce "reform dividends" and to reinvest them into information and communications technology. To ride the dynamic waves of the information technology revolution is to harness one of the significant driving forces of economic growth.

In this chapter, first, we examine the organizational and structural transformations that will be needed to accelerate Japanese economic growth. Then, we consider the policy alternatives. In the final section of this chapter, we will provide an agenda of what Japan might do to realize vigorous economic growth in the next decade.

Creation of a technology friendly competitive environment

The IT revolution and the process of worldwide globalization has created a dynamically competitive environment that transcends national boundaries. These developments place a special premium on organizational and decision-making flexibility. The success of many world-leading Japanese enterprises suggests that some Japanese firms have been able to make the required adjustments and to achieve competitive success and rapid growth. A primary challenge for Japan would be to make the cultural and organizational changes, including a turn from integrated to modular organizational forms, throughout the entire economy to facilitate rapid adaptation to the new global competition.

We do not believe that cultural change can be imposed by government policy-makers. But a society that is freely competitive and open to international trade, investment, migration, and international flows of knowledge can adapt to the global environment. Japan has taken many steps in that direction. Some observers, but certainly not all, see international convergence of cultural and organizational norms reflecting competition in an increasingly global economy (Porter, 2000, Inkeles, 1998). We anticipate that as time passes many more Japanese firms will adjust their organizational form and their culture to better compete. This is particularly important for those sectors of the Japanese economy that have been protected from foreign competition by circumstance or by regulation, such as banking, transportation and distribution, agriculture, and many domestic service activities.

There is a role for government policy in establishing a competitive dynamic environment. We will discuss the policies that are required in greater detail later.

The growth of the economy's total output is a primary macroeconomic objective. Growth can take the form of cyclical recovery in the short-run but long-run growth requires increases in inputs of capital and labor or gains in productivity. An accelerated rate of growth is the basis for a dynamic economy and for rising living standards.

But macro policymakers must balance the emphasis on growth against other critical objectives, such as employment, price stability, and equilibrium in the nation's fiscal accounts and in its foreign balance. Establishing a policy target for growth, say 2 or 3%, calls for a consistent review of the implications of each growth alternative on other dimensions of economic performance, particularly of the effects on price stability and budgetary equilibrium. This is a task best carried out by model simulations like those of the previous chapter.

Alternative policy possibilities

In this section, we will consider alternative policy possibilities for accelerating Japan's rate of GDP growth. First, we will look at policy alternatives from the perspective of supply, then from the perspective of demand, and, finally, we will examine the interactions between the demand and supply-side policies. Some of this discussion will be based on policies of other countries, like the United States, that are also adapting their economies to the new IT technology.

Supply-side policies

As we note elsewhere, policies dealing with a supply-side are aimed primarily at increasing the economy's production potential through increases in inputs, IT and non-IT capital and labor, and improved productivity. On the basis of more sophisticated approaches to the production function, investments in the new technologies will have more than proportionate impacts on growth of output.

Such policies are listed and evaluated for their growth impact relative to their effect on the government budget deficit in Table 13.1. They include general and IT industry-specific stimulus for investment, specialized venture capital institutions, tax incentives for additional labor supply, and incentives for R&D, support for development of fast-growing new high-tech infrastructure, and industrial policies. Improvement of technical education seeking a higher output of new scientists, engineers, and technical personnel is another way to stimulate technical capability. Improvements in the nation's productive potential may also be achieved by structural policies to reduce regulatory constraints. Increasing the competitiveness

Table 13.1 Alternative policies for additional growth

Type of policy	Policy specifics	Supply effect	Demand effect	Growth effect relative to impact on budget
Supply-general				
	Investment tax credit	X	X	High
	Income tax cuts	X	X	High
	Accelerated depreciation	X	X	High
	Monetary stimulus and credit supply	X	X	Low
Supply sector specific				
	IT applications tax credit and accelerated depreciation	X		High
	Easing of regulatory constraints	X		High
	IT industrial policy	X		Uncertain
	Venture capital financing	X		High
	IT infrastructure spending	X		High
	IT education spending	X		High
Demand				
	Public works expenditure stimulus		X	Low
	Government (IT) investment expenditure	X	X	High
	Consumption tax cut		X	Low
Structural				
	Competition policy	X		High
	Trade policy	X	X	High
Industrial	Industry-specific aid	X		Uncertain
Labor market	Increase labor supply	X	X	High

Source: Authors' calculation.

and openness of the Japanese economy promises substantial improvements in productivity.

Demand-side policies

The operation of aggregate demand policy, in the face of the economy's growing potential output requires great care. The principal policy options are summarized in Table 13.1. Typically we think of aggregate fiscal policy governing expenditures, on one hand, and tax revenues on the other. Increases in public works expenditures have stimulus impact but, with the exception of particular cases, many public works do little to improve the economy's production potential. Reductions and increases in consumption tax rates similarly have impact on the demand-side but not on potential output. Fiscal policy may be further constrained by the high level of public debt outstanding. In some cases, however, the expenditure stimulus may have sufficient impact on tax receipts and on growth that the debt to nominal GDP ratio will be improved.

Traditionally monetary policy has focused primarily on short-term interest rates but intervention in long-term rates is another promising possibility.

Japanese experience suggests that a demand stimulus policy orientation may continue to be necessary, if, as in the past decade, there is a serious shortage of aggregate demand, so that demand falls short of the economy's output potential.[1]

Interaction between supply and demand

The policy strategies that can take advantage of the linkages between demand and supply would be particularly advantageous. For example, accelerated depreciation of investment expenses, tax incentives for R&D and for software development, public support for technical education, and similar projects, many of which have been tried in the United States, involve modest additions to expenditures or reductions in taxes on specific types of projects in the expectation that these measures will cause improvements in productivity. Financial incentives to workers or employers to delay retirement or to attract additional workers, including women, to the labor force may also be advantageous. Monetary policy stimulus reducing interest rates, if that is possible, may serve to stimulate business investment which, as noted, represents both a demand stimulus and a force to increase production capacity and productivity.

Microeconomic policies

It is difficult, if not impossible, to dictate cultural or organizational change. Numerous actions intended to achieve technological and organizational change have taken place during the past few years. More will be needed to enable Japanese industry to compete even more effectively in an open globalized world economy. Moreover, much still remains to be done to reduce regulatory constraints in Japan, particularly with respect to finance and distribution, precisely the fields where recent gains in productivity in the United States have been concentrated.

There must be a clear agenda and vision for microeconomic policy, aimed at rebuilding economic competitiveness. The government must facilitate private business investment in new technology to boost productivity and to achieve vigorous economic growth.

The specifics of microeconomic policies can range from privatization of publicly owned firms (and quasi-public companies like NTT) to a reduction of regulatory controls, application of antitrust laws, and reductions in trade barriers. We have already noted the need to reduce regulation of trade and many service activities.

Industrial policies

In some cases, national policies focusing on particular industries that are central to the development of new IT technologies may be important. But, in today's high-tech world, industrial policies may not mean the creation of heavy capital intensive industries, as in the past. Public policies must seek to stimulate competition: "Let many flowers bloom!" taking advantage of private entrepreneurship and business dynamics. Public support for research institutes focusing on particular sectors like health care or advanced technology may be appropriate. Venture capital financing may facilitate the rapid application of new technologies. There may be a need for public expenditure on IT infrastructure, for example, glass fiber networks, WIFI, and additional broadband communications facilities. Public support for an intelligent transport system is another possibility. Much of this spending should be and can be provided by private industry. Public support is warranted only if there are recognizable general benefit externalities. The establishment of an ultrahigh speed network proposed in the e-Japan strategy (IT Strategy Headquarters, 2001) is an example of such a project. The e-government proposal contained in the same document is also an example. Similar efforts can be made to establish an electronically based national health record system. The introduction of computers and electronic communications into small and medium business enterprises may call for public support. Logistics systems supporting wholesale and retail trade still require large quantities of resources not available to smaller businesses. At the same time, they may bring valuable scale economies.

While there may be possibilities for creating and funding publicly supported industrial projects like the policies of MITI in the 1960s, whether to engage in such active and project-specific industrial policy, focusing on and supporting specific industries, is a political decision. Such an approach may be less suited to today's dynamic high-tech environment than at earlier stages of Japan's economic development.

Trade and globalization policies

There is very broad scope for policy measures that will improve domestic and international competitive pressures in Japanese economy. While such policies have little direct short-term budget impact, they yield benefits over the long term.

Opening to the world economy can play an important role in establishing and maintaining a more competitive environment. That means removing barriers to imports and eliminating support and protection for agriculture. Japan can rely more heavily on foreign sources of low-cost consumer goods and refocus Japanese industry even further toward high-tech and capital goods and high-level services. Attracting foreign direct investment is also important, more for its competitive effect and for the technical and management skill that foreign companies bring than for the flow of capital. Most importantly, Japan must establish increased participation in the burgeoning East Asian market.

Labor market policies

Policies to increase the size of the active labor force may help to offset the aging of the Japanese population. The significant step in that direction is to delay the age of retirement. Each additional year worked represents a year of productive activity along with one less year on social insurance.

It may be possible also to increase incentives or other assistance, such as child care, so that a larger fraction of working age women could take employment outside the home. The organization of Japanese employment contracts may also be changed to improve incentives and to increase worker mobility.

The issue of immigration will remain a controversial political and social issue, as in most other countries. Whether and in what way this question can be resolved, perhaps by providing employment opportunities for trained specialists from abroad, is a question for political decision makers.

A strong argument can be made in favor of increased public expenditure on education and training to improve the quality of the labor force. For example, it may be helpful to expand technical institutes, perhaps with an international reach, producing a growing supply of scientists, engineers, technicians, and trained business managers. Improvements in the quality of labor can be achieved not only by providing education and training to young people but also by retraining over the workers' lifetimes.

The logic of externalities, spillovers to the broad interest of the society, will support additional public expenditures at R&D. From a fiscal perspective, these steps incur current costs while the benefits come with substantial delay and are spread over a long time.

Spending on education and R&D. can be directed toward the creation of regional high-tech clusters. Experience in many countries suggests that networks of skilled workers and entrepreneurs and of suppliers and users of equipment and specialized services interact effectively to create regional concentrations of high-tech industries.

Incentives for investment and modernization

Investment tax credits and accelerated depreciation for the IT sectors and applications of IT in the non-IT sectors were part of the policy package provided during the 1990s and early 2000s in United States. It is believed that these policies had a favorable impact on development of the IT industries and on the application of IT particularly in finance, and retail and wholesale trade where the biggest gains in productivity have been made in recent years. Such policy measures can hold down the effective cost of capital at times when interest rates are rising. A tax credit conditional on making investment expenditure can be translated into the equivalent of a reduction in the cost of capital. It differs from a general reduction in interest rates since it requires an expenditure for new IT capital or on programming and management in order for the tax credit to be granted. From a fiscal perspective, such measures are advantageous since relatively small public contributions serve as incentives for large, highly productive, private spending.

Improved credit facilities for small ventures are another opportunity to increase investment. The model of the venture capital firm, perhaps with some public funding, is potentially a good way to encourage and guide the development of new enterprises.

Proposals for policy changes to accelerate Japan's growth rate

In this section we summarize these policy proposals as a menu of proposals for policy changes that will accelerate the growth of the Japanese economy. We seek policies that have maximum impact on the productive potential of the Japanese economy and improve, or at worst, minimize the adverse effects on the government budget. Proposals presented here represent the views of the authors and have not been evaluated by political party experts in Japan. Table 13.2 lists some specific policy proposals.

Table 13.2 Proposed policy measures to accelerate Japanese growth

- *General macroeconomic policies*
  - Reviewing the timing of consumption tax increases
  - Continued low interest rate policy
  - Refocus public works expenditure policy
- *General microeconomic policies*
  - privatization
  - regulatory reform
  - enforcement of antitrust laws
- *Globalization policies*
  - reduction of tariffs and import restrictions
  - policy measures to improve domestic and international competitiveness in Japanese industry
  - attract foreign direct investment
  - participate actively in East Asian cooperation projects
- *General supply-side policies*
  - strengthen intellectual property laws for IT materials and content
  - provide favorable tax treatment for R&D
  - provide favorable tax incentives for work, saving, and investment
- *Specific supply-side policies*
  - support construction of ultra high-speed electronic communication network
  - establish innovation centers for creating new science and technology
  - establish specialized industrial cluster zones
  - promote IT R&D in collaboration with universities and business
  - provide tax incentives for IT investment and modernization
  - realize the application of the intelligent transport system
  - expand e-government initiatives and use of electronic record keeping in health care
- *Labor market policies*
  - postpone the age of retirement
  - promote employment of women and young people
  - promote immigration of skilled workers
  - support graduate MBA education
  - support lifetime education
- *Research and development policies*
  - promote high technology developments, such as fuel-cell, robots
- *IT Industry and Applications Policies*
  - investment tax credit for IT investment and programming applications
  - accelerated depreciation for IT investment and programming applications
  - venture capital support
  - public expenditure for improved Internet communications network
  - expenditure on improved technical education
  - public spending on R&D

14 Accelerating Japan's economic growth

Conclusions

Policy must take account of economic considerations as well as political ones. The rate of growth of GDP is an important economic objective, one that must be reconciled with other aims like price stability and budgetary equilibrium. Achieving the basic economic aims of society is a requirement to maintaining a sound stable political situation.

In this volume, we have examined the forces that lie behind Japan's modest growth record of the 1990s and early 2000s and the basis for official projections of a low 2% GDP growth rate. We have examined the question of whether the Japanese economy can achieve a higher rate of growth along with its objective of fiscal stability.

Japanese growth experience during the past 15 years has been disappointing. This performance reflects not only the insufficiency of demand, but also the failure of Japanese productivity to increase rapidly. Projecting into the future, Japan faces serious challenges: the aging of its population, its growing public debt, and its need to compete in an increasingly globalized world economy. A growth rate around 2% per year will not be sufficient to meet these needs.

Fortunately, the new IT technologies and their application offer many possibilities for improving productivity and for achieving higher economic growth. If the externalities and increasing returns that are implicit in the new technologies of the IT revolution are taken into account by the production functions describing the operation of the economy, higher productivity growth rates can be projected.

In the case of Japan, a low productivity growth projection appears, on the one hand, to reflect a failure of measurement in connection with the production function, and, on the other, to reflect the fact that many Japanese sectors have not fully taken advantage of the potentials of IT investment. While the Japanese economy is highly advanced with respect to cellular telephones, its utilization of IT in some fields does not seem to be as far advanced as elsewhere. In the United States, huge productivity gains have been made through the application of IT and finance and retail and wholesale distribution. There is not evidence of similar gains in the case of Japan. The reasons behind this may lie in the regulatory regime as well as in cultural considerations. The incomplete privatization of NTT used to stand in the way of the development of a complete network economy. More recently, the implementation of the e-Japan initiative is serving to advance IT development and application in Japan. The organization of Japanese industries in an integrated fashion, as compared to modular firms, elsewhere, may also stand in the way of rapid technical change. With the opening of Japanese markets to competition, these barriers appear to be fading.

Our model simulations suggest that the Japanese economy can achieve a higher growth rate than that projected in recent government plans.

We have studied the impact of alternative policy scenarios. Improved growth and moderately higher prices would help to meet the challenge of fiscal stability. On the other hand, return to a higher consumption tax rate would have little long run impact on the central government budget but would slow the growth path significantly. Policies will be needed that will stimulate investment in IT technology, and the application of IT, and improvement of human capital. Stimulus to the growth of IT investment accelerates growth of actual and potential GDP. However, an investment tax credit appears, in our simulations to have little permanent impact, perhaps because a more focused instrument is needed. Monetary policy may have an impact but it appears to be small. Exchange rate simulations suggest that yen appreciation would have a negative impact on growth. Policies will be needed to maintain exchange stability and to open the Japanese economic environment to greater competition at home and from abroad. A more highly detailed model, designed to focus on the special characteristics of the IT industries and of the application of IT in other fields, would offer possibilities for more focused testing of policy alternatives. Such a model is proposed in the Appendix. Finally, we propose a menu of policies that will serve to accelerate Japanese economic growth.

With appropriate policy formulation, the outlook for the Japanese economy has brightened. We hope that Japanese growth can be accelerated so that, despite its aging population, Japan will see continued improvement in living standards and will maintain a leading role in the world economy.

Postscript

The debate about growth projections in Japanese government circles has had a favorable outcome. In view of the fact that it was possible to show growth of Japan's potential real output at a 3% growth rate, the government agreed to reconsider its policy posture. In March, 2006, it had been proposed to raise the consumption tax rate from 5% to over 10% in 2007. The two groups taking opposing positions on growth projections appear to have agreed to postpone the increase until 2009 and then to increase from 5% to only 8%.

Early in 2007, Hiroko Ota, Heizo Takenaka's successor as head of the Council on Economic and Fiscal Policy in the Abe administration, was reported as saying "Real growth is about 2% today. We are striving to raise that over the next five years [to 3%] even as the population sinks. For that we need to raise productivity." (*Financial Times*, January 12, 2007) She visualizes three ways to achieving that goal, all of them presenting challenges. Japan must harness information technology more effectively. While Ota speaks of specific projects, like computerizing medical records, much of the task of computerizing business transactions falls to private business firms. Japan must become a more open economy, in part to link Japan to its fast growing East Asian neighbors. This faces opposition from entrenched interests like the farm lobby. And Japan must make better use of human resources, significantly reforming the labor market's present distinction between temporary and permanent workers.

Perhaps what is even more important is that this represents an important shift in the locus of economic policymaking from bureaucrats to political experts. In Japan, government bureaucrats have been the main players in making economic policy. Traditionally, they have been extremely careful and conservative, unwilling to "think outside the box." This time the projections were made in the framework of the Liberal Democratic Party's own Think Tank. It is too early, however, to predict whether new projections will result in significantly new policy and whether a new approach will be successful in accelerating Japanese economic growth.

Appendix

Modeling faster economic growth – A proposal

The IT revolution and the process of globalization have been changing the Japanese economy. These changes have affected the macroeconomic performance of the economy in significant ways and will continue to do so in the future. The issue is whether, by taking advantage of the profound technological changes of the IT revolution, current improved growth trends can be translated into long-run progress. New strategies must be tested empirically to see if they enable Japan to enter a period of sustained economic growth. As the research and policy planning to accelerate the Japanese growth rate proceeds, the econometric model used for simulation exercises needs to be refined and modified to take into account the special features of the IT economy.

Modeling the new economy

The standard Keynesian macro model with conventional treatment of the economy's supply potential, so frequently used for policy analysis, has important gaps that must be supplemented for policy analysis in the new economy setting. IT investment and the application of new IT technologies affect output and productivity at the sectoral level. In turn, these influence international competitiveness, government revenues, and other important aspects of the economy. The model should be designed to incorporate these developments in the relevant sectors and should be equipped with policy handles that will enable us to test new IT policy proposals.

In our earlier work, we have been able to make some of the required adjustments, but not all of them. Specifically, we have introduced the production function allowing for increasing returns. We have separated out investment in IT from other investment expenditures. We have made adjustments in the model whenever these were required to provide a realistic picture of the policy inputs proposed.

There are, however, possibilities for further elaborating the model for obtaining results with greater precision. The most important of these possibilities would involve sectoral disaggregation and the introduction of an input–output system. Specifically, it is important to further explore the changing structure of the economy, the effect of introducing IT equipment and programs into various sectors of the economy, and the changing utilization of the labor force. Changes in the structural composition of the economy also play an important role in influencing the path of productivity. Hopefully, gains in productivity in some sectors can offset increasing costs elsewhere in the economy so that the relationship between full employment, rapid growth, and price stability can be maintained.

The starting point, a standard econometric model

The standard macro econometric model used for forecasting and analysis over the business cycle focuses on the demand side of the economy and deals with supply largely in order to determine the unemployment rate and inflationary pressures. It may lack a production function altogether, or it may use a simple constant returns production function with total factor productivity in the form of a time trend.

The standard Keynesian model is summarized in Table A.1. This represents the structure of a model with emphasis on the demand/income flows that dominate the business cycle variations, though capacity constraints and price determination are included. We note, also, that such a model lacks sectoral disaggregation. The characteristics of the IT economy suggest the need for a more complex system that we propose below.

A model to accommodate IT and new economy

The rapid changes going on in the world economy as a result of the IT revolution and increasing globalization affect Japan in various directions The proposed modifications of the standard model affect many dimensions of the system but they do not undermine its basic character. The structure of an expanded model is shown in Figure A.1.

Beginning at the left-hand top of the figure, the system's final demand vector determines sectoral activity through an input–output matrix and that in turn determines labor demand and capacity using production functions. These aspects of the economy are disaggregated. Wages, prices, and factor income are determined on the aggregate level. The flow of funds (FOF) represents the monetary sector that determines interest rates. The exogenous variables include external forces, policy changes, and various possibilities for adjustment to fully recognize the impact of IT throughout the economy.

In this section, we will survey the major changes that will enable us to better simulate the outcomes for the Japanese economy in this new environment.

A number of considerations can guide the adaptation of the model:

- a long-term versus a short-term model
- the input–output system
- the extent of disaggregation in the model
- the structure of the production function, and
- emphasis on production versus demand

Table A.1 Structure of a Keynesian model

	Equation	Variable definitions
	Demand	
I	$Y = C + I_b + I_r + G + X - M$	Y = GDP; C = Consumption; I_b = Business Investment; I_r = Residential Investment; G = Government Purchasing; X = Exports; M = Imports; T_c = Consumption Taxes; T_o = Other Consumer Taxes; T_r = Transfer Payments; k = capital stock; % = Interest Rate, Pop = Population, K_r = Residential Capital; D = Depreciation; D_r = Residential depreciation; P = Price level; XR = Exchange Rate
B	$C = f(Y - T_c - T_o + T_r)$	
B	$I_b = f(\%,Y,K_{-1})$	
B	$I_r = f(\%,\text{Pop},K_{r-1})$	
I	$K = K_{-1} + I - D$	
I	$K_r = K_{r-1} + I_r - D_r$	
B	$M = f(Y,P,\text{XR})$	
	Capacity utilization	
B	$Y_p = f(K,t)$	t = time; Y_p = Potential GDP; L = Labor Force; CU = Capacity Utilization
B_{alt}	$Y_p = A,(L^a K^{-b})$	
I	$CU = Y/Y_p$	
	Wage and price determination	
B	$W_{dot} = f(1/U,(Y/E)_{dot},P_{dot-1})$	W_{dot} = Wage Rate Change; U = Unemployment Rate; $(Y/E)_{dot}$ = Productivity Change; P_{dot} = Change in Price level; P = Price level; XR = Exchange Rate; E = Employment; L = Labor Force
B	$P_{dot} = f(W_{dot},(Y/E)_{dot},P_{mdot},(I - CU))$	
I	$P = P_{-1}*(1 + P_{dot})$	
B	$E = f(Y,K)$	
I	$U = (1 - E)/L*100$	
	Income distribution	
B	$WT = W*E$	WT = Total Wage Bill; W = Wage Rate; E = Employment; Y_n = Nominal Y; $\%Y$ = Interest Income; Y_o = Other Income
I	$Y_n = Y*P$	
I	$Y_o = Y_n - WT - D - \%Y$	
	Government budget	
B	$T_c = f(C*P*\text{tcr})$	T_c = Consumption Tax; tcr = Cons. Tax Rate; T_o = Other Taxes; T_r = Transfer payments; GD = Government Deficit
B	$T_o = f(Y_n)$	
B	$T_r = f(Y,U)$	
I	$GD = (G*P) + TR - T_c - T_o - (\%*\text{Debt})$	
I	$\text{Debt} = \text{Debt}_{-1} + GD$	
I	$\text{Ratio} = \text{Debt}/Y_n$	Ratio = Public Debt to GDP ratio
	Monetary sector	
B	$\% = f(MS,Y_n)$	MS = Money Supply, Y_n = nominal GDP = $Y * P$

Source: Authors' calculation.

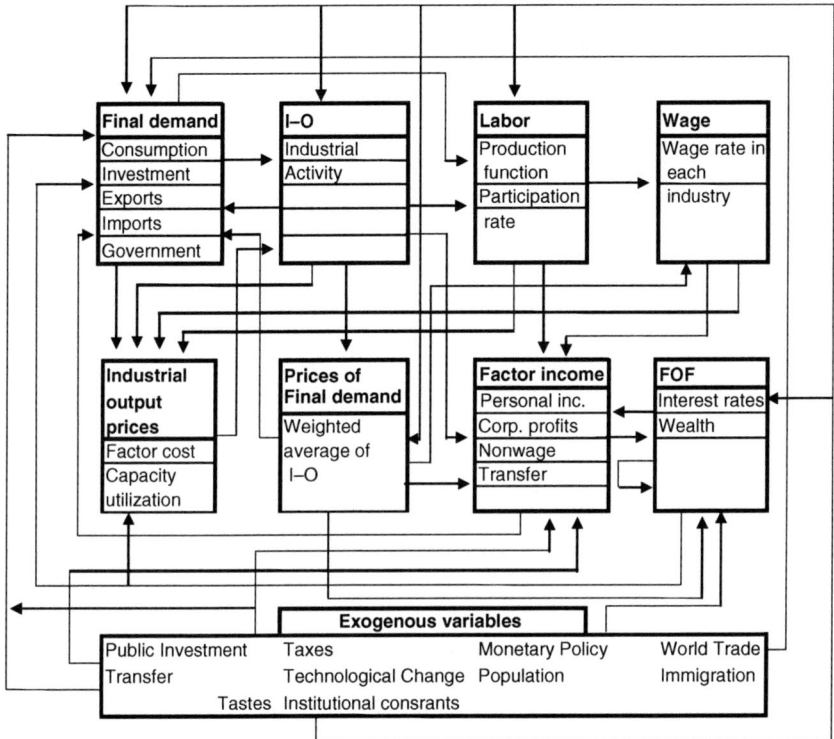

Figure A.1 Flowchart of K–L model.

Long-term versus short-term model

The traditional econometric model is focused on short-term variations of the economy over the business cycle. Technological change related to the introduction and utilization of IT, calls for a longer time perspective, one that will allow structural changes to take place. We want to deal with structural issues rather than focus on fine-tuning macroeconomic policies. An annual model with focus on long-term trends, rather than a quarterly model directed at business cycle swings, can serve the purpose. Such a model can be designed to simulate structural changes and measure the impact of policies that are likely to have a gradual impact on the economy over an extended period of time. It can also be used to study the long-term structural problems facing he Japanese economy

Disaggregation and input–output

There are clearly advantages to using a more disaggregated model to study questions associated with productivity growth and IT. It may be possible to study behavior in sectors that are growing rapidly or declining and between sectors closely associated with the introduction of new technology, hardware and software, and to evaluate their contribution to productivity. It will be necessary to integrate a sector breakdown, one that would distinguish between sectors that benefit from IT and those that do not. Such a breakdown may also help to establish the sources of productivity growth in the economy.

A combination of Keynesian and Leontief type macro model will provide sectoral disaggregation consistent with the structure of the traditional macro system. This will require disaggregation of final demand and of trade consistent with the disaggregation of the input–output system.

As we discuss below, disaggregation imposes considerable costs. The required effort rises by more than the number of sectors, and it may increase the difficulty of estimating meaningful relationships. Existing input–output matrices must be aggregated to identify and distinguish the sectors most likely to be affected by the new IT technologies.

Structure of production functions

Sectoral production functions play an important role in the model framework determining the potential output of the economy. The production functions must incorporate the increasing returns to scale features that we have discussed in Chapter 5. The point here is that as a result of the introduction of IT equipment and the use of IT technology, productivity and potential output are rising rapidly. These gains can be incorporated into the model through increasing returns production functions.

Production versus demand orientation

The IT revolution is not the first time that economists have attached importance to the supply-side. When we analyzed the effect of the oil crisis on the economy, we found that a demand-oriented Keynesian type macro model was not able to fully simulate the stagflation problem. It was necessary to augment the supply-oriented system elements of the system to complement the traditional demand-oriented elements. In the case of the oil crisis, the supply curve shifted upward due to the rise in oil prices. As we look to the future, it is fortunate, however, that as a result of the IT revolution, the supply curve will shift downward, producing pressure on prices.

The emphasis of the model oriented toward long-run productivity improvement should be on the production/supply side. We seek to determine quantitatively the impact of the introduction of IT and/or the impact of policies intended to stimulate applications of IT to boost the productive potential of the economy, that is, growth of output and productivity. In principle one might suggest a model dominated by production, based largely on the production function or sectoral production functions. That would avoid the question of closure. On the other hand, while it would allow us to measure potential output, it would fail to measure the actual growth of GDP since that depends on demand as well as on supply. The analysis of the Japanese economy requires such a linkage since it has been precisely an insufficiency of demand, in many cases, that has prevented the investments in technological change that might have accelerated growth of the Japanese economy.

Suggested modifications in model structure

We are seeking to develop a model structure that will allow us to test numerous alternatives related to the new IT economy. For this purpose, we are adding numerous modifications to the standard Keynesian model. The new system will contain an integrated I/O matrix, a substantial degree of disaggregation, flexible coefficient adjustments, increasing returns production functions, and emphasis on supply-side closure.

Integration of an input–output system

Input–output analysis is a method to integrate output at the sectoral level into a model of the aggregate economy. Traditional I–O analysis is shown by Eqn (A.1).

$$(I - A)X = F \tag{A.1}$$

where $(I - A)$ = I/O coefficient matrix consisting of $a_{ij} = X_i/X_j$, X_{ij} = Input from I sector to J sector, X_j: Gross output of J sector. X = Vector of gross outputs, and F = Vector of final demands.
Solving such a system for X, yields

$$X = (I - A)^{-1}F \tag{A.2}$$

Integrating such a system into a macroeconometric model requires links between the final demand categories at the sectoral level, the Fs, and the final demands at the final purchaser level that make up the GDP as in Eqn (A.3). (Preston, 1975)

$$F = CG \tag{A.3}$$

where C represents the allocation of each final demand category in G to the sectoral breakdown of output.
Finally, we require a link between the sectoral gross outputs, X, and the value added produced by each sector. Since sectoral value added

$$VA_j = X_j - \sum_{i=1}^{n} a_{ij}X_j = (1 - \sum_{i=1}^{n} a_{ij})X_j \tag{A.4}$$

$$VA = Y = BX \tag{A.5}$$

where B is a diagonal matrix whose elements are $(1 - \sum_{i=1}^{n} a_{ij})$.

Then

$$F = (1 - A)X = (1 - A)B^{-1}Y = CG \qquad\qquad (A.6)$$

$$Y = B(1 - A)^{-1}CG \qquad\qquad (A.7)$$

Eqn (A.7) completes the linkage between GDP components (G) and value added (Y). This is the essential step in establishing a Keynesian–Leontief type system.

It is possible to operate such a system to obtain industry outputs consistent with GDP using fixed C, B and $(I - A)$ matrices. One approach would be to maintain constant coefficients based on the I–O statistics. In some cases, these may be modified by estimates of the I–O coefficients derived from the Generalized KLEM Cobb–Douglas production function for some important industrial sectors (see Chapter 5). Alternatively, it is possible to treat them as variable coefficients making explicit adjustments for the impacts of information processing, software, and hardware.

Disaggregation

The extent of disaggregation in a Keynesian–Leontief model depends on the availability of data and on the desired amount of detail. While models can be built with many final demand categories and industrial categories, it is advisable to limit detailed breakdowns to the point required by the planned policy simulations.

IT and non-IT capital inputs and human capital

Since the productivity gains being projected are associated with the application of IT technology, it is useful to disaggregate capital stock into IT capital stock and non-IT capital stock. A distinction between hardware and software may also be appropriate. This means also that investment must be disaggregated into similar categories. Capital consumption allowances will be different, assuming shorter lives for IT than for non-IT capital, and for software as compared to hardware. If suitable data are available, we will also separate employment of skilled workers and unskilled workers to include a human capital component in the production function.

Improvements in the quality of human capital, usually associated with education and training, play an important role in the application of IT equipment. Adjustment for improvement in labor quality should affect the production function. Estimating relationships between productivity and years of schooling will permit adjustments in the labor inputs entering the production functions.

Sectoral disaggregation

It is our objective to provide a breakdown for a substantial number of sectors, particularly those that provide opportunities for productivity improvement with the use of additional IT hardware or software. The precise number of sectors depends on the availability of data and their tractability. We aim for approximately 12 sectors separating out the major industries. For each of the sectors, we want to estimate production, potential output, inputs of IT capital and non-IT capital and labor. It will be our objective to compute productivity measures at the sectoral level. We do not plan, however, to do extensive disaggregation of the demand-side. An illustration of the probable sectoral disaggregation is as follows:

- Manufacturing light
- Manufacturing heavy
- Manufacturing high-tech
- Retail and wholesale distribution
- Raw materials
- Energy
- Finance
- Health services
- Government
- Construction
- Agriculture
- Miscellaneous other

The precise definition of the sectoral breakdown will depend on data available including information from the new input–output tables.

Demand-side disaggregation

Demand-side disaggregation will be carried out only insofar as it is necessary to provide a link between the demand-side and the disaggregated supply-side of the model. It is appropriate to select out various investment categories, as we have noted, and perhaps some major categories of consumption.

Trade disaggregation

Breakdowns of trade between IT goods and non-IT goods and/or between trade with East Asia and trade with the rest of the world will make possible adjustments for changing competitiveness of Japanese products in world trade.

Other potential data breakdowns

There are other possibilities for expanding the model to make it more suitable for studying the problems with regard to demography, fiscal balance, and trade composition faced by Japan. These involve the following possibilities:

- more elaborate breakdown of the population and labor force recognizing labor force participation and the aging of the available labor force

- more detailed breakdown of taxation and government finance to establish guidelines about the budgetary impact of alternative future growth paths, and
- more detailed analysis of international trade by composition and/or by geographic origin in order to evaluate the impact of globalization on the Japanese economy,
- Monetary sector disaggregation will depend on the needs of the structural model—for example a breakdown of interest rates into short-term rates and mortgage rates.

Structure of sectoral models

We consider here the structure of the models at the level of the individual sectors. The challenge of the sectoral models is to reconcile the demand and the supply sides. The objective is to project actual and potential output at the sector level and to aggregate this information for the wage and price determination mechanism.

Actual sector output

The actual output of each sector is determined from the demand-side by the input–output system. The estimated production function is used to compute labor requirements, given available capital stock and technology.

Potential sector output

The supply-side must use the available inputs to establish potential output. on the sectoral level. Using estimates of IT and non-IT capital stock and allocating the available labor supply between sectors, the sectoral level production functions can be used to estimate potential sector outputs. Adjustments in the utilization of labor of various qualities may be required as well.

Price and wage equations

Wage and price determination occur in the model at the aggregate national level rather than at the sectoral level. We will compute wages and prices at the level of the aggregate economy. These relationships can be largely as in the standard model. Aggregate productivity is computed as aggregate Y divided by aggregate employment. Changes in wages are determined in relationship to productivity, labor market pressures (unemployment), and the past trend in inflation.

$$W_{\text{dot}} = f((Y/E)_{\text{dot}}, 1/U, P_{\text{dot}-1})$$

where W_{dot} = change in wages, $(Y/E)_{\text{dot}}$ = change in productivity, U = unemployment rate, and P_{dot} = change in the price level.

Price change is then determined by a markup equation on unit labor cost (ULC), prices of materials, and the inflation trend.

$$P_{dot} = f(\text{ULC}_{dot}, P_{mdot}, P_{dot-1})$$

where $\text{ULC}_{dot} = W_{dot} - (Y_{dot} - L_{dot})$, and P_{mdot} represents change of materials (or import) prices.

Adjustment of labor supply

To allow for policies seeking larger labor force participation and/or, possibly, immigration, more detailed treatment of the labor market is required. Detailed treatment of the age distribution of the population and of labor force participation may be appropriate.

Adjustments to the growth trend of the labor supply are appropriate to account for the impact of proposed policy changes on the age of retirement, incentives for labor force participation of women, and, possibly, increased immigration.

Delaying the age of retirement will mean fewer people on retirement benefits. This needs to be taken into account in determining government transfer payments.

Financial sector

The supply and demand for money are the structural underpinnings of interest rate determination. It is possible to elaborate these mechanisms through the use of Flow of Funds data. But a simple monetary sector may be sufficient in a model where the primary emphasis is on the impact of IT. Flow of funds into IT investment will play a role in the model, The most important factor may be the special incentives that are provided for financing IT investment projects and applications. Preferential financing in the form of venture capital has played an important role. The model will be structured to allow for the influence of such financing.

Potentials for model application

Once the model has been built and tested, there are numerous possibilities for its use. In this section we discuss briefly some of the simulations that we will run with the new model system.

Macroeconomic policy

The objectives of macroeconomic policy involve growth, employment, price stability and fiscal and balance of payments equilibrium. Policy makers seek to achieve these aims by manipulating expenditures, tax rates, and money supply and interest rates. We propose systematically to test alternative tax proposals, such as changes in the consumption tax, changes in corporate taxation including tax credits and accelerated depreciation for investment. We will consider alternative expenditure plans focusing, for example, on education and research or on a variety of focused public works projects. We will consider alternatives to manage short and long-term interest rates in such a way that investment is stimulated without damage to the balance of payments or the price level.

The primary objective of these simulations will be to see what policies can be used to accelerate Japanese economic growth. An important consideration in managing expenditure and tax policy will be the impact on the fiscal situation since Japan cannot afford further expansion of the ratio of public debt to nominal GDP.

Sectoral simulations and industrial policy

Simulations assuming changes at the sectoral level are designed to test the response of the economy to stimulating development in specific directions. We may assume changes in demand, in technological development, investment, and costs at the sector level. We may consider the impact of policies that are directed at the development of particular industries or at research and scientific progress in general. This can be a basis for designing industrial policies to maximize the long-run growth of the Japanese economy.

Trade policy

The integration of the Japanese economy into East Asia and its relationships with other parts of the world economy has potential impacts on many dimensions of Japanese economic performance. The model will offer possibilities for testing alternative assumptions with regard to trade policy and exchange rate policies.

Research, education, and human capital policy

The possibilities for evaluating research and education policies in a model framework present some difficult challenges. The sectoral structure of the system and its inclusion of human and IT capital will permit evaluating impacts of policy aimed at these dimensions on the economy. We may also be able to modify sectoral coefficients to show the effects of specific technical changes on the economy's productive potentials.

Conclusions

We are seeking to build an econometric model in an annual timeframe with substantial disaggregation on the production side with particular focus on industries that are developing or applying the new IT technologies. Such a model will be useful to test alternative long-term growth performance scenarios of the Japanese economy.

Notes

1 Introduction and summary of the book

1 This argument about measurement of the public deficit (and debt) not being fully or clearly stated was the main position of our late colleague, Albert Ando. See L. R. Klein, ed. (2006).

2 The economic growth record in Japan

1 Kokko *et al.* (2001) entitle their article "Japan as Number Three." The reference is to Ezra Vogel's 1979 book *Japan as Number One.* Interestingly, Kokko *et al.* are concerned with the relationship between Japan and the EU. With the rise of China, Japan will soon be Number Four!
2 The principal studies to which we refer include Oliner and Sichel (2000), Basu *et al.* (2003), Bosworth and Triplett (2004), Jorgenson *et al.* (2005).
3 Note that in the United States, continued rapid population growth is in part attributable to immigration. From the perspective of the labor force, as compared to natural population growth, immigration has the advantage that immigrants are largely young adults. Most are unskilled but some of them are highly educated.
4 Gordon (2000) argues, however that the increase in IT investment is in part the result of the hedonic index methods used in the United States to compute the price of IT products.
5 There in no implication, however, that the non-IT industries do not benefit from IT. The distinction between the two groups rests on whether IT represents more or less than 15% of capital inputs (Jorgenson *et al.*, 2005, p. 92).
6 From an article "A productivity prescription: how the U.S. has pulled away from Europe and Japan," *Financial Times*, January 25, 2006, p. 8.
7 A similar conclusion is reached by Bosworth and Triplett (2004), though differences in calculation produce somewhat lower figures.
8 The background of this failure is considered below.
9 The idea of the liquidity trap is that no matter how much money the central bank injects into the economic system interest rates could not be driven below zero since consumers would simply hold the increased quantity of money.

4 The IT/E-business revolution and globalization: implications of the New Economy for Japan

1 Denis Gauthier, at the Conference on "Service Sector Productivity and the Productivity Paradox" in Ottawa, Canada on April 11–12, 1997.
2 See Case 3.1, Adams (2004) p. 38.
3 Like energy inputs, IT inputs are mainly intermediate inputs so that it is often better to measure technological progress in gross output terms rather than in value added (GDP) terms.

4 Mortimer B. Zukerman, Chairman of *US News and World Report*, said "The IT revolution matches the U.S. culture of individualism" in "A Second American Century," *Foreign Affairs*, May/June, 1998.
5 In a recent article, Edmund Phelps, the 2006 Nobel Laureate in Economics, contrasts two versions of capitalism: the European Continental system and the American. He argues that restrictions intended to protect "stakeholders" and "social partners" reduce flexibility and stifle dynamism in Europe as compared to the United States ("Dynamic Capitalism," *Wall Street Journal*, October 10, 2006). Though the details are different, a similar comparison can be made between Japan and the United States.
6 Even if the time used by consumers is longer, as it is in many cases, the consumers' costs are not measured in the national accounts.

5 IT and productivity growth: theoretical and empirical framework

1 Allowing for enough spare labor and capital to accommodate short term adjustments and frictions. For example, traditionally 3 or 4% unemployment is necessary to account for people who are "between jobs."
2 Professor Klein first introduced a generalized Cobb–Douglas production function to analyze the effect of IT on the auto and parts sector in his and his colleagues' paper "Contributions of input–output analysis to the understanding of technological change: the information sector in the United States," pp. 311–36 in "*Biographical Memoir of Wassily Leontief,*" *Proceedings of the American Philosophical Society*, Vol. 194, No. 4 (December 2000).
3 See "IT Revolution and Increasing Returns to Scale in the U.S. Economy" presented at Project LINK Meeting at United Nations, Spring 2000.

6 The East Asian growth process and IT: implications for Japan

1 The systematic discrepancy between exchange rates and purchasing power parities, known as the Penn effect, also plays a role. Countries at early stages of development typically have an undervalued exchange rate in relationship to purchasing power comparisons. This means that their products, which sell internationally on exchange rate terms, are cheap in world markets, even cheaper than a comparison of per capita real incomes or purchasing power would suggest. This advantage disappears as countries reach higher income levels (Samuelson, 1994).

7 Information and communications technology and productivity growth in Japan

1 In Japan, labor statistics, such as work hours per employee or the unemployment rate, do not exactly represent the business cycle effect because work hours tend to decline during business booms to attract workers by offering higher payments for fewer work hours, whereas in a recession layoffs cause longer work hours for the remaining employees. As for the unemployment rate, it is apparent that some of the increase in unemployment in the 1990s resulted from fundamental changes in the labor market, such as reforming the so-called lifetime employment system, rather than cyclical changes. Consequently, labor market indexes may not accurately represent the business cycle effect in Japan.

8 Revisiting Japanese industrial organization and the corporate system

1 Network effects represent the scale merits of the demand-side (consumption), whereas economies of scale represent those of the supply-side (production). Katz and Shapiro (1985) argue the nature of network externalities. For detailed arguments, see Shinozaki (2003), chapter 9.

2 According to an international comparison survey conducted by Andersen Consulting in 1997–8, Japanese senior managements ranked last in web literacy among those in developed countries. Less than 80% of Japanese executives were using the web, while almost 100% of US executives were using the web. To make matters worse, only 15% of Japanese executives felt "comfortable" or "familiar" with web access, and only 13% had experience shopping on the web. In contrast, almost two-thirds of US executives felt "comfortable" and "familiar" with web access and enjoyed on-line shopping (Andersen Consulting, 1999).

3 Similar thoughts are expressed in the culture literature. "Organizational forms that were effective in exploiting one state of technology can turn out to be liabilities with newer technologies" (Pye, 2000, p. 255).

9 Case study of government policy and the telecommunications market in Japan

1 In the mid-1990s, there were 6.5 millions private business establishments of which small businesses run by individual proprietorship, not incorporated, amounted to as many as 3.5 million. On the other hand, there were only 60,000 firms that employ 100 employees or more. Furthermore, about one million incorporated establishments employed only 4 employees or less.

2 For detailed discussions, see Kishimoto (2005).

10 IT-related development and policy: some examples from the United States with relevance to Japan

1 Radio Frequency Identification (RFID) is an automatic identification method, relying on storing and remotely retrieving data using devices called RFID tags. An RFID tag is a small object that can be attached to or incorporated into a product, animal, or person. RFID tags contain silicon chips and antennas to enable them to receive and respond to radio-frequency queries from an RFID transceiver. Passive tags require no internal power source, whereas active tags require a power source (Source: Wikipedia).

2 At this moment, the tags for items still cost about five cents each. Thus, it is likely that the application of the tags will be limited to products with relatively high prices, such as medicines, bags, pets, books, tickets and some non-retail products. To be able to apply RFID tags to cheaper products sold in supermarkets, one must wait until tag manufacture increases greatly and the unit price goes down to less than one cent. Wal-Mart estimates this will not happen until 2020. This means that the next 15 years would be a crucial chance for Japan to take the initiative in developing the new RFID technologies that are applicable to individual items. The advanced tags are now being developed by the companies such as IBM, Xerox, Samsung, and some Japanese enterprises such as Dai Nippon Printing.

3 As we noted in Chapter 7, cyclical forces have a major short term impact on labor productivity. That may simply reflect the fact that employers are reluctant to lay off workers on the downswing and are reluctant to hire them on the upswing of the business cycle. This explains the sensitivity of US productivity data to business cycle conditions, for example, why data ending in 2003 give a somewhat different picture than data ending in 2001 in Table 10.1. However, as explained in Chapter 7, the cyclical movement of work hours may be different in Japan from the United States.

11 Estimating a new economy production function for Japan

1 Calculated by Kumasaka using the estimated Generalized Cobb–Douglas production function for the Kumasaka and Tange (2004) paper.

12 Simulation studies for accelerating Japanese economic growth

1 Detailed model specifications are available from the authors on request.
2 An increase in interest rates has been assumed because interest rates are very low at this time. A reduction in interest rates would have approximately the same impact only in the opposite direction.
3 Assuming an average life of 10 years and a cost of capital about 7%, this is roughly equivalent to an investment tax credit of 35%.

13 Policies to achieve faster economic growth in Japan

1 But our simulations do not suggest that demand stimulus policy has strong or persistent impacts.

References

Adams, F. Gerard (2004) *The E-Business Revolution and the New Economy*, Cincinnati: Thomson Southwestern.

Adams, F. Gerard (2006) *East Asia, Globalization and New Economy*, London: Routledge.

Adams, F. Gerard and Lawrence R. Klein (eds) (1983) *Industrial Policies for Growth and Competitiveness*, Lexington: D. C. Heath.

Agoston, Thomas, C., T. Ueda, and Y. Nishimura (2000) "Pervasive Computing in a Networked World," http://www.isoc.org/inet2000/cdproceedings/3a/3a_1.htm (accessed on June 12, 2007).

Akamatsu, K. (1962) "A Historical Pattern of Economic Growth in Developing Countries," *Journal of Developing Economies*, Vol. 1, No. 1, pp. 3–25.

Andersen Consulting (1999) Press release handout, May 7, 1999, in Japanese.

Anderson, G. F., B. K. Frogner, R. A. Johns, and Uwe E. Reinhardt (2006) "Health Care Spending and Use of Information Technology in OECD Countries," *Health Affairs*, Vol. 25, No. 3, pp. 819–32.

Arrow, Kenneth, J. (1962) "The Economic Implications of Learning by Doing," *Review of Economic Studies*, Vol. 29, No. 3, June 1962, pp. 155–73.

Asian Development Bank (2003) *Asia's Growth Strategies for the 21st Century*, Manila: ADB (draft).

Basu, Susanto, John G. Fernald, Nicholas Oulton, and Sylaja Srinvasan (2003) "The Case of the Missing Productivity Growth: Or Does Information Technology Explain Why Productivity Accelerated in the United States but Not in the United Kingdom?" Federal Reserve Bank of Chicago paper, WP w003–8.

Blomstrom, Magnus, Byron Gangnes, and Sumner La Croix (eds) (2001) *Japan's New Economy*, Oxford: Oxford University Press.

Bosworth, Barry P. and Jack E. Triplett (2004) *Productivity in the US Services Sectors*, Washington: Brookings.

Busom, Isabel (1999) "An Empirical Evaluation of the Effects of R&D Subsidies," Burch Center Working Paper, Berkeley: University of California.

Cabinet office (2004) *Annual Report on the Japanese Economy and Public Finance*, Tokyo: Government of Japan.

Callen, Tim and Jonathan D. Ostry (eds) (2003) *Japan's Lost Decade: Policies for Economic Revival*, Washington: International Monetary Fund.

Chandler, Alfred D., Jr (2000) "The Information Age in Historical Perspective," in Alfred D. Chandler and James W. Cortada, eds, *A Nation Transformed by Information: How Information has Shaped to the Present*, New York: Oxford University Press, pp. 3–38.

Christenson, Clayton M. (2000) *The Innovators, Dilemma*, New York: Harper Business.

Coase, Ronald (1937) "The Nature of the Firm," *Economic*, Vol. 4, pp. 386–405.

Cohen, Adam (2002) "Editorial Observer: PayPal and Other Post-Bubble Signs of Life on the Internet," *New York Times*, February 6.

Committee on Prosperity in the Global Economy in the 21st Century (2005) *Rising Above the Gathering Storm: Energizing and Employing America for a Brighter Future*, Washington: National Academies Press.

Council on Economic and Fiscal Policy (2005) *The Report of the Special Board of Inquiry For Examining "Japan's 21st Century Vision,"* Tokyo: Cabinet Office.

Deckle, Robert and Kenneth Kletzer (2003) "The Japanese Banking Crisis and Economic Growth: Theoretical and Empirical Implications of Deposit Guarantees and Weak Financial Regulation," WP # 1002, Santa Cruz Center for International Economics.

Economic Planning Agency (1990) *Keizai Hakusho: Nenji Keizai Hokoku (White Paper: Annual Economic Survey of Japan)*, August 1990, in Japanese.

Fahy, John and F. Taguchi (1995) "Assessing the Japanese Distribution System," *Sloan Management Review*, Vol. 36, No. 2, pp. 49–61.

Friedman, Thomas (2005) *The World is Flat*, New York: Farrar, Strauss, and Giroux.

Gordon, Robert J. (2000) "Does the 'New Economy' Measure up to the Great Inventions of the Past," *Journal of Economic Perspectives*, Vol. 4, No. 14, Fall, pp. 40–74.

Hayashi, Fumio and Edward C. Prescott (2002) "The 1990s in Japan: A Lost Decade," *Review of Economic Dynamics*, Vol. 5 (Special issue), January, pp. 2067–35.

Hofstede, Geert (1980, 1984) *Culture's Consequences*, Newbury Park: Sage.

Hofstede, Geert (1997) *Cultures and Organizations*, New York: McGraw-Hill.

Inkeles, Alex (1998) *One World Emerging*, Boulder: Westview Press.

Intriligator, Michael D., R. G. Bodkin and C. Hsiao (1996) *Econometric Models, and Applications*, Englewood Cliffs: Prentice Hall.

IT Strategy Headquarters (2001) "E-Japan Strategy" <http://www.kantei.go.jp/foreign/it/network/0122full_e.html> (accessed on June 12, 2007).

IT Strategy Headquarters (2005) "IT Policy Package – 2005 – Towards the Realization of the World's Most Advanced IT Nation" <http://www.kantei.go.jp/foreign/policy/it/itpackage2005.pdf> (accessed on June 12, 2007).

Jasinowski, Jerry J., ed. (1998) *The Rising Tide*, Hoboken: John Wiley & Sons, Inc.

Jorgenson, Dale W. (2001) "Information Technology and the U.S. Economy," *American Economic Review*, Vol. 91, No. 1, March 2001, pp. 1–32.

Jorgenson, Dale W. and Kevin J. Stiroh (2000) "Raising the Speed Limit: US Economic Growth in the Information Age," *Brookings Papers on Economic Activity*, Vol. 1, pp. 125–210.

Jorgenson, Dale W. and Koji, Nomura (2005) "The Industry Origins of Japanese Economic Growth," National Bureau of Economic Research Working paper No. 11800.

Jorgenson, Dale W. and K. Motohashi (2005) "Information Technology and the Japanese Economy," NBER Working Paper No. W11801.

Jorgenson, Dale W., M. S. Ho, and K. J. Stiroh (2002) "Growth of U.S. Industries and Investments in Information Technology and Higher Education" (processed); unpublished paper <http://post.harvard.edu/faculty/jorgenson/papers/jhscriw.pdf> (accessed on June 12, 2007).

Jorgenson, Dale W., M. S. Ho, and K. J. Stiroh (2004) "Will the U.S. Productivity Resurgence Continue?" *Current Issues*, Vol. 10, No. 13, Federal Reserve Bank of New York, pp. 1–7.

Jorgenson, Dale W., M. S. Ho, and K. J. Stiroh (2005) *Productivity Volume 3: Information Technology and the American Growth Resurgence*, Cambridge: The MIT Press.

Katz, Michael L. and Carl Shapiro (1985) "Network Externalities, Competition, and Compatibility," *American Economic Review*, Vol. 75, No. 3, June 1985, pp. 424–40.

Kishimoto, Shuhei (2005) "Perspectives on the Japanese Content Industry and the Government's Policy," *Hitotsubashi Business Review*, Vol. 53, No. 3, pp. 6–20, in Japanese.

Klein, Lawrence R. (2000) "Contributions of Input-Output Analysis to the Understanding of Technological Change: The Information Sector in the United States," in *"Biographical Memoir of Wassily Leontief,"* Proceedings of the American Philosophical Society, Vol. 194, No. 4, December, pp. 311–36.

Klein, Lawrence R. ed. (2006) *Long Run Growth and Short Term Stabilization, Essays in Memory of Albert Ando*, Northampton: Edward Elgar Publishing.

Klein, Lawrence R. and K. Ohkawa eds (1968) *Economic Growth and the Japanese Experience since the Meiji Era*, Homewood: Irwin.

Klein, Lawrence R. and Yuzo Kumasaka (1995) "The Re-Opening of The U.S. Productivity-Led Growth Era," *NLI Research Institute Monthly Report*, unpublished paper.

Klein, Lawrence R. and Y. Kumasaka (2000) "IT Revolution and Increasing Returns to Scale in the U.S. Economy," presented at 2000 *Spring Project LINK meeting*.

Klein, Lawrence R., Cynthia Saltzman, and Vijay G. Duggal (2003) "Information Technology and Productivity: The Case of the Financial Sector," *Survey of Current Business*, Vol. 83, No. 8, August 2003, pp. 32–7.

Kojima, Kiyoshi (2000) "The 'Flying Geese' Model of Asian Economic Development: Origin, Theoretical Extensions, and Regional Policy Implications," *Journal of Asian Economics*, Vol. 11, No. 4, pp. 375–401.

Kokko, A., B. H. Lambert and F. Sjoholm (2001) "Japan as Number Three: Effects of European Integration," in Blomstrom, Magnus, Byron Gangnes, and Sumner La Croix, eds (2001) *Japan's New Economy*, Oxford: Oxford University Press.

Krugman, Paul (1998) "Its Baaack: Japan's Slump and the Return of the Liquidity Trap," *Brookings Papers on Economic Activity*, No. 2, pp. 137–205.

Kumasaka, Yuzo and Toshiko Tange (2004) "The Effect of Information Technology on the Japanese Macro-Economy," Paper presented at the conference of the Japanese Economic Association on June 10 and 11, 2004, Tokyo.

La Croix, Sumner and James Mak (2001) "Regulatory Reform in Japan: The Road Ahead," in Blomstrom, Magnus, Byron Gangnes, and Sumner La Croix, eds (2001) *Japan's New Economy*, Oxford: Oxford University Press.

Langlois, Richard N. and Paul L. Robertson (1992) "Networks and Innovation in a Modular System: Lessons from the Microcomputer and Stereo Component Industries," *Research Policy*, Vol. 21, No. 4, pp. 297–313.

METI (Ministry of Economy, Trade and Industry) (2006a) "Nichi-Chu-Kan no ryuutuu oyobi butsuryu ni kansuru kyoudou houkokusho: Nippon hen (Joint Report on Distribution and Logistics in Japan, China, and Korea: Part Japan)," in Japanese, March, Tokyo: METI.

METI (Ministry of Economy, Trade and Industry) (2006b) "Ryuutsuu bunya niokeru kadai to taiou (Challenges and Responses in the Distribution Business)," handout in Japanese, July, Tokyo: METI.

Ministry of Internal Affairs and Communications (2006) *White Paper 2006, Information and Communications in Japan*, Tokyo: Ministry of Internal Affairs and Communications.

Motonishi, T. and H. Yoshikawa (1999) "Causes of the Long Stagnation of Japan during the 1990s: Financial or Real?" *Journal of the Japanese and International Economies*, Vol. 13, No. 3, pp. 181–200.

National Institute of Population and Social Security Research (2002) *Population Projections for Japan: 2001–2050*, Tokyo, pp. 1–29.

No author, "Accelerated Depreciation of Capital Spending," *The Big Picture* 9/2004, <http://bigpicture.typepad.com/comments/2004/09/accelerated_dep.html> (accessed on June 12, 2007).

OECD (2001) *The New Economy Beyond the Hype*, Paris: OECD, <http://www.oecd.org/dataoecd/2/43/238ch15.pdf> (accessed on June 12, 2007).

Oliner, Stephen D. and Daniel E. Sichel (2000) "The Resurgence of Growth in the Late 1990s: Is Information Technology the Story?" *Journal of Economic Perspectives*, Vol. 14, No. 4 pp. 3–22.

OMB (2005) "E-Gov: Powering America's Future with Technology," Washington: Office of Management and Budget, <http://www.whitehouse.gov/omb/egov> (accessed on June 12, 2007).

Policy Research Institute (2000) *Nippon Keizai no Koritsusei to Kaifukusaku*, Ministry of Finance, June 2000, in Japanese.

Porter, Michael E. (2000) "Attitudes, Values, Beliefs, and the Microeconomics of Prosperity," in Harrison, L. E. and Samuel P. Huntington, eds (2000) *Culture Matters*, New York: Basic Books, pp. 14–28.

Preston, Ross. S. (1975) "The Wharton Long-Term Model: Input-Output in the Context of a Macro Forecasting Model," *International Economic Review*, Vol. 6, No. 1, pp. 13–19.

Pye, Lucian W. (2000) "Asian Values: from Dynamos to Dominoes?" in Harrison, L. E. and Samuel P. Huntington, eds (2000) *Culture Matters*, New York: Basic Books, pp. 244–55.

Robertson (1992) "Networks and Innovation in Modular System: Lessons from the Microcomputer and Stereo Component Industries," *Research Policy*, Vol. 21, No. 4, August 1992, pp. 297–313.

Saito, Mitsuo (2000) *The Japanese Economy*, Singapore: World Scientific, p. 10.

Samuelson, Paul A. (1994) "Facets of Balassa-Samuelson: Thirty Years Later," *Review of International Econmics*, Vol. 2, No. 3, pp. 201–26.

Schick, Allen (2000) *The Federal Budget: Politics, Policy, Process*, revised edn, Washington, D.C.: Brookings Institution.

Schumpeter, Joseph A. (1926) *The Theorie der wirtschaftlicher Entwicklung (Theory of Economic Development), 2. AuFL*, Japanese translation, 1997.

Schumpeter, J. A. (1942) *Socialism, Capitalism, and Democracy*, New York: Harper and Row.

Shinozaki, Akihiko (2003) *Joho Gijntsu Kakushini no Keizai Koka* (The Impact of Information Technology on the Economy: A comparative study between Japan and the United States), Tokyo: Nippon Hyoron Sha, in Japanese.

Shinozaki, Akihiko (2004) "Aggregate Productivity Growth and the Contribution of Japan's ICT Assets: Isn't it Another Puzzle?" *RCSS Discussion Paper Series*, No. 20, September, 2004, Research Center of Socionetwork Strategies, Kansai University, pp. 1–23.

Shinozaki, Akihiko (2005a) "The Nature of Productivity: Historical Perspective on an Aging Japan," *Journal of Political Economy (Keizaigaku_Kenkyu)*, Vol. 72, No. 1, June 2005, Kyushu University, pp. 1–26, in Japanese.

Shinozaki, Akihiko (2005b) "How Does Information Technology Pay Off?: Firm-level Evidence in Organizational Structures and Human Resource Management," *ESRI Discussion Paper Series*, No. 127, February, 2005, Economic and Social Research Institute, Cabinet Office, pp. 1–34, in Japanese.

Shinozaki, Akihiko (2006a) "Effective Corporate Reforms with Information Technology: Logit Model Analysis on Business Process Reengineering, Business Unit Restructuring, and Human Resource Management," *ESRI Discussion Paper Series*, No. 164, June, 2006, Economic and Social Research Institute, Cabinet Office, pp. 1–21, in Japanese.

Shinozaki, Akihiko (2006b) "Can the Sun Rise Again in the Ubiquitous Information Age?: Feasibility of a Three Percent Economic Growth for Japan, which is Dealing with Aging and Diminishing Demographics," *Journal of Political Economy (Keizaigaku=Kenkyu)*, Vol. 72, No. 5–6, March 2006, Kyushu University, pp. 99–124.

Shoch, John (1999) "The US Environment for Venture Capital and Technology-based Startups," in *Harnessing Science and Technology for America's Economic Future*, Washington: National Academies Press, pp. 119–24.

Sidorov, Jaan (2006) "It Ain't Necessarily So: The Electronic Health Record, an Unlikely Prospect of Reducing Healthcare Costs," *Health Affairs*, Vol. 25, No. 4, pp. 1079–85.

Thurow, Lester (2003) *Fortune Favors the Bold*, New York: HarperCollins.

United Nations (2006) *World Economic and Social Surveys*, New York: United Nations.

Warsh, David (2006) *Knowledge and the Wealth of Nations*, New York: Norton.

Weinstein, David E. (2001) "Historical, Structural, and Macroeconomic Perspectives on the Japanese Economic Crisis," in Blomstrom, Magnus, Byron Gangnes, and Sumner La Croix, eds (2001) *Japan's New Economy*, Oxford: Oxford University Press.

Wolff, Edward N. (2001) "Has Japan Specialized in the Wrong Industries?" in Blomstrom, Magnus, Byron Gangnes, and Sumner La Croix, eds (2001) *Japan's New Economy*, Oxford: Oxford University Press.

Woo, Wing T. (1999) "The Real Reasons for China's Growth," *The China Journal*, No. 41, pp. 115–37.

World Bank (2006) *Information and Communication for Development: Global Trends and Developments*, Washington: World Bank.

Index

CPSIA information can be obtained at www.ICGtesting.com
Printed in the USA
268173BV00002B/11/P